On Losing the Soul

D1571349

On Losing the Soul

Essays in the Social Psychology of Religion

Richard K. Fenn
Donald Capps
Editors

Center for the Study of Religion, Self, and Society
Princeton Theological Seminary

STATE UNIVERSITY OF NEW YORK PRESS

BL
290
.05
1995

Published by
State University of New York Press, Albany

For information, address State University of New York
Press, State University Plaza, Albany, N.Y., 12246

Production by E. Moore
Marketing by Theresa Abad Swierzowski

Library of Congress Cataloging-in-Publication Data

On losing the soul : essays in the social psychology of religion /
    edited by Richard K. Fenn, Donald Capps.
        p.   cm.
    Includes bibliographical references and index.
    ISBN 0-7914-2493-6. — ISBN 0-7914-2494-4 (pbk : alk. paper)
    1. Soul. 2. Religion and sociology. 3. Psychology, Religious.
    4. Spiritual life. I. Fenn, Richard K. II. Capps, Donald.
    BL290.05 1995
    306.6—dc20   94-31494
                                                                      CIP

10 9 8 7 6 5 4 3 2 1

Contents

RICHARD K. FENN

Introduction: Why the Soul?

This volume is an attempt to expand the discourse of the social sciences about the self by reintroducing the word soul. 'Reintroduction' is the right word to use; there was a time when such usage was rather ordinary. Very few professional sociologists or anthropologists use the term, despite its currency in the days of Levy-Bruhl and Raymond Firth. Of course, a few therapists like Thomas Moore define their work as the cure of the soul, and the psychiatrist Leonard Shengold (1989) does not hesitate to speak of the loss or even the murder of the soul. Even the therapeutic community, however, has needed to be reminded about the importance of the soul. Bruno Bettelheim contended that, especially on the American side of the Atlantic, a great deal of Freud's meaning was lost in translation. What was lost was not only the notion of a soul, but also all that the term implies: myth, mystery, essential being, and the common, ordinary, human struggle for a real, even an essential self. As the essays in this collection by David and Bernice Martin indicate, however, much of that meaning is still accessible on the other side of the Atlantic, and a number of our contributors are mining their own traditions for a comparably rich semantic vein. It is Daniel O'Keefe who has made perhaps the most persuasive and thorough-going case for studying the soul and soul-loss in his unparalleled work in the sociology of religion, *Stolen Lightning*. As Bernice Martin puts it, in a footnote to her contribution to this volume:

> The word 'soul' suggests to me the possibility of recognizing—hinting at—a level of discourse which accords some ultimate significance to the person beyond what can be said by the expert social scientific disciplines. The metaphysical and theological connotations of 'soul' suggest a dimension of the integrity of persons, which is not fully captured by the vocabulary of 'self' and 'selfhood.' The death of the soul is of greater

moment than the death of the self. The poetic language of love
and its corruption says more than, and different from, the scientific analysis of 'the self in relationship.'

We are not alone in discerning a void in the language of the
social sciences where the person, in his or her depth, should be.
Take, for example, Mary Douglas's comment that "The first source
of our troubles as anthropologists is that we have no adequate conception of the individual," (1978, 5). She agrees with those who crit-
icize both sociology and anthropology for seeing the individual as a
mere outcropping of an underlying social granite. The bedrock of
social life may be thought to be rules, roles, and relationships, or
beliefs, values, and general conceptions of what it means to be a
good person in a variety of specific contexts. In any event the individual ends up as a case in point, a more or less serious or tongue-in-
cheek performer of a script that has cast each and every one in some
part or another. Unfortunately, as we shall have occasion to point
out, Mary Douglas herself seems precisely to reduce individuals to
points on a social grid.

In this volume we are proposing to use the notion of the soul as
an end-term: a word that comes at the end of a series of terms like
the individual, individuality, the person, personality, self, selfhood,
and even beyond the inner or essential self. The soul represents a
hypothetical point in the individual's subjectivity: the point from
which it is possible to become aware of the existence of an essential
self or of its possible loss and corruption. Standing at the end of a
series of such terms the notion of a soul points both backwards along
the semantic range thus travelled and forward into an uncertain ter-
rain of meaning and significance. Pointing backwards, the notion of
a soul suggests that there is something about an individual that cannot be subsumed under the headings either of 'nature' of or 'society':
something beyond sheer vitality and relatedness. Pointing forward
into uncertain territory, the term 'soul' taps the mythic and philosophical meanings that inhere, for instance, in Freud's use of the
term *psyche*. Applied to Western societies the notion of the soul
speaks to a dimension of social character that has embodied and
endured often untold suffering.

The notion of the soul, then, opens the possibility of going
beyond conventional discussions of alienation. It raises new questions about the costs and possibilities of social life and about the
limits and potential of selfhood in modern societies. Thus we agree
with Bernice Martin's insight on the function of the term, the soul,

to indicate "the possibility of recognizing—hinting at—a level of discourse which accords some ultimate significance to the person beyond what can be said by the expert social scientific disciplines."

If social scientists think of individuals as social creatures or products, the soul (if they think of it at all) is precarious and ephemeral: laboriously created through social interaction and far too easily either crushed by social pressures or starved to death for lack of social nourishment. Take, for example, Susan Nelson's contribution to this volume. There one will find the the soul struggling to survive either in a sterile environment devoid of affection and response or in an atmosphere polluted by abusive, intrusive, and demeaning relationships. The notion of sin simply adds cultural insult to such injuries to the soul, Nelson suggests, by creating a climate in which the victim is easily blamed. If the notion of sin transfers to the individual a sense of personal failure and responsiblity for the failings of others on whom the individual has necessarily depended for sustenance and for life itself, would it not be better entirely to discard the notion of sin? Nelson addresses that question directly. For social scientists who think of the soul as moth-like and ephemeral, the soul is far too easily either enthralled by the products of its own social imagination, confused by a multiplicity of ambiguous and conflicting images and symbols for the self in society, or surfeited with a glut of meaning. Thus the fate of the soul depends on the individual's willingness to surrender the projections, identifications, and delusions that have given the illusion of quality and depth to social life.

In this collection we wish to use the term soul to point toward a mystery at the heart of social life. By 'mystery' we mean to say more than that the natural and social depths of the individual need to be explored if we are to understand the consuming passions and the capacity for relatedness of the individual. Like the black hole around which neighboring galaxies slowly revolve, but which emits no light of its own, the soul can only be hypothesized. It is the immaterial substratum of social life that can only be imagined at this stage, like the hypothetical matter of the universe, most of which still remains to be seen. In this book we are inquiring into depths within the individual which are only partly understood or coded by communities and societies but which remain crucial to the interpretation and explanation of the individual and of social life itself.

To speak of the soul it will be necessray to rescue the term from too close an associaton with notions of 'spirit' or 'heart.' Capps's contribution to this volume vigorously defends the notion of the soul

from the enchroachments of the spirit, and he argues that the soul has
claims of its own which the spirit can neither successfully preempt or
deny. Furthermore, heart and soul are not two words for the same
thing even in Western societies; neither are they identical for a wide
range of so-called "primitive" communities. Some societies see only
a body and a source of animation within; others, however, believe in
a protective genius that guards one against danger over time. At the
very least, we have to account for what it is that renews the person
from within (a mystery, as Capps points out, that is often expressed in
folklore as stemming from that self-regenerating organ, the liver.)
The soul is thus a residual category, but it is not composed merely of
the residues of convention and desire, object-relations and fantasies.
The soul is implicit, suppressed, or even buried in social life, waiting
for the discerning eye of the anthropologist. Even within the self, its
presence, like a black hole, can only be inferred from its effects, since
it cannot be seen directly.

For some sociologists, like Mary Douglas, it is clear that the
individual is largely a social product: merely a subset of social
residues. Within such Durkheimian assumptions, indeed, the individual is only a little animal unwittingly adding a small increment to
the coral reef without which the animal itself would hardly exist. For
Durkheim, and for those writing from Durkheimian presuppositions
about the derivative character of the individual, societies are *prior to*
the individual in every sense of the word: that is, in moral as well as
causal, in ontological as well as in epistemological priority.

For others, however, social life itself is only a screen invented
by the individual in order to have something on which to project
the unexamined and intolerable aspects of the self, which otherwise
cannot be seen at all. The clue to this thinking is the notion of the
double: a chimera, a mere fantasy, which nonetheless has very real
effects indeed. Social life takes on the quality of a double for the
soul simply because the individual is fundamentally unsure of, and
frightened by, the shadow of his or her own existence. Freud, too,
found the individual to be frightened at the prospect of losing the
self: a fear that could easily become attached to particular organs
like the eyes or the genitals. "Castration anxiety" is not only the fear
of losing one's genitals; it is the fear of being "cut off" from the land
of the living—the fear, that is, of extinction. That fear can take the
form of what later analysts have called "persecutory" or "depressive" anxiety. In either event, the prospect of not-being drives the
individual to make a double of himself or herself: anything, quite literally, that will stand the test of time.

Thus, for social scientists of the latter, non-Durkheimian persuasion, social life is composed merely of doubles—in the Rankian sense—of the individual. The 'double' may take the form of a divine or ancestral spirit, or it may take a more animistic form, as in the case of the burning bush. The double may become an ideal, in relation to which the individual acquires selfhood and confidence in his or her own being. The double inevitably, however, becomes a rival: like Abel to Cain. Such a rival comes to stand for one's own mortality, the very thing from which the double was initially supposed to protect the self. In the long run, as in the *Portrait of Dorian Grey*, the double becomes recognizable as death itself, and the mask is dropped. For social scientists who see the individual as real and social life as an extension, projection, and effect of individual consciousness in action, the psyche or the soul is the mystery which lies buried in the heart of social life.

While not seeking to mystify discussions of the individual in relation to society, we do intend to point to elements of mystery yet to be explored in social scientific discourse about the self.

For instance, one of our authors, Owe Wikstrom, indeed finds a mystery to be plumbed: the interaction of autonomy and spirituality, the unpredictable and the socially constrained, in the depths of the self. It is out of this mystery, he argues, that anthropologists, psychologists, and sociologists must gather their data, and by that mystery their work is judged:

> I see in modern psychology a risk that the individuality of man can be *reduced* to metanarratives like physical laws, semantic structures, psychodynamic forces or social processes. The necessary *methodological reduction* can—if unobserved by the researcher—be translated into *ontological reductionism*. The consequences are professional loss of soul.

Note that it is the researcher who is hurt by this reductionism. Wikstrom takes his point from Dostoyevsky, who finds the criminal killing himself in the act of murdering others. Reductionism is a two-edged sword and pierces to the heart of the reductionist. Technicians may be without a soul, as Weber put it, precisely because they have ignored or lost track of the soul in those whom they study, (and, of course, vice versa). Unless social scientists respect what Wikstrom calls "man's longing for the unseen," they will not know what it is that they are missing in their pursuit of knowledge about human beings.

Not all of our contributors, however, are convinced that the social sciences will be improved by extending the semantic range of our words for the individual, the person, and the self to include the soul. Contrast Wikstrom's interest in the mysterious aspects of the self, related to the divine, for instance, with Kwilecki's understanding that religious experience and belief are both curative and pathological. With friends like the gods, she implies, individuals do not need enemies, and yet many individuals, like the two in her case studies, have found their innermost selves realized, for good or ill, in struggle with or surrender to powerful, supernatural presences. At the very least, as I argue in the first essay, these dramas of the soul can be observed, and the place to observe them is in ritual. It is in ritual that one can observe the movements of the galaxy of personal and social factors, so to speak, around the putative black hole which is the psyche or the soul.

Not all our contributors, therefore, would agree that a quasi-scientific vocabulary for speaking of the self has deprived professional discourse of access to what is essential about the being and development of the individual. For Kwilecki, as we have noted, there is no use in talking of a soul, except perhaps as a metaphor for aspects of the self for which psychoanalysts in fact already offer relatively clear and useful concepts. Self-object theory, she argues, helps to explain why some individuals see and experience the divine in one way or another: the divine being a more or less transparent version of their own inner dynamics, repressions, and self-images. The linkage between the images of self and of God, she notes, is often precarious and idiosyncratic, but in the confusion of the self and its ideas she discerns patterns that have helped individuals to make sense of themselves and their experience of the world, even if that sense is an unhappy one. Much depends on whether one is examining hysteria or neurosis, of course, but in her view nothing really stands in the way of a fairly clear psychoanalytic version of the individual's mental economy. As for the soul, she argues, the notion itself does not have the flexibility or specificity of psychoanalytic concepts and is a bit of conceptual baggage that we would be better off without.

Many social scientists would agree with Kwilecki on this point. For example, let us return to Mary Douglas, who typifies the strong program in Durkheimian sociology. Douglas, unlike Wikstrom, does not present us with a mystery in the form of the individual. True, she would have us see individuals as being nimble, inventive, pragmatic, resourceful, and even a bit canny in the way they create the world in which they live. But her metaphor for the individual is a miniscule animal on the coral reef, (1978, 6). Every little worm on that reef is simply adding to a process that has been going on for many, many years. On the other hand, were it not for the inventive and laborious work of each individual, social life would be dead of its own weight, inert and maladaptive without the contribution of the individual making choices, playing games, getting by, making do, and making it up as he or she goes along.

According to Douglas, what is missing between the concept of a culture, with its deposit of instructions and memories, and the individual who negotiates more or less freely in terms of that culture, is a social context:

> a context conceived in strictly social terms, selected for its permitting and constraining effects upon the individual's choices. It consists of social action, a deposit from myriads of individual decisions made in the past, creating the cost-structure and distribution of advantages which are the context of present-day decisions. We will pick from the coral-reef accumulation of past decisions only those which landscape the individual's new choices: the action is this afternoon, the context was made afresh this morning, but some of its effects are long, slow fibres reaching from years back. With such a view of the social environment we can try to make allowance for the individual's part in transforming it, minute to minute. (1978, 6)

It would seem from this passage that individuals seldom have a reason to take the long view: to look at their work and their choices *sub specie aeternitatis*. Instead, they are busy making choices, maximizing utility, electing alternatives, exercising options. Indeed, Douglas says that just such a shortened time-perspective describes what she calls "low-grid" societies. These tend to leave a great deal of discretion up to the individual, who is therefore continuously engaged in a process of bargaining and negotiation to control more and more resources, to widen the circle of useful acquaintances, and to keep options open for the future. Each individual thus constructs a social system in which he or she gets by. The formal differences between individuals, for example, in age, gender, status, or religion, matter far less than they do in "high-grid" societies; social life is more open, complex, and uncertain. One must therefore, like a recent U.S. presidential candidate, continue to work the crowd, shake hands, maintain one's network, and add to one's store house of opportunities as best one can in order to acquire status and power for the somewhat longer haul. This intensification of the immediate time horizon, Douglas argues, links industrial societies in the West with preindustrial societies in New Guinea, for instance, or in West Africa. Perhaps it does.

I would argue, however, that the extended present of modern societies, in which the future is a constantly receding horizon and the past has indeterminate boundaries, is quite different from the present of traditional societies in which ritual establishes the boundaries of the present and creates both the past and the future. Time in traditional societies is thus renewed, and the soul is thus granted temporary exemption, pardon, and release from the weight of society. The seasons of the soul, as it were, are determined by the cycle of ritual, whereas in modern societies the burdens of social and emotional debts persist into the indefinite future. The past is never created, and hence old obligations and injustices continue to weigh on the present. Thus without the benefit of rituals which can cancel social and emotional debts, the future does not arrive.

The experience of time, we would suggest, both forms and expresses the innermost life of the individual. Unfortunately, however, Douglas avoids any discussion of the fate of the soul in modern societies. Her metaphors are uniformly spatial, whereas the soul swims, as it were, in the sea of time. Time is a projection of the soul, the medium for its self-realization, and yet also its rival and mortal enemy. It is not sufficient to imagine the self as working in a spatial field composed of drives and relationships, symbols and structures, internal space and external environment, nature and society. Individuals do not merely reproduce and extend the social structure of which they are a part into the indefinite future. The individual does not simply mirror both in body and spirit the network and grid on which personal experience is based. Yet for Douglas one can only see the coral reef of society forming from the small increments of time and energy invested by the little animals that briefly contribute their vital energies to its formation:

> The one single cultural value that justifies the movement towards low grid is the unique value of the individual person. Calling on an ethic of individual value, each person can be justified for breaching constraints upon his freedom. This principle is basic to low grid because it extends the individual's scope for negotiating. Each basic principle, the value of the group, the value of the individual, is the point of reference that justifies action of a potentially generative kind. When one winds heav-

ily against the other, the slide starts toward strong group or toward low grid. When each pulls against the other the tension is a dialogue within society. (1978, 13)

Note that the opposite of low grid here is not high grid but strong group: a clear indication that Douglas is working not with two dimensions (grid and group) but with one. Integration (group) and regulation (grid) are fundamentally the same processes, as critics of Durkheimian theory have long alleged. The result is that there is a polarity at work: at one end of the spectrum the impulses and prerogatives of individuals prevail over those of social groups, organizations, movements, institutions, and other systems; at the other end the requirements of those systems for maintenance, continuity, and succession prevail over the claims of the individual. In the tension between these two poles, Douglas argues, individuals' choices create a more or less focused, clearly defined, well-articulated and enduring social fabric. *What is missing here is any notion of the self that moves beyond nature and society, beyond sheer relatedness and vitality, into the metaphoric range of discourse about the soul.*

We spend this much time in discussing Douglas to highlight the way in which many of the contributors to this volume have departed from conventional ethnography. Take, for example, Bernice Martin's study of her own daughter's experience of abuse at the hands of a "common-law" husband. Professor Martin makes it clear that one pole of her daughter's existence was in the world of the university, where she enjoyed considerable freedom and responsiblity, while at the same time her daughter was also confined by her husband to an increasingly oppressive world in which not only her movements and relationships but thoughts and feelings were constantly under surveillance. Bernice Martin could have contented herself with exploring the fate of individuality in two such different contexts: contexts that could easily be typified in Douglas's schema of high and low "grid" and "group." Instead, she goes on to discuss her daughter's as yet untold suffering. When subject to the social world dominated by her husband, she was humiliated and beaten for whatever her husband considered to be an infraction, whereas in the world of the university she was expected to think for herself, take responsiblity for her studies, and do original work in a collegial and highly professionalized setting. In this process she came dangerously close, we are told, to losing the integrity of the self which is Professor Martin's interest in employing the connotations of the term soul.

To describe her daughter's experience of alternating between these two very different social worlds requires a language that goes far beyond Douglas's notions of the social body, let alone of social worlds that are relatively low or high on their grid and group characteristics. Professor Martin does not hesitate to describe her daughter's experience as a drama of the soul. Only such a language, it seems to us, can articulate the depths to which social life can impress itself on the innermost recesses of the individual; conversely, discourse about the soul can suggest the resources which an individual must summon to withstand pressures which can literally crush both body and spirit. Many women have indeed died, both physically and spiritually, under the conditions described by Professor Martin. Soul loss, as I will suggest in my essays, is a clear and present danger even in modern societies.

Like Douglas, Bernice Martin knows that ritual encodes what may become the individual's own moral center, but she goes beyond Douglas in pointing to the moral and spiritual tragedy that can ensue from rituals that work all too well. Professor Martin argues that the domestic rituals of the household, and the responsiblity for nurturance and caring which originate there, are so impressed on women in particular that women become defenseless against abuse from men. Not only do these domestic rituals render women defenseless against abuse; they make women prone to feeling responsible and guilty for such abuse. The result is that women tend to sacrifice their integrity in order to respond to appeals for assistance from the very men who are subjecting them to physical and emotional torture. If the demonic is anywhere to be found in modern societies, it is in this corruption of ritual, and not merely in its decadence. Ritual can impress social obligations on the self with sufficient force to crush the soul. Inevitably, then, the most oppressive social systems create a demand for charismatic, that is, magical sources of redemption and release from the weight of duty. It is no wonder, then, that there is such a demand for magical antidotes to the threat of soul-loss: a problem which I take up in my discussion of the seminal work on this subject by Daniel O'Keefe (1983).

The use of moral argument to intimidate, and of physical abuse and social isolation to punish the victim, gain entrance to the soul through the rituals of everyday life. Like Mary Douglas, Bernice Martin also is concerned with social structures and with the way an individual's life moves in and out of them: with "modes of social control" and with the ways in which individuals actually do organize their lives as they participate in a relatively wide range of more or less constraining and limiting contexts (Douglas 1978:16). Professor Martin's story of the social worlds of her daughter would satisfy Mary Douglas's interest in "the combinations of beliefs in all the possible social contexts in which the individual has to operate" (1978, 15). But whereas Douglas is interested in the mixture of actuality and possibility defined by the social map, Professor Martin raises the question of how individuals may extricate themselves from the labyrinth of social control. Not only does she know a labyrinth when she sees one; she knows that there is a minotaur at the center, and that it is capable of consuming the youth of the city.

In seeking to recover professional discourse on the soul, of course, we are not alone. Others have returned to this concept to express the notion that something essential to the individual is endangered in modern societies. In the hands of certain ethnographers, however, selfhood is still being reduced to the merely social. Take, for example, Michael Fischer (1986), who argues that ethnicity is carried like a mystery within the soul; it is a mystery to be brought to the surface through struggle, through the difficult arts of memory, and through the signal effort of lifting the veil of repression that puts one's own ethnicity in the impersonal darkness of the unconscious. His criticism of sociology is exceedingly well taken:

> *ethnicity is something reinvented and reinterpreted in each generation by each individual and . . . it is often something quite puzzling to the individual, something over which he or she lacks control . . .* Insofar as ethnicity is a deeply rooted emotional component of identity, it is often transmitted less through cognitive language and learning (to which sociology has almost entirely restricted itself) than through processes analogous to the dreaming and transference of psychoanalytic encounters. (1986, 195-196; emphasis added)

In reporting on the work of Maxine Hong Kingston, for instance, Fischer (1986, 208ff.) notes that the Chinese have long regarded foreigners as ghosts; in America no less than in the homeland, the world around them was a source of spiritual threat and invasion. In Kingston's reminiscences of her Chinese-American childhood, however, it is Chinatown itself that seems like a corpse, dying, or haunted: the imagery of death having been internalized and related to one's community of origin. For the ethnologist, as we have noted, the core of the individual is incurably social, even when the society in question is moribund. From the Rankian viewpoint, however, Kingston's sensitivity to the moribund aspects of the Chinese community of her origin is better understood as a projection of her own mortality onto the screen of social life; the Chinese community becomes her double: an ideal, a rival for selfhood, and finally a sign of her own mortality.

There are indeed profound ties between social life and the soul, but they may not be what Fischer has in mind: the residues of communal and ethnic life. On the contrary, Susan Nelson points out that the conviction of an inner shamefulness or fault, of sin, is a sign of partial soul-loss. To negate those parts of oneself which seem dangerous or shameful is to collude with one's victimizers in crushing the soul; psychic splitting is not only a cause but a sign of soul-loss. Nelson urges us, therefore, to rethink the doctrine of sin in such a way as to demand, first of all, the truth about social life, and especially about the abuse of children. It is a truth which can account for psychic death. Without it, the doctrine of a fundamental flaw, of sin itself, can like the theory of drives be used to place responsibility for soul-loss on the victim rather than on the victimizer. There is an indictment of the Christian tradition and of the church in Nelson's account, and it is not to be missed.

The soul can also be lost not only in abuse but in acts of reverence and worship. Women who were sexually abused as girls by their fathers may have tended to idealize and revere these same fathers, may have sought to become like them, and may have adopted a male alter ego in order to protect themselves from feelings of powerlessness and rage. Those emotions, that would otherwise be directed at their abusers, are turned toward themselves. Thus these victims have learned to hate their own femininity in the same way as any oppressed group learns self-hatred. Their souls are lost, therefore, both because they idealize their victimizers and loathe themselves. To know this much, it seems to us, is essential if we are to get beyond cardboard cutout images of individuals as reflecting social categories. Women may adopt masculine roles, not only because these roles model power and status, but because their own souls have been violated.

In the same vein, Capps argues that the soul is visceral. His essay in this volume also reminds us of the importance of the body as the scene of the soul's struggle with passion and loss. The battlefield of the soul, metaphorically speaking, is the liver or the spleen: somewhere beyond reach of symbols and social categories. There the soul struggles for embodiment, long before and after the individual's spirit has soared in various encounters with people and places, with society and nature. Not that the soul is immune to the individual's attempt to acquire a self or to transcend his or her limitations. On the contrary, Capps argues, the soul is often held in abeyance, ignored, defeated, or rejected by the individual who becomes transported in various relationships or lost in grandiose imaginings. *It is in the soul, however, that one experiences loss and panic, abandonment and rejection, as well as quietude and the inner certainty of one's own being.*

Capps insists that the soul has a life of its own. The individual's spirit, so carefully nurtured by Christianity, is therefore for Capps almost a sideshow. While the spirit may be the object of pastoral attention and professional advice, it is the soul that determines the individual's possible healing. Only the soul can regenerate itself: Capps's point being that there is more to the individual than priests and pastors, not to mention sociologists and psychologists, ever dreamed of.

This volume, then, parts company with mainstream ethnology at a crucial point. We would agree with an anthropologist like Victor Turner that, deeply rooted in the psyche, there is a "root-paradigm" that governs a person's sense of the sequence, order, duration, and outcome of one's life. We would also agree that, when structured by a society, that root-paradigm is acted out in pilgrimage and festival: in dramas of the soul. No doubt we would agree also that, when individuals seem most caught up in sheer temporizing and negotiating, these generic models for human life may assert themselves and may even call for self-sacrifice.

We would not agree, however, that the individual is—at the core—defenseless against the power of these root-paradigms. Turner's language leaves no room for the autonomy of the soul or for its capacity to fill and move beyond its own inner space:

> the main actors are nevertheless guided by subjective paradigms . . . [that] affect the form, timing, and style of those who bear them. (1976, 158)

For Turner, these root paradigms in the self come from beyond the usual social horizon that limits an individual's sense of what is possible or obligatory, and when they assert themselves it is always the human community that prevails over individuality and the self. Especially in the world of the marketplace, where everything is "up for grabs," subject to negotiation and dealing, and of only limited and temporary value, the timeless requirements of the human race assert themselves. Call them "fate" or "destiny," Turner argues, "this implicit paradigmatic control of human affairs in public arenas, where behavior appears to be freely chosen, resolves at length into a total pattern" (1978, 159).

It is as if, for ethnographers like Turner, Fischer, and Douglas, the individual is simply possessed and enthralled by social structures or, worse yet, by root-paradigms that assert themselves when social controls are weak or lacking. Try as they might to redeem themselves, individuals will only exhibit their enslavement to forces that are beyond their ken and control. How is it, then, that individuals do find within themselves the resources to withstand abuse and to overcome their oppression even by individuals to whom they have given themselves?

In answering this question we can turn to a sociologist like David Martin, who documents the liberation of the soul from the powers that plague it. For Martin the soul "is inwardly tuned and it resonates to an harmonic structure intrinsic to the world of being." It is an inner space, although it can be occupied by others who leave the person with no space of his or her own. Indeed, Martin tells the story of Vera, whose inner space was occupied by her own passions, which threatened to consume her; she was also preoccupied in defending her inner space from ministers and psychiatrists, from her family and from believers who tried to define her, to pronounce on her ills, and to limit her prospects. Lacking an inner space of her own, Vera had to go out in the company of others. Conversely, external spaces seemed inhospitable and threatening since she had no inner dwelling place of her own. Psychoanalysts would call such a loss of soul 'displacement.' For Martin, soul-loss

> is the dethronement and incarceration of that which should be sovereign, the erasure of essential markings, the averting of the face from the summit of being, the atomization of integrity, the deterioration in the realm of spirit of vital 'presence,' and a repulsive occupation by powers or turbulences making for destruction, darkness, and death.

Others besides David Martin have focused on the soul's struggle for its own sovereignty. Victor Turner, for instance, has studied Thomas a Becket's struggles to possess his own soul in spiritual combat with his sovereign, Henry II. Whereas David Martin, however, would see Becket's struggle as fighting against "the dethronement and incarceration of that which should be sovereign," that is, his own soul, Turner argues that Becket's life can only be understood as the slow manifestation of an internalized cultural model, the root-paradigm of martyrdom. Again, whereas Martin finds the soul struggling against "the erasure of essential markings," Turner locates the struggle as being between a cultural root-paradigm (martyrdom) and Henry II for possession of Becket's shifting allegiance and self-identity. For Turner there is nothing remaining to be explained in the individual beyond the workings, however subtle and protracted, of longstanding social and cultural forces. For David Martin, however, there is always the possibility that the individual will obey its own sovereignty.

Turner argues that it was the breakdown of normal communication, of smooth and ritualized patterns of action and decision making, that called forth this root-paradigm in Becket's spirit. At a fateful conference, where "prelates and magnates" lost their usual reserve and became injudicious or even exceedingly dramatic, it was not individuality that emerged in Becket but this root-paradigm of martyrdom that began "to dominate his development from that time forth" (1976, 162). In his contribution to this volume, Martin finds in contemporary Brasil similar cases of spiritual confusion among authoritative voices:

> The old monopolies and sacred canopies collapse in pluralistic confusion and people are caught by this and that wind of the spirit, above all by a Pentecostal wind that is adaptable and capable of combination with other elements, like protection against witches in Nigeria, or shamanism in Korea, or ancient cura divina in Brazil.

But Martin ascribes to Vera, one no less beset by spiritual powers than was Becket, a soul of her own. Turner finds only a "myth of martyrdom," a cultural root-paradigm, slowly asserting its control over Becket, from the time of his installation as Archbishop of Canterbury, through his struggles with Henry II, and the chaotic falling-out of the ecclesiastical authorities with one another over the issue of arch-episcopal authority vis-a-vis the sovereign. David Martin, on the contrary, finds in Brasil no root-paradigms further enhancing their control over the soul of the individual. On the contrary, through the Universal Church, Vera slowly gains the freedom and certainty of an inner space that is not subject to sovereigns either of church or state, of demonic or ecclesiastic origin, but one that is truly her own. As that space becomes more certain, along with her control of it, so does her ability and willingness to make offerings and even sacrifices, but these, we are reminded, are of her own free will:

> People see themselves (or others) as taken over by the potent Enemy and in the ensuing melee they themselves and a supportive human chorus have to call upon the potent Friend to liberate them. The UC is the supportive chorus, shouting out 'burn, burn, burn' as the demons are named and come forth, and dancing or singing at the scenes of victory.

Of course, every form of exorcism or initiation contains within itself a principle of violence (hence the Universal Church's need to fight demonic fires with spiritual fires of their own—'burn, burn, burn'). What varies from one society to the next, or over time in a single community, is whether the rituals of transformation and initiation can turn the individual from a "prey" into a "hunter," (Maurice Bloch 1992). For some the process of initiation is aborted midway; a root-paradigm for transferring the victim into the aggressor fails to come to full flower, perhaps because individuals have wills of their own and may refuse to become aggressors on behalf of the community. Vera, as Martin points out, refused to be preyed upon either by the Assemblies of God or by various practitioners of spiritual cure or of psychiatry; she experienced herself as preyed upon by demons and by religious or medical helpers, all the while exercising a will of her own. Turner, too, points out that Becket, however beleaguered by internalized root paradigms or by his sovereign, refused to carry out the will of King Henry II against the clergy and the courts of the Church.

For Turner, instead of an extraordinary act of will on Becket's part, there was only a man "propelled along this path or passage by certain images and ideas" (1976, 163). For David Martin, Vera is no less beleaguered by "spiritual terrorism," but she finds her own social space and helps to create it by choosing the remedies of the Universal Church and by following its courses. Thus she acquires additional space for her soul by adding to the physical as well as social space that she can occupy. At last the spirits have room to "come out." "They leave her head and stomach and come roaring helplessly into the open air." Nature and society, as it were, are sent packing and leave the soul intact and sovereign in its own sphere.

It would therefore be a mistake to underestimate the power of ritual even in modernizing societies such as Brazil. Indeed, as David

Martin notes, there are strong material forces against which the individual must still seek the sure defense of a spiritual Friend: forces such as the overwhelming power of drugs. What matters is finding an arena for the drama of the loss and recovery of the soul. In that space, the soul finds and creates for itself its own spiritual venue. Martin does not—and need not—evoke the fatal mastery of ethnographers' root-paradigms to name the demons. Indeed, he credits the believers with the capacity "to assign the correct names to the 'operative agencies.'" In the end, one has to choose between the ethnographer, who claims to know these agencies and who therefore calls them by the professional names of grid or root-paradigm, and the individual who claims—perhaps with the help of shamans or a chorus—to know how to name the demons themselves.

What are we therefore to make of a society like the United States that lacks strong root-paradigms, where individuals are asked to leave behind the cultural traditions that have given them support and sustenance? How fight for the sovereignty of the soul against sovereigns that are notable by their absence? How to struggle against animal spirits in a society that is highly rationalized? What can one say of the inner struggles of a soul in an environment which does not exercise strong pressures for conformity or have clear and distinct social categories by which to mark and define individuals in their various capacities? To answer such a question would take more than another volume in this series.

Some would agree with Durkheim that anomie is bad for the soul. Americans would therefore lose their souls because their society itself lacks the images, the communities, the relationships, and the self-understanding that foster the development of the soul. Immigrant communities, to be sure, arrive on these shores with strong traditions, a cultural music, so to speak, for the words by which individuals come to terms with others and with themselves. In the end, however, these traditions dissipate themselves into the rather thin air of American society. No longer able to live according to what one knows or to treasure what one loves, the individual learns the dessicated speech of modern corporations and professions: the language of rationality, of goals and objecives, of procedures and processes. The same process of secularization which, as Bettelheim noted, once deprived Freudian psychoanalysis of spiritual substance when it was translated to American shores now has resulted in a disenchanted and anorexic soul.

Add to this insult to the soul the injury sustained by Americans who have been separated from their homes and who must now face a frontier which itself offers only an empty space in which to expand the self or seek one's fortune. Never has American society been a comfortable or supportive environment for the soul. In an anomic society Americans continue to be wrenched from familiar sur- roundings and to be sent into a world which, like the old frontier, is not only promising but unfamiliar and threatening. To survive in such a world takes a soul with substance: not one deprived of the nourishment of religious belief, of folk traditions, and of enduring ties to people and place. Unfortunately, as I have argued, that spiri- tual substance is no longer administered by rituals and impressed upon the soul.

Are Americans indeed facing a social and cultural vacuum: nothing against which to exercise the sovereignty of their own souls? Or is the United States better conceived as a society which system- atically suppresses and eliminates any individual who lacks the capacity to resist from within his or her own depths? In *Stolen Lightning*, O'Keefe argues that individuals in societies such as the United States are seeking the protection of magic not against an anomic social order but against social pressures that threaten to overwhelm and crush the soul. The prevalence of New Age religios- ity and of a myriad popular therapies attests to the demands for such bulwarks against social pressures. Drawing an analogy between voodoo death and the apathy, depression, despair, and suicide that afflict individuals in American society, O'Keefe finds that individu- als know when they are not wanted and, unless they find magical support for their individuality, their very existence is threatened. His term for what is ailing Americans makes our argument exactly; it is "soul-loss."

However, in his discussion of Updike's character, Rabbit Angstrom, Roger Johnson argues that O'Keefe got it wrong (and by implication, that Durkheim got it right). It is the absence of rela- tionships that anchor and nourish the soul that afflicts Americans like Rabbit: not soul-loss and voodoo-death but death from a worn- out heart. Rabbit is a man who has spent his life 'scoring': selling cars, shooting hoops, and sleeping with women. He dies trying to outscore a younger black man with whom he has been playing bas- ketball. That young man, seeing Rabbit nearly exhausted, tries to call the game a tie; he offers mutual recognition, even praise for Rabbit's shooting, but Rabbit insists on playing out the remaining points and has a heart attack. His heart—like his soul—simply could not get enough nourishment; no wonder that Rabbit had precious little to give to his family and to the women with whom he had slept over a lifetime of scoring. We should note, moreover, that Rabbit died after being excommunicated from his family: a form of voodoo-death, perhaps, although Johnson does not make the comparison. Had there been either a ritual of transformation or sufficiently charismatic sources of support for the soul, would Rabbit have been able to protect himself against the threat of soul-loss? At the very least, the basketball game is a decadent form of ritual. His is not the first society to witness its rituals secularized into spectacles and games as they lose their power to forge and sustain the soul.

Americans—like Rabbit Angstrom—may well be facing the threat of soul-loss because their society crushes or ignores, extrudes or malnourishes them. Under these conditions, however, the individual may be in a better position to see social structures as counterfeit. Indeed, human relationships are largely a matter of 'projections' until and unless there is sufficient mutuality and exchange of feeling that these projections can be replaced by more accurate perceptions of the other and, therefore, of the self. That is precisely McDargh's point in his essay on "Desire, Domination, and the Life and Death of the Soul."

For McDargh the soul—the inner and essential self—can best come into play when there is enough leeway for the self to be somewhat playful. That latitude is provided when children find themselves in the company of others who are able to bring their differences into play without either masking them or merely mirroring back the children's own feelings. The element of difference arouses in children an essential sense of themselves. With that sense they will be able to enter into mutual experiences with others without imagining themselves to be fused in a specious sort of spiritual or emotional communion. In the same way children need to experience the presence of adults as being part of their internal life without having their souls obliterated by too much feeling or sensation. To internalize an adult who is controlling or damaging, invasive or overwhelming is to make friends with the devil, as it were: that is, to open the door to lifelong torment. Neither control or submission but a surrender of the false self and the expression of the true self are necessary for the soul to come alive, according to McDargh. Masochism and sadism, conversely, are the expression of a hunger for knowing and being known that can never be satisfied while one seeks control rather than mutuality, fusion rather than recognition.

What is needed, I would argue, is a morphology of the soul: a map for charting its vicissitudes even in late modern societies. It is crucial that sociologists, anthropologists, and psychologists come to understand the literature on the development of the soul: from the vital energy or protective genius imagined by 'primitive' societies, and from the phantasm or 'free soul' of archaic civilizations, to the 'unitary' soul of classical antiquity. Only such an understanding can ground the range of potential variation of the soul in late modern societies: from individuals who are profoundly open to suggestion and hysteria, on the one hand, to those on the other who experience themselves as possessing a soul in relation to which everything else appears secondary if not actually counterfeit. In the latter category may be those who hold fast to religious or metaphysical convictions, but I would hold open the possibility that a large proportion of modern individuals do not need such reassurances to affirm a soul which emerges from and yet transcends the interaction of nature and society within themselves.

PART I: SOUL-LOSS AND RITUAL

RICHARD K. FENN

1

Soul-Loss in Antiquity

One can lose one's soul in a variety of ways: through being abused and tortured, enslaved and humiliated, or by becoming attached to persons and objects that seem to have a magical or potent presence of their own. To defend the soul against such influences individuals may seek to become like some other person or thing that is filled with a comparable potency. Individuals make psychic compromises with those whom they fear and with those to whom they turn for support; they identify with their enemies and their sources of magical help, and thus lose their souls, as it were, in their efforts to save them. All of these possibilities are considered in some depth in what I consider to be the primary source on the subject of soul-loss, De Martino's *Primitive Magic: The Psychic Powers of Shamans and Sorcerers,* on whose account I will be relying heavily throughout this discussion.

In this discussion we will encounter two quite different sets of assumptions about the deeper reaches of the self. On the one hand are those who feel the soul is a relatively modern invention;

that is, anthropologists who have found the outward and visible signs of the soul in so-called primitive societies are on this view projecting their own Christianized assumptions on to peoples who lack such a notion of their own. A variation of this view suggests that modern societies at least have enshrined the individual as a bundle of legal rights and duties. The person is also a Western product: the focus of cultural expectations that favor the emergence of people who can think for themselves, trust their own perceptions, and make their own decisions about big issues as well as about the details of everyday life. While the "individual" and the "person" may be well institutionalized in Western societies, however, it does not follow that the self is any stronger in the twentieth than in the first century, in "modern" societies than in "primitive" or "traditional" ones.

A second set of assumptions, then, focuses on the ephemeral and vulnerable aspects of selfhood. This is an aspect of personal identity to which the individual subscribes and can be distinguished from the person and the individual as social institutions. Selfhood is a matter of personal identity, and confusion about one's own identity can as well be found in college undergraduates or the middle-aged as among native Americans, in contemporary Western societies as well as among the societies of antiquity. Doubts about the self, however, converge on another, 'deeper' level of self-awareness: a level at which it is possible to speak of psychic death, the death of the ego, or, as I prefer, of soul-loss. Indeed, O'Keefe (1983) argues that soul-loss or psychic death is a widespread phenomenon in American society, regardless of how well established are the more readily visible and sociable aspects of the self. On this view, despite the social supports for individuality, personhood, and self-identity, the inner self is still vulnerable to social pressures, rejection, emptiness, and psychic death. Indeed, along with a spate of books condemning individualism in a variety of forms, there is a growth industry of books on the narcissistic self, the hungry or the depleted self, and on the burdens of rejection and shame.

These reflections on the vulnerability of the self and on soul-loss may seem odd to those convinced that American society is being torn apart by an excess of individualism. There is no doubt that the institution of the Individual is highly developed in Western societies, which have enshrined the individual with an unprecedented panoply of legal protections, cultural honors, social institutions, and everyday practices. O'Keefe (1983, 293) notes that "the Individual with a capital letter is a complex of institutions" which includes laws governing persons and contracts, the rights and duties of citizenship, responsibilities and rewards for production, the prerogatives of conscience and practices for sustaining the self, and individualism as an ideology. There is no doubt that modern societies, at least in the West, justify themselves on the basis of the protections and services that they can provide for the individual; in turn, enlightened individualism justifies the freedom of the individual as a prerequisite for civic responsibility and cultural innovation.

What is good for the "Individual," however, may not be good for the self. That was Durkheim's point in his studies of complex societies and patterns of suicide. An open society requires much of an individual in the way of time and energy, creativity and competition, but promises relatively little in the way of security. Some individuals find the burden of becoming creative, special, or unique very heavy indeed and suffer from being labeled as ordinary. Indeed, it is these pressures on the self that may very well be responsible for high rates of psychosomatic illness, some of it fatal. Society not only weighs heavily on the individual but permeates the self where it leaves various imprints in the form of low self-esteem, hypertension, tachycardia, and other stress-related illnesses of the spirit and the flesh (cf. O'Keefe 1983, 296ff.). Individuals whose selves are literally thus impressed with social expectations are most vulnerable to social judgements. Note the high rates of illness and death following divorce, forced retirements, lay-offs, commitment to nursing homes, and other forms of social rejection. O'Keefe (1983, 296ff.) compares these illnesses to "voodoo deaths." The question, then, is how much the self has flourished or been overwhelmed in modern societies that enshrine the Individual.

The question is central to this book, since it focuses our concern once again on the use of ritual, both personal and societal, to shore up the otherwise empty and fragile ego. In societies that rely heavily on ritual not only to support the ego but to socialize the self, the failure of ritual may have disastrous consequences. For the ego, the failure of ritual may heighten anxiety that time is running out. Debts to those from whom the self has withdrawn emotional credit may fall due; certain passions may demand more immediate satisfaction; the possibilities of making up for lost time may seem even more remote. Individuals may panic at impending disaster, fear that they are coming under the control of alien influences, or feel that they themselves are doomed to wander restlessly as aliens in a land far from their own spiritual homes.

In societies that have sought to gain a monopoly on magic, individuals may turn to popular sources of healing outside the control of the priesthood. In those societies, however, such a choice may be regarded as seditious or even blasphemous. In modern societies, however, where there are many more degrees of freedom for the self, the choice of deviant therapeutics may not be regarded with so much suspicion or be so heavily penalized. Under these conditions individuals may pursue their own salvation without the benefit of clergy or other, more secular priesthoods, without being accused of negligence in making the appropriate sacrifices. Nonetheless, as O'Keefe and others have pointed out, the self even in modern societies remains precarious, and the ego is still vulnerable to potent suggestion, since all egos are born both empty and hungry, live for many years on borrowed or stolen emotional credit, and issue promises to pay that can eventually bankrupt the self. Modern societies are better at recycling emotional debts than at canceling them, unlike more traditional societies that have ritualized means for the forgiveness of obligations both to the living and the dead.

The question I have raised about the relative security of the ego in modern, as compared with traditional societies, goes to the heart of a debate on how to understand the self in societies that are more highly ritualized and less structurally differentiated than our own. The question is sometimes posed in terms of "the fate of the soul." Some have argued that the members of primitive societies indeed have souls, and that individuals in modern societies, on the other hand, may be like Weber's specialists without a heart, technicians without a soul, with weak, impoverished, and empty egos. Others, however, have argued the reverse proposition; it is the member of a traditional society that lacks anything as substantive as a soul. Such a person possesses a sense of self so fleeting and precarious that it can easily be destroyed by imposing presences or overwhelming passions. I would argue that the ego or innermost self even in modern societies is dangerously close to extinction even when it is shored up by the institution of the Individual. As O'Keefe puts it:

> The ego is easily invaded and taken over from outside. It is easily hypnotized, stolen, fascinated, entranced. And like magic itself, ego is permeated with the feeling that it has constructed itself out of crimes—the destruction of the father buried in the Oedipal repression, the abandonment of loved objects, the release of the death instinct to strengthen itself.

> Ego is a magician riding wild horses, doing a balancing
> act, making itself out of things it throws away, full of conflict
> and increasingly complicated and barely adequate in focusing
> the action of the self. (O'Keefe 1983, 283-284)

Thus the ego is always running out of time even in modern societies,
where the individual is buttressed by such rituals as "elocution
lessons, assertiveness lessons, dancing lessons, swimming lessons or
sex therapy lessons . . . work party rituals, sex party rituals, play
rituals" (O'Keefe 1983, 291).

Are there no differences, then, between traditional and modern
societies where the innermost self is concerned? On the face of it, it
would seem that the soul was precarious in traditional societies which
lacked the institution of the Individual. In this regard, O'Keefe seems to
agree with De Martino, who has most eloquently argued that soul-loss
is a danger far more serious among "primitives" than among "moderns." On the other hand, O'Keefe's own discussion of the fragility of
the ego and the prevalence of voodoo deaths among the civilized suggests that the innermost self, the soul, is as precarious among moderns
as among primitives. I am arguing that traditional, even primitive societies have forged, fashioned, and buttressed the soul with potent rituals,
whereas I question the adequacy of contemporary rituals for protecting
the fragile soul. Modern rites seem more like games or spectacles: far
less impressive and potent than the rituals which strengthened and
tried the souls of Greek soldiers or Jewish pilgrims in antiquity. Before
we can enter into the discussion of antiquity, however, and long before
we can proceed with an inquiry into the fate of the soul in complex,
contemporary social systems, we need to have more clarity regarding
the terms for the soul and the meaning of "soul-loss." It is to that subject that the remainder of this chapter is devoted.

In arguing that the innermost self was better off in antiquity, I
am clearly rejecting the assumption that the soul was more vulnerable
prior to modernity because there was no institution of the Individual
to buffer the soul from social pressures. On the face of it, the innermost self may have been in far more danger in, say, Palestine of the
first century than it is in contemporary American society. Indeed,
what Bourdieu calls 'symbolic violence' was more direct and personal
in antiquity, and individuals' souls were at stake in the way they
responded to challenges to their honor. The same sort of symbolic
violence created debts and obligations that had to be "satisfied."[1]

Not only was the soul put in bondage to such external challenges, but individuals, in the case of those who had been made

slaves, were subject to cruel measures aimed at the murder of the soul; I will return to this subject shortly. Even those who were not enslaved or subject to direct challenges to their honor, however, were faced by many powerful and attractive symbols: gods and goddesses, powerful politicians and military heroes, wandering prophets and hermits, evanescent but potent demons and spirits, and the wealth and power of the Roman Empire itself. Finally, the severity of the times produced conditions that are known to make the soul begin to disintegrate: loneliness and fatigue, hunger and thirst, exile and imprisonment. It was hard enough to survive under conditions of famine and drought, economic hardship and debt crises, the expropriation of land and the selling of one's family members into slavery to redeem debts; it was even harder to overcome the threats posed by conquest and banditry, sedition and guerilla war, or mass murder and collective punishment.

As a means for the creation and formation of a community, it was necessary for ritual to impress upon the individual the society's temporal order. Ritual worked this wonder, I would argue, through the intensification of the meaning and experience of time. In that intensification individuals were moved to experience their own critical moments as though they were also decisive for the community or society in which they lived. They were also taken from a passive experience of the inevitable approach and fatal passage of time into a more active and dynamic, however dangerous, passage of their own. In this way the larger society forged an individual, as it were, in the crucible of ritual: an individual who could be relied upon to be present in time, on time, in the face of death, and to take his or her place in the society's own temporal and social order as a member of a generation. Indeed, the rituals of Greek and Jewish antiquity can be seen as collective dramas in which the soul was both risked and saved.

De Martino emphasizes that, in societies which we would regard as traditional or even primitive, these dramas may be enacted by individual holy men and women, but the community as a whole takes the journey into heaven or hell. In the struggle with evil spirits and demons, in the journeys of the soul through alien lands or wilderness, in the soul's exposure to elements and wild beasts, the community as a whole participates in—and in the end triumphs over—the forces of chaos and evil:

> In this sense the sorcerer becomes a kind of *magical Christ*, the mediator for the whole community, through whom the

'being here' may be redeemed from the danger of not being here. It is a cultural redemption in the sense that the individual experiences connected to the magic existential drama do not remain isolated and without inter-relation, but are moulded into a tradition and, as such, form the ideological and institutional expressions which will be the starting-point of new individual experiences; through these, the dangers, audacities, failures, and victories which characterize the magic world shall arrange themselves and unfold in their own unique way. (De Martino 1988, 90)

The soul was therefore part of a drama in which the entire community was at stake: a cultural achievement that survives in the notion of a 'cloud of witnesses' comprising both the living and the dead.

A community of spiritual presences was able not only to shore up the soul but to test and to torment it. For instance, demons and ghosts were a pervasive threat to the innermost self, against whose influences individuals often turned for help to shamans and sorcerers. There is evidence in such writings as the Testament of Solomon that popular religion found Solomon a veteran shaman and sorcerer: one who could name and control the demons and use them to build a temple without employing any manual labor whatsoever. That Jesus also was believed to have claimed that he could build a temple without hands, and was believed like a son of Solomon to have command over the demons, is ample evidence for magic in popular religiosity. The point here, however, is that even Jesus's use of exorcism was a communal act in which his followers could experience their own redemption from the forces that would otherwise crush the soul of the people. As De Martino puts it:

The fact that the sorcerer is able to *create* the spell, intentionally, and that another person can *un-do* it, makes the existential magic drama a kind of struggle-one that will be won by the stronger presence. Spell-binding and exorcism, taken as historic institutions, as a collection of forms, experiences, practices and counter-practices that have been consolidated by tradition, drag the entire community into the struggle—an enforced participation." (1988, 100)

I dwell on this point in part because so much of the literature on magic has relegated it to the realm of the individualistic manipulation of divine or supernatural powers, as opposed to religion which is presumed to be collective and freed from the pragmatic, instrumental, and individualistic aspects of popular devotion. The drama of the redemption of the soul from slavery to alien forces, then, was *both magical and corporate,* no matter whether it was only one person's liberation that was principally effected.

The soul was indeed the ground over which religious movements and the central institutions of the household and of the state fought for spiritual and legal possession of the individual. The point needs to be made, if only because there is a certain premature celebration of the achievements of the West in both guaranteeing the status and rights of the individual and in providing cultural anchors for the self. O'Keefe, following De Martino on this point, provides an unusually clear example of the assumption that the battle for the soul was won in the West:

> Our Christian civilization assumes a soul; it is based on centuries of Christian philosophy, institutions, legal guarantees, the reward of a long struggle. In the magic world of the primitive, soul is not guaranteed, but must be fought for in heroic struggle. (1983, 311)

The fragility of the soul in antiquity was heightened, I would argue, not only by the failure of ritual but by its successes. Rituals attempt to model the magic by which individuals buy time, renew their lease on time, or seek to restore a sense of primordial timelessness. In so doing, however, they add a new set of social obligations to the psychic ones which individuals incur through their own magical thinking. Rituals not only confer on individuals a new dignity, mark a milestone in the lifecycle, avert disasters, or claim to incorporate the individual in a society transcending time and space. They also confer a fortified self-awareness and a new set of obligations to be discharged over time. Soldiers have to be made ready to enter into battle. Men and women have to leave behind their single estate and their families in order to marry. The young have to leave youth behind in order to be transformed into adults, but the young also returned to their communities wearing masks or brandishing spears. In Jerusalem prior to the civil war in the first century, the presence of daggers under familiar cloaks at Passover meant that the angel of death was not passing over the city but had entered its gates. Those who had been initiated into adulthood returned through the gates not as hunters and warriors but to prey upon their fellow citizens. Also returning through those gates were free spirits who had been in the desert envisaging the destruction of the walls of Jerusalem and the end of its days. The dying have to be ushered into the land of the dead lest they trouble the living, yet they must return on demand when the needs of the living require their presence. What is required is a theory which spells out the conditions under which ritual both frees and yet also binds the soul.

Moreover, under certain social conditions, ritualized transformations may not have been complete. Soldiers, for instance, could panic and flee, or they could lose their heads and engage in indiscriminate killing of friend as well as enemy. Rites of initiation or enthronement could turn into fratricidal killing, as indeed they still do in some parts of the contemporary world. The citizen could become an industrious bee or domesticated drone, but bees also are known to escape their hives and set up societies of their own. Some citizens might never become bee-like, but might regress to the flight of the moth or the erratic and clinging habits of the bat (Bettini 1991). The polis required an individual whose soul could be counted and counted upon, as opposed to the more unpredictable and evanescent soul of the individual whose transformations have not been subsumed within the larger society's temporal order. What is needed, then, is a theory of rituals which also accounts for the conditions under which rituals succeed and when they are likely to fail to forge and sustain the soul.

Such a theory would account for the various ways in which the dialectical relationship between individual and society can be mediated by ritual. The unreconstructed, 'free' soul was a danger to the polis. The tendency of that soul to move freely in and out of the present into other times (and therefore other places), enabled the individual to inhabit several times while apparently remaining in one place. This capacity for spiritual journeying through time had to be turned to useful social purpose. Ritual enabled the larger society to present itself to the individual as a community in which one could be present to others in the past and the future: a community in which past and future generations were still present and could be accounted for. The polis, whether Athens or Jerusalem, presented itself in liturgy as a temporal model for a soul reliable, industrious, and accountable.

An adequate theory would also account for the ways in which rituals defeat themselves by their own successes. The more civic duty is impressed by ritual on the individual, the more demand there is for magic, and especially for witchcraft, to defend the fledgling soul. Pilgrimage might begin as a form of liberation from the mundane and the domestic, a time for putting industry and ordinary duty aside, but it ended at the temple, where sacrifices and tribute had to be made to a society that claimed to subsume all times into its own transcendent order. The charisma of the pilgrim is initially a defense against the weight of social obligations; the pilgrim is at first exempt from mundane obligations in order to obey a higher calling. Nonetheless pilgrimage ends in sacrifice and the renewal of obligation. Therefore note the dialectical tension between ritual and charisma, mediated by religion.

The dialectic of religion and magic or charisma appears in the fact that pilgrimage is both a religious institution and a personal project. The institution of pilgrimage creates a social space for the self to walk in: a time for the self to emerge in the encounter with other selves who were also separated from their usual forms of social support and self-definition. Few knew anyone's origins on a pilgrimage; the person was alone in the face of others along a way filled with unique perils and opportunities. Pilgrimage offered a larger gap in the social structure through which the self could emerge: a space far larger than the narrow openings offered by the temple itself for those who had passed the tests for eligibility and purity. The temple cult allowed partial entry and a limited vision of god, whereas pilgrimage offered a wider vision without guarantees that one would enter into a new and more sacred status. In the dialectic between pure magical self-assertion and the weight of social obligation, ritual forges a compromise that exhibits and yet manages the ambivalent relationship between self and society. Pilgrimage was just such a compromise, since it balanced the will of the individual with social duty. The end result is to enable the magical processes of the mind to be less antisocial, but in this compromise the self is partially defeated. Thus rituals can not resolve but only sublimate the desire for a self unconstrained by traditional obligations or by the reality-principle. The desire for such liberation was often expressed, of course, in a demand for charismatic leadership. "Historically," O'Keefe reminds us, "magic bought time for the Individual to emerge and develop more lasting defenses for the self." One of these defenses was the notion of the soul.

Rituals tend to fail, I would suggest, the more one enters into a range of personal experience for which there are few cultural maps; there is also a danger to the self in expanding personal experience without the limits and the comfort of a substantial human 'other' in whose presence one can come to terms with one's own being. In psychoanalytic terms, the ego is an expansive but also a hollow space seeking to fill itself from what ever lies to hand. Hence the ego stuffs itself with the powers and attributes of fathers and mothers, siblings and rivals, from an early age. These attributes interpreted to others may be largely symbolic; hence the ego becomes stuffed with images of itself that range from the grandiose to the despicable, from the benign to the diabolic. In the absence of more or less substantial 'others' with whom to interact, the ego can become consumed by its own experience as it tries to satisfy its longings with the symbolic objects of its own passions.

In the end the question is whether rituals will not only provide the substantial other on whom the hungry ego can feed, but whether ritual will also enable the ego to pay its emotional debts. Rituals not only create emotional obligations, they also help to liquidate them. As I have noted, the ego builds itself up at the expense of others and accumulates enormous debts not only to the world but to the emotions it has promised to satisfy. These debts may be compared with promissory notes; they are aspects of the self that must be satisfied over time. Lying near the core of the self, they are referred to in psychoanalytic terms as the superego or the ego-ideal. The ego is thus mortgaged to people and to projections or parts of the self; that is one reason why the ego is always running out of time. Its meter, as it were, is always running.

I would argue that when rituals fail to enable individuals to discharge their psychic debts, the individual will experience time as being weighted with unfulfilled obligation. The child who steals or borrows the parents' lightning or a sibling's thunder understandably knows that a time is coming when it must pay back what has been taken. The ego's dread of such a day of reckoning may take the form of an acute sense of obligation to pay back the gift of life, as if one's life is not rightfully one's own. To make such a payment, however, is to forfeit one's own existence. The ego therefore creates a way of giving and yet withholding, of paying and at the same time taking back in order to work out a compromise with its creditors. The ego temporizes, and the soul is therefore placed in a sort of limbo.

As an emergent property of the individual's self-awareness, the psyche or soul becomes a potential to be realized and redeemed in and through time that is heavy with the weight of unpaid social and emotional debts. That is why Freud noticed the tendency of the obsessive to do and undo, to repeat over and over again the ritual of taking and giving back, time and time again. These strategies are a way of buying time, and they resemble, as Freud noted, the rituals by which religious communities have kept themselves alive while staving off a day of reckoning.

To avoid the date at which one's credit expires, as Rank observed, the ego will settle for a compromised and diminished existence. The ego that makes partial payments avoids running out of time, but in the mean time the ego cannot fully call its psyche its own. Neither giving up the past or fully entering the future, the ego temporizes. In developing its own resources out of what rightfully belongs to others, the ego may feel as if time is running out, as if a dreaded day is coming, and as if one will be called upon to have something to show for the time that has been spent. Awake, the self may become especially scrupulous about paying back debts and about productivity; in sleep the self may dream about being unprepared to pass an examination and having nothing to show for the time that has elapsed during the school year or semester. It is a very common dream indeed. I take it that the dream indicates an emerging self-awareness of the self as being untested and possibly fraudulent. At the very least, the self that is overly scrupulous about time indicates a psyche or soul that has not yet been fully possessed.

The sense that a day of reckoning is coming may also derive from the withdrawal of affection and emotional investment from others. Indeed, it is a commonplace of psychoanalysis that the ego does take back the emotions and credit with which it has endowed others, if only to make the self feel more capable of satisfying its own longings. The drive for self-esteem may therefore also produce a sense of emotional obligation to those from whom affection has been withdrawn: a foreboding that there will come a time when that debt also has to be repaid. Until that day comes, of course, the innermost self is mortgaged, as it were, to others for an indefinite period of time.

On the other hand, at the core of the self we can also find something like a river or a reservoir. Like any river, it can swell up and flood its banks, leaving residues, debris, and destruction in its wake but also opening up new channels. This is one way of understanding what Freud meant by Eros: a powerful passion that indeed sweeps away obstacles that lie in its path as it seeks new outlets. Under the pressure also of these longings, the ego can feel that time is running out.

As unsatisfied longings press against the levees of the self but fail to find outlets, the ego may feel as if it has somehow missed an important appointment or an opening. In the waking hours, the individual may become especially scrupulous about keeping appointments or concerned not to miss an opportunity. During sleep, however, the individual may dream about being late for the scheduled departure of a train, perhaps, or of a plane. The fear of 'missing the boat' comes partly from the failure to catch the tide of emotion when it begins to flood. The ego can therefore require itself to keep imaginary but serious appointments: actions to be undertaken after serious preparation and exactly on time. Such rites, whether performed in secret or in the open, ensure that the ego will not fail to make important connections and will not miss crucial opportunities. In this way the self is deceived into believing that it has satisfied its obligations to desire.

Precisely because it is vulnerable to passions and longings, it is easier for the ego to imagine that it is being threatened by outside influences. It is others who are greedy and malignant because they are leading a blighted existence: the ghost of someone who has died prematurely, perhaps, or someone still alive who has been cheated of his or her satisfactions in life. The bereaved, the spirits of the dead, and individuals living on the margins of a community and enjoying only a few of its benefits are typically thought to be dangerous and grasping. That is why a vast range of rituals has been developed to fill the need to satisfy such longings: for example, gifts, memorials, food for the dead to eat, flowers at shrines, and food sacrificed for the gods at harvest time. Important days and seasons are turned into a fetish for unfilled desire.

In this effort individuals are often aided and abetted by their communities, which have a common interest in controlling the passions and limiting the consumption of their members. Many traditional societies have ritualized defenses against strangers who may arouse longings for consumption and other forms of prohibited satisfaction, just as many societies also develop ways to control the sexuality and longings of their own members. In ritual, societies can act as if the dangers to their continuity are external or at least can be externalized; conversely, the same rituals can suggest that only one's own community provides the sources of true satisfaction at the time prescribed.

The fact that the ego borrows so heavily from outside sources makes one particularly open to suggestion and vulnerable to being possessed. As I have suggested, the ego remains heavily indebted to those from whom it has taken sustenance or whose powers it has stolen. Once these sources thus become internal to the self, they keep the ego under pressure to prove itself and to have something to show for the time it has spent. Despite the repeated attempts to recycle these obligations over time through various rituals, the ego still faces the danger of being taken over by its creditors, that is, possessed or, more exactly, repossessed. That is why it is easier for the ego to imagine that these powerful presences are external. Demons, avenging angels, and dissatisfied ancestors are easier to fend off and placate than a spirit that has taken up residence in one's own soul. That is why there is an element of voodoo in every ritual that attempts to satisfy the presumed greed of the dead, of the spirits, and of the gods. Feed them, as it were, and they will go away at least for a time.

The sense that one is living on borrowed powers means that one is living on borrowed time. A day will therefore come when one is tested, and on that day it may appear that one is in fact a fraud with no rightful claim to one's honors. In its efforts to avert a day of reckoning with the sources of its psychic strength, to avoid a day of trial, moreover, the self is sometimes aided by a society's own rituals for averting various disasters.

When the ego withdraws its affection or emotional investment from a person, however, and returns that love to itself, it faces a more difficult day of reckoning. As I have suggested, withdrawal is seldom wholly complete. Like a spurned lover, the other becomes a part of oneself with a right to make demands and to reclaim certain satisfactions. It is the soul that still incorporates those no longer loved who has the heaviest debt to pay and stands in the greatest need of purification. Where voodoo has failed to ward off a day of reckoning, and where other rituals have failed to strengthen the soul for a day of testing, there is still recourse to exorcism to expunge unwanted presences from the ego.

It is not enough, of course, to ward off, temporize with, or seek to eliminate such presences from the innermost self. Within the unconscious there flow rivers of desire that continually press upon the banks of the ego. As I have suggested, passions continually threaten to tear down the levees that have been erected to keep desire within certain channels. In this situation the ego faces what is essentially a no-win situation. If the ego allows itself to be displaced by passion, it literally is in danger of psychic death. On the other hand, the ego may fail to satisfy these desires simply because they are unrealistic. In either event, the ego is running out of time, either because it is about to be pushed aside by desires or because it must frustrate them. Under pressure from the reality-principle the ego may experience itself as too late to keep an important appointment or make a connection; that is, it misses the boat.

Shamans and priests may provide individuals with rites that offer enough satisfaction to ward off the threat of being overwhelmed by desire. A person on the verge of being swamped by desire or rage, fear or longing, can thus go into prescribed ecstasies or trances and may be temporarily flooded or suffused with libido. The ego remains in sufficient control, however, to terminate the ecstasy or the trance after a sufficient (and proper) time. Indeed, the trance is a form of symbolic action that is far more creative than mere voodoo or exorcism. In ecstasy there are no sacrifices to make, debts to pay, presences to ward off, or tormenting inner spirits to be exorcised from the self. However, the ego also knows that such a trance-state is dangerous, and must only be temporary lest one fail to make the journey back. Societies with an investment in controlling the energy and attention of their members may regularize such periods of immersion into temporary timelessness; indeed rituals of immersion in water may simulate a return to the undifferentiated state of union with the infant's first matrix. Such rituals also serve the purpose of initiating the individual into a new period of life with its particular duties.

Baptism, for instance, clearly has aspects of voodoo and exorcism; evil is warded off, and the individual renounces the power of Satan. The ritual allows the individual to feel that he or she has been restored to the time of origins, that is, born again. As original sin is removed, the individual begins again with the innocence of Eden before history, time, and sin had separated the self from God. In thus making up for lost time, societal rituals seek to monopolize the means of salvation from evil and death in order to ensure that their members will consent to certain duties and make their sacrifices of the mind, the heart, and of the body.

The ego is thus in a no-win situation. The ego, as I have noted, is perennially threatened with collapse or death and needs to borrow sustenance and power from outside sources. The ego's attempts to buy time, however, create new duties that must be discharged over time. The same dilemma applies to the ego's attempt to make up for lost time by restoring a primordial world of timelessness. That very effort to recover the timeless matrix of infancy, however, threatens the ego with death, since the ego exists only in the act of separation from that very matrix. That is why Freud eventually found it necessary to relate the pleasure principle to the putative death instinct.

It is of crucial importance not only to the social system but to the individual to regulate this romance with death. To that end societies create times at which it is permissible or even obligatory for the self to imagine itself restored in an unmediated relationship not only with other human beings but with nature. The Sabbath is one such institution in which the individual is enjoined from engaging in any of the activities that normally signify a bounded self in competition with others for scarce resources. Indeed, the creation of the Sabbath is an instance of making up for lost time, but it clearly has a beginning and an end in accordance with the reality-principle. That is why it must be repeated as an antidote to the temporal panic of the individual faced with the abyss that separates the self from its original matrix. The failure of an institution such as the Sabbath, I would suggest, might well initiate a temporal panic that could result in the paralysis or death of the ego or in hysterical aggression and flight.

NOTE

1. Scott Lash, *Sociology of Postmodernism*, pp. 247-248, 254-258.

REFERENCES

De Martino, Ernesto. 1988. *Primitive Magic: The Psychic Powers of Shamans and Sorcerers*. Prism Press, Dorset, England.

Rank, Otto. 1950. *The Psychology of the Soul*. Philadelphia: University of Pennsylvania Press.

———. 1971. *The Double: A Psychoanalytic Study*. Chapel Hill, NC: University of North Carolina Press.

2

Bedeviled

Prior to the discussion and presentation of documentary testimony, it helps to indicate how 'soul' and 'soul-loss' are being identified and understood. In doing so it is not necessary to make assumptions about the real existence or otherwise of souls. They exist phenomenologically by being talked about in the context of the life of the spirit, not in the sense that fairies might be said to exist by being talked about, but as one might conversationally locate an 'outpouring of soul' in Mozart's C minor Mass. This outpouring is, of course, a semi-secularized variant of the idea of soul, and the point of making the reference is to distinguish all kinds of 'markings' considered as an uncovering of inwardness, from suppositions about entities and sprites like fairies or hobgoblins.

Most talk about soul implies that soul is (with or without definite article) the essential or animating element of any human being, and the spiritual quiddity, characterized ideally by reason and integrity and wholeness considered together. Soul is inwardly tuned and it resonates to an harmonic structure intrinsic to the world of being. By being turned as a whole and resonating to a vaster horizon of perfection it is both itself and more than itself, unique but having commerce with the One. By contrast 'self' is the mere fact of identity, generated linguistically and grammatically by the apodictic nature of recollection, reflection and reflexivity. It is the usual standard experiencing subject manifested over time.

From all the above it would seem that soul-loss is the dethronement and incarceration of that which should be sovereign, the erasure of essential markings, the averting of the face from the summit of being, the atomization of integrity, the deterioration in the realm of spirit of vital 'presence,' and a repulsive occupation by powers or turbulences making for destruction, darkness, and death. This last-named aspect of soul-loss is very prominent in the testimonies utilized here, and can be reversed by recourse to the higher powers. Perhaps one has to add that turbulence and occupation can to some extent manifest themselves on the surface: the inner chambers are not altogether violated by outward negativity and dissolution. This paradox is paralleled by others: soul is immortal but open to destruction, manifest yet hidden, unique but sharing the same perfection.

The two interviews presented and discussed here were conducted by our research associate Paul Freston (P), the one with Vera on his own, and the one with Wander with my wife and myself present. The place is Campinas, Sâo Paulo, Brazil; the time 1991-92. Vera belongs to the Universal Church of the Kingdom of God (UC) and Wander to the God is Love Church (GL), both of which offer 'cura divina,' combining exorcism and healing. These churches subsume—and attack—the spiritism of Brazil, and they also subsume and rival classical Pentecostalism. They draw converts from the spiritist and classical Pentecostal faiths, as well as elsewhere, and have their greatest success among the very poor, more particularly the black poor. Vera and Wander have been attracted to cura divina in preference to the relative sobrieties of the Assemblies of God (AG). However, as will be seen from the texts, the GL Church requires what is called a 'heavy' doctrine in terms of restrictive moral practices while the UC begins with an easy yoke before tightening up.

The religious scene in contemporary Brazil is replete with alternatives each in spirited competition: Catholicism—more or less Roman and proper, syncretic Catholicism—more or less traditional, Catholicism—more or less charismatic, Catholicism—more or less liberationist, Spiritism—more or less Afro-Brazilian (and whitening and blackening by turns), and Evangelical Protestantism, mostly

Pentecostal of some variety or other. Amongst these competitors the Pentecostals are probably the most successful. They are the principal option taken by the poor, along with Spiritism, and they probably outnumber liberationists by ten to one.

It is important to see these Pentecostal movements not as archaic intrusions from a bygone world or as curious exotica somewhere over *there*, but as a major and massive response to the megacity and to urbanization the world over. The old monopolies and sacred canopies collapse in pluralistic confusion and people are caught by this and that wind of the spirit, above all by a Pentecostal wind which is adaptable and capable of combination with other elements, like protection against witches in Nigeria, or shamanism in Korea, or ancient cura divina in Brazil. The movements of the spirit deal with diabolically induced loss of soul and disablement of body *together*, holistically, through collective action, by prayer and fasting on the New Testament model. Most of these movements are not only responses to modernization but themselves self-consciously modernizing, shifting whole groups from hopelessness to empowerment, from a sense of being acted *upon* to the control of free social space and the creation of rudimentary social security.

What is particularly interesting in the Brazilian context is the way Pentecostalism adapts to different layers of Brazilian society. The AG, which is the oldest and largest group with a constituency of about ten million, is most effective among the respectable poor. Indeed, it is the AG which helps make them respectable and enables them to raise their sights into the lower middle class. However, some of those who reach the lower middle class devise—and encounter—a free-floating charismatic style less legalistic and less authoritative in approach, and they jostle with other charismatic evangelicals expanding very rapidly within the huge nascent white collar class. That constitutes the competition *above* the normal social milieu of the AG and it is very recent. But there is also a competition below the normal social milieu of the AG coming from the groups practicing cura divina, in particular the GL Church emerging in the sixties and the UC emerging in the seventies. These have expanded with a speed which bears comparison with the amazing explosion of shamanistic Pentecostalism in Korea (The Christian churches in Korea and Brazil have achieved what they always purported to desire: an indigenous Christianity within the terms of the local culture. They are, of course, less than pleased with the results).

Cura divina is frequently to be found in liaison with a prosperity gospel, which some critics identify as a North American import but which is, in fact, indigenous to the black faiths underlying Catholicism, and exhibits a general tendency among impoverished third world peoples to create and to prefer faiths which offer some goods. How can things get better in *every* way? The UC in particular offers goods, but to some extent does so by short-cutting the sober 'blessings' achieved by the discipline of the AG. It is both more modern and more ancient than the AG, modern in its rather 'sharp' self-presentation and in a style of building and service that owes a lot to discos and television, ancient in the pursuit of health and wealth by the expulsion of malignant and obstructive demons. It is controversial in many ways, on account of acquisitions in radio and television and because it sometimes uses an antinomian rhetoric in offering open acceptance to all and sundry, but above all because it expels specifically Afro-Brazilian deities in dramatic confrontations labeled 'wars of the gods' by a hostile press and intelligentsia. The trouble is that the intelligentsias in Brazil and Korea are becoming well disposed to shamanism as a 'pure' cultural resource for the people, but the people themselves often disagree. The most obvious feature of this controversy is the huge surplus of misinformation and disinformation over mere inquiry. If evangelicals in general are 'everywhere spoken against' in the prestige press, the cura divina groups are doubly so.

There is an important further difference here which can be put in terms of a rather bumpy continuum running from suffering accepted to suffering rejected. In the world of everyday catholic existence, the goddess of fortune rules, and one may circumvent ill-fortune by recourse to the Virgin and the Saints. Suffering is part of the fated disposition of things. In the AG one may, by God's grace and healing and by personal discipline and hope, achieve some betterment, seen by believers as blessings. But clearly the world is still resistant. In the various movements of Pentecostal cura divina, however, all suffering in health and in wealth is seen as contrary to the divine intention and it can be engaged across the *board* by spiritual warfare. These differences between the Pentecostal faiths connect with varied responses to medicine. Of course, even devotees of cura divina attend doctors, but they will seek spiritual assistance to each and every exigency or problem. The AG however, include the availability of a doctor as part of providential assistance and will simultaneously pay for a member's operation and pray for his recovery.

The object of our research was to explore evangelical life worlds in Brazil and Chile, from the point of view of 'betterment,' in particular economic betterment. That involved a broad contrast between Catholic and Evangelical life worlds but more specifically it involved gradations in styles of betterment which run through the classic discipline and blessings of the AG to the free-floating 'close spiritual encounters' and charismatic spiritual therapies of the new middle class and also to the search for 'goods' (in the widest sense) among the impoverished followers of cura divina. The aim of the research as we devised it was to elicit the interplay of material, spiritual and bodily betterment in everyday life through conversion and change of life. People live in universes, not discrete orders of being, material, corporeal, and spiritual. For complicated methodological reasons control groups were rejected as useless and the research concentrated on narratives, that is on life-stories which were inevitably also testimonies. We elicited testimonies reconstructing changes of life. The texts presented here are memories and reconstructions offered as 'testimony' or witness in response to probes by researchers interested in all the interlinked dimensions of 'betterment' and wanting to know how faith and hope deliver 'the goods.' The texts are, of course, fragments of a much wider whole. Vast areas are effaced or partially effaced by the specific thrust of our concern, so that one often has to engage in imaginative guesswork.

The relevance of these texts to the theme of soul-loss is precisely in the phenomenon of diabolical possession, which here means those things which 'assault and hurt the soul' through the ills of the body and through capsizing the frail barque of moral responsibility and reason. As will be seen, it is difficult to break the phenomenon down into its elements precisely because this is an animated spirit-filled world of dreams, visions, malignant visitations and beneficent leadings, which resists western divisions into body and spirit, or into the natural and the spiritual. People see themselves (or others) as taken over by the potent Enemy and in the ensuing melee they themselves and a supportive human chorus have to call upon the potent Friend to liberate them. The UC is the supportive chorus, shouting out 'burn, burn, burn' as the demons are named and come forth, and dancing or singing at the scenes of victory. Victory or liberation may be achieved spontaneously or in a series of engagements or else through attendance at 'correntes' held for seven weeks on a given day of the week, which vary according to the malady. The word correntes means 'chains' because through regular attendance the lost and imprisoned souls are found and unbound. Here then is the witness of Vera to her liberation through the UC:

V: I've been in the UC for four years. When I arrived, my life was totally destroyed. I was considered practically crazy. I'd even been to a psychiatrist. There seemed to be no hope. I had a very strong headache at the top of my head and I was very nervous. I suffered from so much fear that I didn't even go out on my own. For about ten years I didn't go out on my own. I couldn't even be alone at home. I used to see shapes and hear voices. I was totally disturbed. I'm twenty-nine years old.

P: So you were like that from fifteen to twenty-five?

V: Yes. As a child I was already very nervous, agitated, disturbed. But this began at twenty. At nineteen, when I got married. That was when it got more serious. But even when I was single I had a lot of fear. But I still used to go out on my own. Then I got married and I had practically ten years' suffering. Because even when I was in the UC it wasn't easy to get free. I took a long time, practically three years and seven months. My total liberation from everything occurred just last August.

P: How did you come to the conclusion that finally you were totally liberated?

V: When I first came to the UC I had strong headaches. That was when I went to the psychiatrist, to the neurologist, I did electros on my head. X-rays, the lot. The psychiatrist said there was nothing wrong with me, that I was a normal woman, he even said "I can't give you any medicine." But I was already taking sedatives that a neurologist had prescribed for me. When I left he told my sister, "she should be interned in a clinic. There's no solution to her case."

P: Were you interned?

V: No. I was too afraid and I asked my family not to intern me. Instead of getting better I'd get worse . . . and I couldn't sleep. I went almost two years without sleeping properly. My family took me to several different places, including several evangelical churches, and I couldn't find a solution anywhere. Only in the UC.

P: How was your contact with the UC?

V: Through television. I used to get up at night because I couldn't sleep (I used to live in a little house at the back of my mother's yard), and I'd walk about the house with that horrible headache. It was as if my brains were burning. I'd put my hands on my head and walk around the house in the yard . . . Sometimes I felt like screaming or throwing something or attacking someone. Or hitting my head on the wall. I suffered so much, it was horrible. So one morning, at about 6 o'clock, I turned the television on. My sister had already been to all sorts of places with me, and I said to her, "I want to go to São Paulo." Because we were living in Brasilia and they didn't have a UC there at that time. And that was when they said, "Now she's really gone mad, she wants to go to São Paulo just to go to a church." But when I turned the television on and saw the pastor talking, it was Pastor Paulo Roberto, it was something from God. I felt the touch of God on my heart. I felt, "it's there that I'm going to find the solution for my life." I began to insist with my sister for us to go to São Paulo. And then about two weeks later they inaugurated a church in Brasilia. So the next week I went there. From the first day I put my foot in the church I felt my life getting better. I felt calmer, I began to be able to sleep. My headache wasn't as strong as before. I started doing a corrente. And I did campaigns, which were the whole week. And I began to be liberated. My headaches disappeared. I stopped taking tranquilizers. But there was still one thing impeding me, a horrible, terrible thing, which was the disturbance in my mind, the devil spoke a lot in my mind. And a great fear I had. Fear of going out alone. So I still felt a prisoner. Often I felt worse than a paralytic or blind person, because I was physically normal but spiritually my life was ruined. I kept on struggling at church, doing correntes. The Friday corrente which was for liberation, and then when I came to Campinas, I started to manifest.

P: Why did you move to Campinas?

V: My husband was transferred. We spent a year in Ribeirao Preto first and then came here. We've been here for three years. He is the head of a sector of the Carrefour supermarket. And I kept on struggling, but with that certainty that I was going to be victorious. That my total liberation would happen. By total liberation I mean the liberation of my spirit, my soul, because my soul was a prisoner of the devil. I felt I was a prisoner of the devil. Fear of going out, fear of being alone. I used to see shapes and hear voices. The devil tried to make me go mad through this. I used to say to my mother, "Can't you hear it?" and she'd say, "no, I can't hear anything" . . . Once I tried to kill myself, I got a knife to slash my wrist. The devil told me to kill my husband and children and then kill myself. I couldn't go up high because I used to hear that voice in my mind telling me to throw myself down . . . I'm sure that if I hadn't found Jesus through the UC I'd be dead today, or else dying slowly in a mad-house.

P: Does anyone in your family belong to the church?

V: Now, yes. My mother, my two sisters and my father. My mother used to go to the AG, now she's in the UC. She spent 13 years in the AG.

P: So you were brought up in the AG?

V: No, because I wouldn't accept it. I told my mother I wouldn't go there because I didn't like their manner. I used to say, "Mother, if I go to this church I have to let my hair grow and my legs get hairy and dress like they do, I don't want to." My mother's been in the UC for four years now, same time as me. And she's blessed too. She'd had a problem of high blood pressure for over thirty years and now she's been healed. The doctor said, "your blood pressure is just like a young person's." I tell you, I've been born again. For ten years I was just like a dead person. Now I feel like living. Before, I just felt like killing myself.

P: Has your husband already come along to the church?

V: No, he doesn't accept it very well. He doesn't prohibit me because he saw my state before.

P: Do you have children?

V: Three. When I had my second child was when I got worse. The doctors say it had to do with a problem in giving birth, a psychosis that you get after having a child. But my case was spiritual.

P: Do your children come to church with you?

V: I used to bring them, because when I didn't go out alone my sister used to come with me. But not now. On Sundays they prefer to stay with their father. Whenever I can I bring them, but it's not often. The oldest is eight.

P: Is there any special activity at the church for his age?

V: Not as far as I know. On Sundays the female workers look after the children but I don't know if they have any activity for them.

P: Does the fact that your husband doesn't come create any problems for you in taking part in some aspects of the church, for example, giving the tithe and so on?

V: He doesn't accept it. He doesn't allow it, says it's not right. Says it's something the pastors invented because they want money. I've been four years in the UC and I can count the number of times I've given an offering. Because he doesn't accept it, and I don't work. But it's not because of money that I'm going to stop coming. Whether I give an offering or not I've always been very well attended to by all the workers and pastors.

P: Do you consult the pastors frequently?

V: Yes, because of my husband being an unbeliever. I often need their advice on how to act with him. They give me good advice.

P: What sort of advice do they give?

V: They teach that above all you have to be obedient to God. And they say I have to be ready for him at every moment. To give lots of love and affection and be understanding with him and be obedient to him. Of course, in the first place to Jesus. But also to him. For example, if he doesn't want me to come to church, I always try to come during the day when he's working. So they advise me, "come at a time he's not at home so you can be at home with him in the evening and give him attention. You must give him as much attention as possible, treat him with a lot of love and be obedient." Because a wife has got to be obedient to her husband, it's in the Bible. Even if he doesn't believe, even though he has a living testimony at home which is my life. So I try to be as affectionate as I can, and it's got to work.

P: What did your father work in when you were little?

V: We always lived on a farm. He was a farmer in Minas Gerais. When I was thirteen we went to Brasilia and he worked on building sites.

P: How far did you study?

V: Until the first year of high school, then I married and had children.

P: Would you say you have a reasonable standard of living?

V: Yes. God has blessed us a lot. Even though my husband is an unbeliever, the money he puts into my hands, even though it's not much I give the tithe, I've been faithful with the tithe and I've seen God's blessing. We have a rented house because we're always being transferred. In Brasilia we've bought a commercial lot. So we've improved a lot since when we lived with my mother in Brasilia. Since I joined the UC I've been more blessed each day financially.

P: Has your husband been promoted since then?

V: Yes. In the correntes I've prayed a lot for that. When he entered Carrefour he was a butcher. There were people there who hadn't been promoted in ten years. And he's been promoted to manager of the butcher's after only three years. I've also had physical blessings, because I used to feel a lot of pain in the stomach, also a lump on my head which the doctor said was a nervous problem. Today, they're all cleared up. I've been in the UC for four years and I've never taken medicines again for headaches. And also I'm a calm person now. Sometimes at first when I was on the street I began to feel ill. I couldn't be in the midst of a crowd because I felt like fainting. That's all finished. I've been totally transformed. I used to feel hatred for my father and I couldn't get on with him. I felt I wanted to kill him. I don't know why, I think it's something from the devil.

P: How old were you when you started feeling that?

V: About ten. Maybe it was a lack of affection, but I don't think that justifies it. And today, a married woman of nearly thirty, I feel like sitting on my father's lap and kissing him. But maybe out of shyness . . . But I think I will do it when I go to Brasilia next. I asked his forgiveness, because we used to quarrel a lot. I used to live in a house at the back of his for five years after we got married. Because when we got married we weren't in a good financial situation. So my father suggested we build a little house at the back of the yard. Now I live in a rented three-bedroom house in Campinas. So I've been very blessed.

P: Before, you were saying that in the AG you would have had to let your hair grow long. Isn't there any of that sort of thing here?

V: No, one of the things I liked a lot when I came here is the freedom they give you. But a lot of people don't understand this freedom and say bad things about the church. For example, it was in the papers that here they teach people to prostitute themselves. On the contrary. They teach that if you are single you mustn't do that. They teach a lot that a wife should love her husband and respect him. And the same for the man with his wife. They let the Holy Spirit speak in your heart, not like the other churches. One thing I thought was very wrong at another church I went to three or four times in Brasilia (I can't remember the name) was that a woman prayed for me with laying on of hands and had a revelation. And this woman said, "God is revealing to me that you have an insoluble problem." So you can imagine the effect on me, I was already desperate! I felt crushed. It was a small church which only exists there, there aren't several around the country. It's a woman who prays. She made me kneel down and said, "Give your life to Jesus, sister. Why don't you?" In the UC they don't do things like that. I only gave my life to Jesus a year ago. I came to the UC seeking healing, not to give my heart to Jesus. But in the prayer where they say, "You who want to give your life to Jesus . . ." I felt God touch my heart, but it wasn't because the pastor forced me. In the UC you don't have to do things because the pastor tells you, like at that church.

P: Have you been baptized here at the church?

V: Yes, I was baptized in Brasilia, in May 1988. And I renewed my baptism here just recently.

P: What do you mean by renewing your baptism?

V: I went through the waters again.

P: You've been baptized more than once?

V: Yes. The pastor says that there is only one baptism. But if you feel in your heart that desire to get baptized . . . because the first time I got baptized I felt like I was going to the gallows, because I hadn't been set free. I hadn't given my life to Jesus. I just wanted a solution to my life. But when I renewed my baptism now, I did it joyfully, I felt renewed.

P: Can you only renew your baptism once or several times?

V: Several times. As often as you feel in your heart . . .

P: Had you never been baptized in the AG?

V: No, because I didn't accept their way of doing things. I . . . I don't want to speak ill of any religion, you understand, because I don't want to follow religion, I follow the living God. But I thought their way was all wrong. They used to come round to our house and say, "if you're thinking your mother is going to save you, you're wrong, you're going to hell." So I used to tell my mother, "when these sisters come round, don't call me." When you're suffering you don't want to hear that sort of thing, do you? They used to tell my mother that if I didn't go to church I'd go to hell. So I always say they vaccinate a person against God. Now, I evangelize, but I'd never say that to a person.

P: Do you read the Bible regularly?

V: Yes, I read it like they teach us here. I don't read pages and pages. But every night after my children are asleep I try to read some verses.

P: And what about your children? It's difficult for them to come to church, but do you try to get something across to them?

V: Yes, I do. And to my husband too. Not in that sort of way, of course, getting on his nerves. But I try to take advantage of the opportunities to show him it isn't a fanatical thing. I'm a normal person, after all, well, normal up to a certain point, of course, because as someone who has Jesus you can't smoke or drink, or lie, things like that. But I'm a normal person, I wear clothes like a normal woman. But I tell my husband that if I had to serve Jesus the way those women did, never, because they don't serve a living God, they follow a doctrine. Today I can see that the transformation God has done in my life has nothing to do with clothing, hair, and so on. Lots of people don't come to an evangelical church because of that. People say, "Oh, no, be a crente, no!"

P: So the UC doesn't see any problem with make-up and so on?

V: No. As long as you do it because you like it. In my case, my husband likes it and asks me to wear it. So as long as you don't use it to provoke, there's no sin in it.

P: Are there people in the church who drink?

V: As far as I know, no.

P: The church doesn't forbid it, but orients . . .

V: That's right. In a liberation meeting they don't preach that sort of thing, but in a members' meeting they do. Not forbidding, but teaching truth. Even so, it isn't in the way those crentes used to speak to me. Here, they leave you at liberty.

P: You've been in the church some time. Do the members meet much outside the church? Do you have contact with other members?

V: Well, I haven't been living in Campinas for very long. I know almost no-one. But there are members who live near my home. There's one lady who's always round at my house. Another one as well.

P: Outside the services, do the members have the custom of getting together and doing things together?

V: I don't know because I'm rather a closed person. And I have children. But I think so. I hear people talking. Whenever I can, I go to people's houses. We're always giving testimony to each other.

P: But there aren't any meetings in the house?

V: No.

P: All the meetings are here in the church?

V: Yes. Sometimes they say, for example, that people with husbands who are converted, if he agrees to have meetings in the district . . . But I can't do that. But there are people who do that, and the pastors or the workers go there.

So then, (to reconstruct), Vera is twenty-nine and has been in the UC for four years. Even as a child she was very nervous and disturbed, and she clearly had a poor relationship with her father. But from mid-adolescence on she began to fear being on her own either in the home or outside. She had headaches at the "top of her head," had stomach pains, saw shapes, heard voices, and was overwhelmed by generalized fear and by hatred of her father. At different times she had physical treatment from neurologists and from a psychiatrist who (apparently) concluded she was beyond his assistance and should be incarcerated. When nineteen she married and within a year everything was much worse. Things reached a low pitch of misery after her second child when a doctor concluded she suffered from post-natal psychosis, though in truth (in her view) the problem was 'spiritual.'

She would walk about the house holding her head while her brains 'burned' and she felt like screaming or throwing something or attacking someone . . . or hitting her head against the wall.

All this she described, retrospectively of course, after her liberation, as imprisonment by the devil, especially the fear of going out and being alone. (The metaphor of imprisonment is coherent and precise). 'My soul was a prisoner of the devil.' The devil assaulted her sanity through shapes and voices, and then incited her to kill herself by slashing her wrist. She feared heights because the same diabolical voice urged her to throw herself down.

The background to this is that the family was very poor and her father suggested that she and her husband build a little house in his backyard in Brasilia. It seems that Vera spent quite a lot of time with her mother, who belonged to the AG. Vera had bad experiences of the AG and other evangelical churches they tried. The sisters would come round from the AG and say "If you're thinking your mother is going to save you, you're wrong, you're going to hell." Vera ruefully comments that her suffering was not ameliorated by this. She rejects spiritual terrorism and with it all the legalistic framework of the AG concerning dress, hair, make-up, and so forth. As for other churches, a woman prayed over her with laying on of hands and had a 'revelation' that Vera suffered from an 'insoluble problem.' Once again her suffering was not ameliorated. The woman then told her to give her heart to Jesus. (Here we probably see retrospective framings, at least in part derived from UC teaching. The UC (she says) *first* seeks out your suffering and later gives you a chance freely to offer yourself to Jesus. Moreover, by contrast with other churches, the UC offers 'liberty' not a doctrine, and the Living God not religion. One may add that the UC deploys a liberal hermeneutic relativizing the New Testament as context-bound, but mainly in relation to some New Testament moral prescriptions not to demonology and miracles. It uses liberal methods to reverse liberal priorities.

Then one morning at six o'clock after a sleepless night, Vera turned on the television and heard a UC pastor speaking from São Paulo. She 'felt the touch of God' on her heart and knew this was going to be the place where she found the solution to her life. Immediately, she wanted to set off for the UC church in São Paulo, which her family circle saw as final proof of her madness. Happily the UC came to Brasilia, setting up a new church, and the moment she set foot inside it she began to feel better and calmer. She took a 'corrente'—several in fact—and everything improved, even to the point of dropping her tranquilizers. Yet the devil still spoke in her mind and she was still afraid of being alone or going out on her own.

But then she and her husband were able to move to a sizeable apartment in Campinas and at *that* point a new phase in her liberation began because she started to 'manifest' (externalize) the spirits inside her. Her mother now followed her into the UC and was cured of a thirty years problem of high blood pressure. (Are both of them now better for their separation?) Vera now begins to feel differently about her father and desires to seek reconciliation and his forgiveness. As for her husband, he remains unbelieving but the UC counsels her to come to church only when he is not at home and to give him much attention and love. Vera prays for her husband's material success, she tithes a tenth of what he gives her, and he receives unexpectedly rapid promotion. Clearly her payment into the spiritual treasury is emerging in the material treasury as well. Moreover, in the matter of spiritual exchange she has made further progress towards liberation: her first baptism was 'like going to the gallows' because she simply wanted her problem solved, but her second baptism was joyful and free because it was the gift of her heart to Jesus.

Perhaps a further reconstruction can be added by playing with her key metaphor of incarceration. Vera rightly describes her initial problem as spiritual since she has lost her soul for lack of any space where her soul might be, and because it—or she—has been consumed by rage at her father's lack of affection. She is immobilized by her feelings, and her evident lack of personal space presents itself as an inability to exist or move without somebody being present. Purely local evangelical help in Brasilia only compounds her problem by further spiritual menaces and demands. But on the television she hears a call at a distance, from São Paulo, which makes no such demands and she desires to go there on a journey to find a solution. This is regarded as further madness because the UC is labelled as 'mad' and also labelled open and permissive. Happily the UC comes to Brasilia and offers her a space in which the struggle may occur. (The verb is passive, because although she herself struggles, the conflict is carried on by rival agencies in her soul's space, and when it is resolved she will not have to bear guilt for what occurred previously. As will be seen later, people can be reconciled to each other more easily because neither of them offended the other of their own free will.) Once Vera moves to Campinas and acquires her own space, the final phase of liberation can begin because the spirits can 'come out.' They leave her head and stomach and come roaring helplessly into the open air.

Here now is the text of Wander (and of his wife Benedita).

P: When you came from Minas did you have any religious practice?

W: No. I heard the gospel in Brasilia. I lived six months there with my brother. He was already converted. They took me to an AG and there I accepted the gospel for the first time, I raised my hand, accepted Jesus. But I didn't go on. When I went back to Minas I didn't go to any church. Then, when I was already married. I accepted again. In 1978, in the AG of Vila Industrial, in Campinas. But I didn't go on again. I congregated there for four years, then I had a spiritual failure and separated from the Lord's ways. And so did she. Then I spent at least four years away.

P: Had your wife been converted with you?

W: Yes. From about '78 to '83, we went to church. Then we left.

P: Why?

W: I didn't have spiritual life. I was always despondent in my faith, I already had a wife. I think it was a frivolity on my part. I allowed myself to be carried away by a weakness which I think was lack of experience. So I left. And I regretted it a lot afterwards.

P: Your wife as well?

W: Yes, she left too. And it wasn't good.

P: So how long were you away?

W: From '83 to July '89. And things got much worse for me. I went a way which, as the Word of God says: "He who leaves the ways of the Lord becomes seven times worse than before." I became a completely different person, and I started to practice things that I'd never done before. Since my reconciliation I think: "How could I have done those things?"

P: How did your reconciliation take place?

W: It was on June 15, 1989, in the GL church. Not because I'd planned to do it there, but it just happened. But I don't think it was just a coincidence. And since then I've been congregating there, participating in the church.

P: Did you have a friend there?

W: No, I didn't know anyone there.

P: So why did you go there? Why not go back to the AG?

W: This time it was the Lord himself who showed me. I go to the main church, but during the week I congregate here in the suburb. All the suburbs have one.

P: What differences are there between the God is Love and the AG?

W: I perceive a difference in terms of consecration. GL prays a lot, the prayer requests are pinned up. They pray more than the AG. And they fast. A lot of fasting. The ministers demand this of the members. They demand it. They really want people to be consecrated, to fast, pray, seek. As the Word says: "He who seeks, finds." They do a lot of campaigns. And I've done several campaigns at the church. And I've received wonderful blessings through these campaigns, fasting and prayer. Campaigns of fasting, campaigns of prayer, campaigns of seven Sundays, seven Saturdays, fasting, prayer, that objective with God. And seeking. With the object of receiving that blessing, and I have done. And I've found it very important. I'm satisfied.

P: How are these campaigns of seven Sundays, seven Saturdays, and so on?

W: It lasts for that time. If you have a problem, you take it before the Lord and you say: "Lord, my problem is this or that, you know about it, and I'm going to do this campaign with faith, believing that you are going to provide a solution to my material or spiritual problem." And the person goes to church for those seven Saturdays with that intention. In fasting and prayer. He fasts for that whole day.

P: At the level of the family, economic, financial, work and so on, how has your life changed?

W: I had so many problems. When I left the AG I went back to drinking. I was addicted to drink. I even used drugs, marijuana, cocaine. I sank right down. I had no hope left. I felt as if I was in a well of quicksand. I kicked around, but I felt chained. Chained by a malignant force. I used to lie down in bed and I couldn't sleep, I just had bad visions. When we harden our hearts, God touches those he loves. He who isn't brought back by love is brought back by pain. And there was a time when I had a problem with a chap. I had an argument and a fight. I was taking drugs, drinking, a lot of bad friendships of the world. And I had a fight with this chap, and his fourteen year old brother got it in for me. Two years later he came to get revenge. It was New Year's Eve 1988/89. I was in a snack-bar. I was leaving. At the time I had a Jeep. When I sat down to drive off, he came along with a billiard cue and hit me in the eye. I lost the sight of the eye completely. So they put an artificial eye in. About two months later my reconciliation took place.

P: Was your wife going to church at this time?

W: No. During these two months when I was having treatment for my eye I felt revolted. I thought of killing the boy. My friends said: "You've got to buy a revolver and kill him." And that was my intention. But the Lord said: "My ways are not your ways." We make a plan but God makes another one. About two months later, I woke up one morning transformed. I arrived home late one night, very drunk, drugged, and I lay down. I tried to sleep and couldn't. I began to sweat and see different things. And I felt something talking to me.

P: Had you spoken to any crentes (believers) since the accident?

W: No. I know that when I woke up I was drenched in sweat. And the day was breaking and I felt transformed. Repentant. I cried so much. And the world seemed to be different. My wife went off to work. And I went to the room and turned the radio on. There was an evangelical program on. I began to listen. The pastor preached and preached. It seemed as though he was right with me in the room, talking to me. I still remember the message, he said: "If you're at home listening, if you have an insoluble problem in your life, deliver it into the hand of Jesus and he will solve it. Accept Jesus! I reconcile myself with Jesus." So right then I knelt down and got reconciled. That afternoon, after I left work, it was two o'clock, I went to the GL church.

P: Why there? Was it the first church you found?

W: No. It was the first one I thought of. It was near my route to work.

P: Was the radio program from the GL?

W: No, I don't know whose it was. So I went to the church and got reconciled. The presbyter made the appeal: "Who wants to accept Jesus? Who is addicted and wants to get reconciled to the Lord?" So I got up crying and went forward, they laid their hands on me and prayed. It was like a wash. I even left there breathing better. And I went away thinking: "Now I'm going to have a better life. Things will get better with my family." We'd been sleeping in separate beds for the past six months, in separate rooms. She didn't even speak to me any more. It was deep darkness. And then, just as I was thinking things would get better, they got worse. A testing came. God tests those he loves. My wife was revolted when I told her I'd got reconciled. She wouldn't accept me at all. So we had to separate. Just as I'd come back to God six months later we separated. She left home with the children, and went to live with some relatives.

P: Did she have a job?

W: Yes, she's a nurse. She went to live in a tiny basement.

P: Didn't you leave the church because of that?

W: No. I stayed firm. She was used by things. She said to me: "I'm going to leave you to see if you stay firm with this Jesus. I want to see if you're really a crente. Thirty days from now I want to see you in the bar drinking. You're going to fall." "Well I tell you in the name of the Lord Jesus Christ that I'm transformed, I'm free. You can go but I'm not going to leave Jesus." It was hard! She was away for two years, until last July. It was a testing of fire. There were times when I . . . and then, in February 1991, she started to have more to do with me. We began to build the house in May 1991, before she came back. I humbled myself and said all right, let's build the house. I got all my money, I had an old car. We used to come here every weekend and build. And when the roof was on the house, things started to get worse again. She was different again. That oppression of the past. That malignant oppression. And I had to seek the Lord a lot in prayer and fasting. I didn't have any money, and there wasn't much service. I started to get a bit nervous. And the enemy got into me. We had arguments. I got a bit revolted. It seemed as though I could see the forces of darkness beside me. I used to arrive home and feel the enemy around me, preparing traps for me. I got desperate. One day I arrived from church and I felt ice-cold. I felt a tingling from my head to my toes. A bad thing. A force, an oppression. I had no strength left to pray, I just asked for mercy. I lay down, and the enemy started to attack me on the bed. I felt as if something was coming from under the bed and taking hold of the mattress and lifting it up. I felt the mattress fluctuate. I cried out to the blood of Jesus. I lay down and there it came again. And when I got to sleep my mind was totally dominated by the enemy, I had only bad dreams. I'd been about 20 days without eating. I couldn't eat, just drink milk. I felt really resentful. That morning I felt like taking poison. I came here and said to her: "Give the children a hug, I'm going home to kill myself." I went home and prepared a poison. I took it and was taken to hospital. I was interned for two days. When I was back home, I regretted what I'd done. Because it's not from the Lord. I was tempted. I asked God's forgiveness and felt pardoned. Then my brother got some very big service for me, in seven buildings, and he got me an apartment to live in, right next to the job. The apartment was his. A blessing from God. And God began to open doors. A brother from GL went to live with me so I wouldn't be on my own. He stayed four months with me.

P: What was your wife's reaction?

W: She felt defeated. And I was praying, fasting for her. Every day at two or three o'clock in the morning I got up and prayed for her. Through a brother at church the Lord had told me he would work in her. A prophecy. But the enemy was very revolted. Then later there was a revelation at church that within five days God would operate. Two weeks later she telephoned me. She was already living here in the house. And I moved in with her.

P: Is she going to church now?

W: No, she's still away from the Lord. But I can't complain of anything. An excellent wife, attentive, affectionate, compatible in everything. Happy that I should go to church. Seems to feel happy to see me serving God.

P: Do the children go?

W: The oldest goes more. Two months ago she raised her hand accepting Jesus. There have already been two prophecies that my wife will come eventually. The Lord said: "Let her be. Don't speak to her, just to me." God is blessing me materially as well as spiritually.

P: Even though service is slow . . . How far have you studied?

W: Only up to the third year of primary school. I think my wife finished secondary school.

Benedita (his wife): I finished secondary last year. I've been a nurse nearly five years, I just did a two month course. At first they put me in the cleaning section of the hospital, then they transferred me to nursing. What I wanted was the money. I used to keep it hidden from Wander because he was crazy. That was how I managed to buy this piece of land here. And now he's come more to his senses again.

P: Are the children studying?

B: Yes, they are at school in Campinas, they have to get four buses a day.

P: Have you ever had your own home before?

W: No. We always rented. I used to spend my money on other things.

P: What about when both of you were at the AG, was life better then?

W: Not materially. We got by. It wasn't as good as today. Now, God is blessing, he promised to bless.

P: I didn't really understand why you left the AG.

B: (Gap on the tape. I think she tells a story about a woman at the AG who used to humiliate her). And then she came out with that comment. And that made me mad. To tell the truth, I already felt very weak. I was pregnant and had a hard life, and instead of helping she just put me down all the time. So I saw that people outside the church were better than those inside. And my faith went on getting weaker. And then I left. And he got much worse. But I know my responsibilities, I know about my home, my children. So nothing affects me. But men, you know how they are. God help me!

P: When you left the AG, did you lose your faith completely or did you just leave the church? How do you define yourself now in terms of religion?

B: I respect religion a lot. I left everything, but I respect it a lot. I let him go to church, if he wants to go. I don't have anything against it. Each one should follow . . . but I don't feel at home in any church. Neither in the Catholic church nor in the AG or any other. But I believe a lot in God.

P: Does this belief in God help you in your life?

B: Look, I don't think God has abandoned me. Despite everything I do. Because everything I earn gets multiplied. But, it's not that I have any rancor, but there's a little pain inside me, I can tell you!

P: Against the church?

B: Not against the church. Against the people, their tongues.

W: She felt very offended.

B: I used to like the AG. I respect it a lot. I think it's a very beautiful religion.

P: Were you baptized there?

B: No, because of this problem.

P: What about you?

W: No, I haven't been baptized yet. I'm going to get baptized now, next year. I'm getting prepared.

P: During the bad period, did you get any sort of help from religious people?

B: No. I got by on my own. I never got any help from anybody.

P: Don't you have relatives in Campinas?

B: No. My sisters arrived, but too late. And she's in no state . . . but we got by. One has to have a difficult life, doesn't one, in order to value God. If you get help from everybody you don't know how it is . . .

P: Wander, what's it like in the GL?

W: The doctrine is very heavy. They really demand from you there. They live like the primitive church. The women can't . . . (this, that and the other). And the men, I cut my hair every two weeks. Can't wear a moustache.

P: So I couldn't go there!

W: Paul, I think all this may be from man. I used to go to the AG, now I'm in the GL, I like it, I've no intention of leaving. But I follow the rhythm of the church. I think it is a duty. I can't be there and disobey the doctrine.

P: But I can imagine it isn't very attractive for you, Benedita.

B: Ah!

W: But all this comes from God: the desire to be transformed. To be in a church like this, with its rigid doctrine, there must have been a liberation. . . . I considered myself dead. I was reconciled and came alive again. . . . Today I'm in the GL and I think it's wonderful. I'm disposed to obey because I can see that it's for my own good . . . So I'm there, but I don't believe that if I let my beard grow or if a woman wears trousers or jewelry, that she won't get into the Kingdom of God. If you want to congregate in the Presbyterian Church, Baptist, the Christian Congregation . . .

B: When he was away from the church, I went for a while to the Presbyterian church with the children. And he used to make fun of me!

In commenting on this text, there is no particular point in reconstruction in a different mode. Rather some discrete observations are in order. This is, after all, a culture where people are *possessed* by drugs. At every level of Pentecostal activity there is a warfare against drugs and alcohol, and the dramatization of this warfare in terms of possession not only corresponds to the reality but enables people to repossess themselves.

The point is that Wander has a soul without strong boundaries. He responds to the company he is in and its requirements. On one side is the macho company which requires whoring, drug-taking, violence, and feuding. In that company Wander does things he can barely credit, though the demand that he kill a boy as part of the reciprocal violence of a feud creates a crisis in his soul. But in order to sustain his recovery of his soul, he has to have an alternative group supporting him, and needs demanding rules to let him know where the limits are. His wife comments that she *knows* her responsibilities, but that men like Wander need the restrictive requirements of the GL church to ward off spiritual anarchy and recidivism. Indeed, she concludes that men as such have to be molded by strict rules and sanctions if they are to persevere and to act reasonably.

Benedita is, in fact, quite a contrast to Wander in mode of being and in language. He needs rules and communal support, while she is inwardly aware of responsibilities and is made uncomfortable by the pressures of the community, whether it is the censoriousness of the AG or the restrictive rules and practices of GL. Her language simply contrasts taking leave of your senses with coming to your

senses. His language, however, is much more colorful. There are
phrases like the 'malignant oppression . . . of the past.' There are
lively metaphors like 'deep darkness' and 'sinking' and phrases
which evoke loss of soul: 'I felt as if I was in a well of quicksand. I
kicked around but I felt drained by a malignant force.' At the deepest
layer there is the source of this malignant pull or chain, who is the
Enemy. The Enemy is 'revolted' and attacks physically and psychically until you hang over the abyss and call on the blood of Christ to
wash you clean.

   This whole interview recounts a fluctuating battle between
the Enemy of souls and the Friend of souls for the internal forum
of Wander. Ideally, Wander would need to be juxtaposed with his
brother who 'gave his life' to the Friend of souls early on, after a
youthful bout of mayhem, and never deviated thereafter. His
brother lives by the book and is firmly defended against demonic
visitation or diabolic occupation. For him spiritual and material
progress have marched hand-in-hand so that his life constitutes 'a
miracle' and himself a God-made/self-made man. By contrast
Wander has experienced spiritual and material fluctuation and
alternation, also marching hand-in-hand. Of course, there are problems about this symmetry of material and spiritual in Wander's
life since it can never be quite clear how far material deterioration
plays into a spiritual decline and how far spiritual decline makes
for material deterioration. The point is important, and not only
with regard to Wander, because it is a key nexus in evangelical
motivation. There *is* a positive relation between spiritual and
material uplift, both from an external empirical viewpoint and in
evangelical 'accounting' but experience of the slings and arrows of
fortune has to build in fail-safe understandings to cover a certain
range of material difficulties, excluding total penury. Here lies
the rub: just how *much* difficulty is to be understood as inevitable
on God's testing ground and is there a point in the spiral of material loss where one receives the due reward of spiritual failure?
The evangelical conscience constantly works its way around this
conundrum, allotting some situations to providential blessings,
some to the tests set by divine love, and some to divine judgment.
Blessings are, of course mostly divine, though God can use prosperity as a trap, but tests and disasters can be assigned to the devil
as well as to God. The dramas in the soul of people like Wander,
swaying as they do between heaven gate and hell gate, are in part
composed of attempts to assign situations to one or the other.
These assignments are, to some extent, standardized according to

the teachings of the religious group, but they are also quite personal and even emanate from the heart of the conflict itself. In other words, the soul crying out in the heat of conflict and suffering alternating occupations tries to assign the correct names to the operative agencies. In that context a religious group is a chorus to the action helping the soul identify who is acting behind the masks of trials and events. In the (literally) maddening maze of things, the soul needs a chorus, and some souls need a very firm chorus.

It needs to be emphasized that externalization of the demonic in terms of possession by the Enemy and in concrete rather than abstract language leads to an increase in personal freedom and an ability to recommence de novo. The weight of personal guilt no longer paralyzes the future with the past and you do not accept the definition of incurable offered by the psychiatrist. This helps in the re-formation of relationships, especially when relapse can be seen as repossession. This is where Benedita's vocabulary of 'coming to' and 'leaving' your senses is less helpful than Wanders. She, after all, *blames* him as a recidivist, whereas he sees her virulent blaming as due to demonic agency taking *her* over. The paradoxes of freedom and responsibility are numerous: The Pentecostal group enables problems to be projected in scenarios that enable both participants to begin all over again unburdened and unbedevilled by past mistakes. There is also here a moral seriousness stemming from the direct personal address of evangelical speech which requires that *transactions* in the soul be pursued and completed. Here, after all, are vast numbers of people crowded intolerably in the great mega-city, literally and metaphorically unable to breathe, literally and metaphorically unwashed, comprehensively disabled, universally nameless and anonymous, who are suddenly called by name and offered a space to be in which to experience power and liberation.[1]

NOTE

1. Research by David Martin into Latin American Pentecostalism has been throughout financed by the Institute for the Study of Economic Culture (ISEC), Boston University under the direction of Peter Berger. The first phase was completed in the publication of *Tongues of Fire* (Oxford: Blackwell 1990). The second phase is concerned with 'betterment,' especially economic betterment, among Pentecostals in Chile and Brazil and it has been pursued in cooperation with Arturo Fontaine and

his colleagues at the Centro de Estudios Publicos, Santiago, and in cooperation with Paul Freston, Campinas, Brazil. Bernice Martin has been a consultant throughout this second phase with a specific interest in the cura divina groups and issues relating to women and the family.

PART II: ABUSE AND SOUL-LOSS

3

Whose Soul Is It Anyway?
Domestic Tyranny and the Suffocated Soul

I can't even call my soul my own!
                    —English folk saying

Nay look not big, nor stamp, nor stare, nor fret;
I will be master of what is mine soul:
She is my goods, my chattels; she is my house,
My household stuff, my field, my barn,
My horse, my ox, my ass, my anything.
                    —Petruchio's description of
                    Katherina after their wedding,
                    from The Taming of the
                    Shrew *by Shakespeare*

Whenever my mother reached the end of her tether she would exclaim: "I can't even call my soul my own with you lot!" She was bringing up five children in a damp, insanitary four room terraced cottage in the early 1940s while my father fought in the war. The last straw was usually when she found she could not even go to the lavatory, (a leaky shed in the back yard,) without a crying toddler beating on the door, screaming to get her out or to be allowed in with her. It seems to me, in retrospect, significant that she never said, "I can't call my *body* my own." It was her selfhood that was battered and beleaguered when importunate infants denied her even that much separate existence.

Her use of the word "soul" was more than a metaphor. Long before modern psychology and social theory mapped the functional constellations of "the self" customary language discriminated for ordinary people, those features and attributes of the self that concerned them. Soul, to my mother and the people with whom I grew up in that working class industrial town, was a word used unselfconsciously to mean the ultimate core or essence of the individual's being. Few would have been able to define it; the meaning lay in the usage and the usage, as often as not, involved the telling of stories and the repetition of "sayings." People talked of the soul as if it were the irreducible, indestructible part of the person which, perhaps, continued to exist after death.

The soul had a paradoxical relationship to the body. The accidents of ugliness, deformity, and decay which afflicted the body did not automatically disfigure the soul, though people also talked as if the soul would always be recognizable from the physical body of which it was the animating center. Yet beauty of soul was something quite different from the physical beauty of the body. That was a regular theme in the Victorian and Edwardian popular novels which, with more stealth and subtlety than formal religious teaching, had laid down these taken-for-granted understandings which I absorbed early from books like Hesbah Stretton's *Little Meg's Children* and *Jessica's First Prayer*. Apart from newspapers, these old novels were often the only reading matter in homes like ours. They were the Sunday School prizes given for regular attendance to generations of children of the working classes. In my turn, I pored over these chronicles of poor, sick but heroic children battling, with virtue as their only weapon, against adult alcoholism, violence, despair and abject poverty. *Their* souls were glorious though their bodies were stunted, crippled, and clothed in rags.

Such tales were undoubtedly important and unacknowledged sources of the *moral* discourse of selfhood in the culture I inherited. Every individual was held responsible for his or her own soul. It took the imprint of a person's life experiences but what it crucially reflected were the moral choices made. The soul was the *true* "self" with its experiential and moral record inscribed as if on a body: Pinocchio's nose or Dorian Gray's picture are close to the idea of how this "moral inscription" was thought to operate. I have never lost this sense that *the soul is the selfhood for which one takes moral responsibility.*

Whenever my mother said that she could not call her soul her own she was repeating, with feeling, a folk saying which existed within that constellation of moral meaning which I have crudely summarized above. This meaning was also, of course, gendered. Inscribed on my mother's soul was undoubtedly, "good mother" in shining letters. No one was more committed than she to the moral injunctions of "good motherhood" and she battled womanfully against real hardship in a spirit not wholly unconnected with that of the old Sunday School prize stories. She was a heroic mother, praised by neighbors for her selflessness, for always putting her children first. That was her pride and her validation. So, when she and women like her—for it was usually the women—cried out that they could not call their souls their own they were uttering a *strong* protest against a level of domestic harassment that left them feeling self-less in a double sense. They were protesting against an *excessive* demand that they be "selfless," that is, that they give without stint; and against the sense that they were being denied their own essence, their own boundaries, that they were literally *without self*, dispersed, eaten up, erased, consumed, extinguished by insatiable domestic pressure.

At the same time, however, the angry repetition of the "saying" was a kind of magical defensive incantation. It was a way of drawing a final line between the self and the demands which were bombarding it. The exclamation itself acted to reverse the state of overload. It was a *claim* to have the right to a self at the same time as being a complaint about the threat to the sacred core of that self. If you could say it, you were still in there fighting! In one short phrase those women had condensed both an analysis of a well recognized chronic threat to women's sense of ownership of themselves and a prophylactic against it.

This eloquent old formula of my mother's came to mind as I wrestled with the problem of how to shape the material I wanted to present in this essay. My primary intention was to write about the "soul-loss" involved for women who are the victims of domestic violence. I chose the subject because I wanted to explore my own daughter's reaction to this experience.[1] She was subjected to two years of unremitting coercion and intermittent violence by the father of her child. Having taken himself off when the child was born, he reappeared when she was almost six years old and took over their lives until my daughter finally summoned a strength born of desperation and left him just over two years ago. There is nothing unusual in the case; indeed, of its kind it is relatively mild. My daughter and granddaughter escaped with their lives and have been able, slowly, to "become themselves" again, though the healing has been slow and uneven and the process has dominated all our lives. My daughter will ultimately write her story herself but it is too recent for that to be yet bearable. She is still stunned by the acuteness and completeness of the loss of selfhood that she experienced. I am aware of the dangers in my writing about her experience, even with full encouragement.[2] Jane Flax, for one has warned how important is the conflict between nurturance and autonomy in mother-daughter relationships (Flax 1978). But that, too, is part of the wider problem which is in fact the ultimate unanswered question of my inquiry, that is, the problem of what *female* "autonomy" might be like.

Thoughts and images which occur simultaneously in the mind have to take a tediously linear form when transcribed into prose. I arrived at the long forgotten saying of my mother through a moment of frustration which suddenly superimposed three pictures on each other, of myself, my mother, and my daughter. This had the effect of opening up the subject from the narrow focus of domestic violence to a broader area which I will provisionally call domestic tyranny. It happened this way. I spent the summer tending my very needy granddaughter while my daughter finished the Ph.D. thesis which had been interrupted by her attempt to "make a proper family" by living with Stella's father. Stella was in a state of some distress after her father had unexpectedly tracked her down when she had thought her whereabouts unknown to him. She was afraid—haunted would be a more accurate term—not only because of her own experiences but because she knew that soon after she and her mother escaped he had sexually abused two of his younger children during an "access" weekend. Social workers and police had interviewed her about whether anything similar had happened to her.[3]

Stella's neediness quickly made me feel harassed while she lived with us during her school holiday. She demanded round the clock attention and reassurance: her needs were real; I had no valid protection against her pressure. I lost my private space. My study became her play space and TV room. Her bedtime, and therefore my precious evening became a boundary routinely subject to guerilla incursions. My nights were regularly disturbed by her inability to sleep and her need constantly to make sure we were still *there*. When she did sleep she had frequent nightmares, sleep walking, and shouting. This in turn justified her demand to sleep in our dressing room with the light on and the door ajar.

Such heavily pressured maternal episodes are not a new experience but this one was an extreme, though brief, example. My reaction to them is always the same. I become invisible. I forget to groom myself, I don't notice what I wear and feel that "I" have disappeared. My body ceases to be a source of pleasure though I fuel it with too much "comfort" (nursery) food in what I suppose is displaced self-nurture. I resent the suspension of my "adult" life—music, reading, writing, friends—and begin to feel trapped, my physical body reduced to a work horse while the main mediators of my independent self-hood float away to an unreachable distance and lose their meaning. After a while I no longer even *want* to make music—normally the passion of my life.

One has to have a heavy investment in maternal and matriarchal roles as validating the (female) self in order to bear these periods of partial extinction, for that is what they are. It is clear to me that I early inscribed on my own sense of self my mother's model of heroic motherhood.[4] I was, after all, as eldest daughter, an apprentice "little mother" all through my childhood. Unlike my mother, but like my daughter, I also however have a second model of self, that of the independent woman with an intellectual and social existence as well as a demanding career all of which are quite distinct from my family roles. The two selves are, of course, far from distinct in reality and their imperatives have been in chronic collision all my adult life. I have undoubtedly bequeathed the same collision to my daughter, a fact which leaves me uneasily aware of *my* responsibility for the fragility of *her* selfhood—but that is precisely the moral double bind of motherhood which is the underlying concern of this essay.

The image of my mother and her "I can't call my soul my own!" was obviously waiting just below the surface of memory. After all, a good part of my frustration lay in the fact that I was supposed to be writing this essay on soul-loss instead of spending all my time on heavy-duty mothering. It took only a moment of extra exasperation when Stella pursued me right to the lavatory and continued to shout to me through the door for the click of association to happen. I recalled how it was the invasion of that last resort of her privacy that had always pushed my mother over the edge. I remembered, too, that in the crowded working class homes of my childhood, the *man* had the privilege of retiring to the lavatory— the only place where anyone could be alone—to read the newspaper "in peace." And I recalled my sister-in-law's joke term for my eldest brother's habit of spending hours reading in the bathroom as "meditating"! Indeed, after Leonard Bloom's famous internal monologue in *Ulysses*, conducted on just such a backyard lavatory as the retreat of my childhood, the secret has long been out. An earlier code of

shame and reticence about body functions has constructed the lavatory as a "private" space within the domestic architecture of the
modern home and thus turned it into the last retreat of privacy.

Why does the invasion of that particular privacy, for such an
irreducibly animal purpose, act as the symbol marker of a threatened selfhood? Whatever does it tell us about the relations of body
and soul? Certainly there are hints in accounts of women's refuges
that one of the first things which delights and surprises battered
women is the possibility of tending to even the most basic of their
own bodily needs unmolested. Beatrix Campbell makes a telling
observation in her account of a visit to such a refuge:

> A few of us sit around talking into the night, women's talk
> about operations and illnesses, birth, blood and death. The con-
> vention of body talk among women creates an impersonal inti-
> macy, *by means of our bodies we bare our souls.* (my emphasis)
> (Campbell 1984, 85)

Perhaps there is an important connection between being able to
claim space and privacy for one's body, even for the most basic of
functions, and the ability to say "it's *my* body—*and* my soul!" more
particularly if you have had that body abused.

This brings me to my third picture, that of my daughter in
retreat from her abusive partner. When they lived together he policed
her every moment—an unremitting surveillance which, even more
than the episodes of actual violence, was the key to her loss of the
sense of self. He quite openly sought to control her "body and soul."
(This is why Petruchio's offensive claim to own Katherina has so
reverberated in my mind.) Reading books was her worst crime
because she "disappeared" into them and he was blotted from her
consciousness. She salvaged a remnant of autonomy by smuggling
books into the lavatory. By the end of their time together she knew
precisely how many pages she could race through before he began to
shout and beat on the door in a jokey fashion which was nevertheless
also a genuine threat. Looking back and forth from myself to my
mother and my daughter I realized that the continuities are as striking as the more obvious discontinuities between the "ordinary"
threats to female selfhood involved in traditional motherhood and
those more extreme threats posed by domestic violence. The abusive
partner is a recognizable variant of the insatiable infant or needy
child. He is often, a grown man still experiencing acute infantile
rage that Woman, the original source of his life, pleasure, nurture and

comfort, could dare to have purposes unrelated to his immediate needs and desires. Indeed, there is a powerful tradition of feminist psychology, stemming most notably from Nancy Chodorow (Chodorow 1978) and the unjustly eclipsed Dorothy Dinnerstein (Dinnerstein 1977) which argues that the psychodynamics of child rearing in a culture where women take primary or sole responsibility for child care, will inevitably produce such a pathology as an extreme instance of the "normal" pattern of gendered identity.

Chodorow stresses the male fear of re-absorption in the mother and the consequent imperative of separation, individuation and counter-definition so that none of the characteristics and values derived from mothering shall appear in the male gender description. Men, therefore, according to Chodorow and her many followers, tend to acquire strongly bounded selves, even over-fortressed egos. Women, by contrast internalize those values expressed through mothering and develop less strongly bounded selves. They never fully separate from the mother but internalize her instead: for girls, the process of individuation is limited by the imperatives of nurture, cooperation and the duty of creating harmony and connectedness with others. Female selves are therefore typically more fluid, their boundaries more easily permeable than male selves: they look for connection not separation. Carol Gilligan takes the argument a further step and claims that the result is a different set of moral priorities for males and females (Gilligan 1982).

Dinnerstein's version lays more stress on the importance of the young child's rage when he (or she) moves from the earliest experience of seeming to be part of the mother's body and of receiving unconditional love and unbounded pleasure, to the first stage of separation. As the mother starts to discipline the infant, the child's feelings of love and involvement mingle with strong emotions of anger and hate for the mother, stimulated both by a sense of loss and by the frustrations of dependence and powerlessness. Males never fully resolve these ambivalent feelings, according to Dinnerstein. The best they can hope for is to achieve identity with the father who has mysteriously escaped the power of the mother, but who is also a threat to the infant's pleasure because he can command the mother's attention more powerfully than the child can. The ambivalent feelings of males towards both men and women are thus typically displaced and perpetuated rather than fully resolved. According to Dinnerstein the female infant also experiences rage and hate for the mother but ultimately submerges these feelings by identification with her. This in turn creates the potential for displacing hate and punishment from the mother to the self. Of course, changes have taken place in the domestic sphere since the 1970s when these ideas were first propounded. Yet it is clearly far too early to replace these feminist retellings of the Freudian story by some new model based on equal parenting which, so far, is more rhetoric than reality. Despite all their flaws, one merit of these revisionist accounts is that they recognize and begin to describe the *different* constitution of selfhood for women and for men and provide us with some models—metaphors, myths, "just-so" stories—to act as a vocabulary with which to explore the differences even the different moral constitution of the gendered soul.[5] I am concerned here with the distinctively female vulnerability to soul-loss which women experience through commitment to the female gender ideal itself. These theories go some way towards accounting for the well documented loss of selfhood which abused women display and they offer a more convincing argument than the old canard of "female masochism" to explain why women find it so hard to leave abusive men.

There are many situations in ordinary women's lives which bring with them the possibility of partial extinction of the self and in the worst cases the kind of total extinction which leads to suicide, mental breakdown, and even murder. These situations have three main components. The first and most common is simply chronic overload in the demand for the women's caring activities. All unpaid careers—including mothers and all those caring for sick, disabled, and elderly relatives—are chronically exposed to caring overload (Finch 1989).

The second component is the withdrawal of love by the primary object of a woman's love—usually a man—through connection with whom she experiences herself as worthwhile. This is a commonplace of the feminist critique of the feminine gender role but no less important for being so familiar. The bereavement entailed in loss of love usually leaves the woman grieving for a lost self as well as a lost love object. The mirror in which she saw herself as having value has been taken away and, perhaps, replaced by a distorting glass in which she appears as unlovable and thereby worthless as a woman. The feminist movement has worked very hard to convince women that their selfhood is not in the ownership of a man in this way, and with some success, but few women emerge from the breakup of a relationship without going through this experience even if they eventually create for themselves a more soundly based selfhood. Moreover, divorce or the end of an established relationship, even when the woman has herself initiated the split, as is typically the case today, still leaves many women coping simultaneously with filling the vacuum left by the loss of an old self while coping with an acute bout of maternal overload as they strive to stabilize the world for children. Women coping with the depression or alcoholism of a partner often also experience the double threat to self involved in taking blame and hatred from a partner who is nevertheless needy and dependent.

The third component is abuse, which can itself be broken down into two elements, coercion/control and degradation. Abuse both destroys a woman's ability to call her body or soul her own and, in a particularly devastating way, brands her as worthless as woman and as human being. She experiences herself as garbage. Most abused women suffer all three at the same time: caring overload, loss of love, and abuse. It adds up to a murderous assault on the soul.

Consider the following description of the typical condition of abused women:

> . . . agitation and anxiety bordering on panic were almost always present. Events even remotely connected with violence—sirens, thunder, a door slamming—elicited intense fear . . . nightmares were universal, with undisguised themes of violence and danger.
>
> In contrast to their dreams, in which they actively attempted to protect themselves, the waking lives of these women were characterized by overwhelming passivity and inability to act. They were drained, fatigued, and numb, without the energy to do more than minimal household chores and child care. They had a passive sense of hopelessness and despair about themselves and their lives. They saw themselves as incompetent, unworthy, and unlovable and were ridden with guilt and shame. They thought they deserved the abuse, saw no options, and felt powerless to make changes.
>
> Like rape victims, battered women rarely experience their anger directly . . . Aggression was most consistently directed against themselves. (Beechey and Whitelegg 1986, 39; quoted in Hilberman 1980)

Hilberman calls this "specific stress syndrome" but if that is not loss of selfhood it is hard to imagine what is (Hilberman 1980, quoted Beechey and Whitelegg 1986, 39).

How does it come about? That was the question above all which seized me when I discovered that my intelligent, cultured, tough, competent daughter had been reduced to just that condition. Even after her escape she was like a newly released hostage, jumpy, fearful, expecting recapture at any moment, not even sure of her right to be free and desperate not to have to be in the same room as the man in case his very presence, even across a court room, should be enough to extinguish all her intended fight. She tutored herself in her waking hours to cope with confrontation which she dreaded, working out techniques of defending herself and her child. But at night she dreamed incessantly that she had let him into her room and could not remember why she was supposed to keep him out, though the only emotion she felt was a dreadful fear of extinction.

About the time that she and her daughter fled into hiding and were seeking a court protection order, my attention was caught by a newspaper report of the death of a young woman, her two children, and the violent ex-boyfriend from whom she had been hiding and against whom she was seeking the same kind of court injunction as my daughter had applied for. All four had been found locked in the sealed interior of the man's car, asphyxiated by carbon monoxide from the exhaust pipe. There were no signs of struggle. The woman's parents were devastated by the coroner's verdict of suicide on *both* adults. They could not believe that their daughter would consent to her own and her childrens' deaths (the man was not their biological father). They protested that she feared him, she was in hiding from him, she wanted to escape, they had spoken to her only the previous evening, she *must* have been coerced.

I discussed the case with my daughter, not then but later when she was "becoming herself" again. Yes, she said, it is very easy to imagine that happening. There comes a point where you believe there *is* no escape, not just because he hounds you and invades any refuge you may find, forcing you to move on endlessly, to live your life in fear of discovery, to have no *home*: but even more crucially because eventually coercion doesn't come from outside you but from within. For months after she was effectively safe from him my daughter would catch herself operating *his* surveillance on herself as his proxy—suppressing and censoring all the activities, responses, expressions of self, which had been dangerous in her life with him. Her accounts of how it feels to be in this condition remind me sharply of the Dibbuk legends: it is a state of being possessed by the will of another.

There are still times when she believes that only when the man dies will she be truly safe from reinvasion. I sense that this is more a measure of the intensity of the soul loss which was involved in the original experience than a realistic likelihood of his ever being in a position to repeat it. After all, his power over her derived in the first place from her decision to make a total commitment to him, something that she is most unlikely to give again. Nevertheless, I make the point here because I think it illuminates the rationale of those desperately abused women who kill their partners. In British law, a woman who kills her violent partner, even after years of degradation at his hands, has no defense in law under the head of "provocation" or "self defense," if she does not act in the heat of the moment. Those women who wait until the man is asleep, drunk or drugged before they attack him are judged to have committed premeditated murder. I believe, having seen my daughter's acute fear, that what is often happening here is not simply a rational judgment—"he's stronger than me: I'll never defeat him in a fair physical fight"—but the *magical* effects of finding the self invaded and taken over. Only when the man is unconscious is he unable to reclaim possession of "his" woman's soul and paralyze her resistance. This is surely the purport of my daughter's nightmares about opening the door to let him in and finding herself face to face with extinction. In the worst cases the only exorcism possible is the exchange of his extinction for the release of your own soul. It is a terrible magic that operates in such situations, illustrated, not least, in the woman's frequent ability to mourn the man she once loved only *after* she can reclaim a self with which to grieve and through which to feel remorse—and for some women his death is the necessary condition of that recovery.

The processes which result in acute loss of selfhood build up slowly and it is often some time before the state of affairs is apparent to outsiders, even, perhaps especially, to family from whom the woman typically tries to conceal the shame for as long as possible. In many cases the woman feels she is protecting the man from disgrace by this concealment, although many battered women find that when they do try to alert other people to the truth they are not believed, especially when the man's public face belies the private reality (Stanko 1985, 53). Often the abuse creeps up on the woman slowly: how bad do things have to get before she allows herself to recognize let alone name the problem to herself?

The first stage is normally the apparent exchange of mutual trust at the outset of the relationship. This brings into play all a woman's desire for connectedness and for the opportunity to express love and her own womanliness through care and concern for the other. The memory of this stage of having been "in love" is one of the things that holds back many battered women from making the final break—the need to hold on to the assurance that once, however briefly, the state of loving vulnerability had been *mutual*. As one of Elizabeth Stanko's informants said:

> I loved him and we had happy times. I guess he'll have to put me in a hospital before I'll go to the police. (Stanko 1985, 55)

In my daughter's case this early stage laid her open to a continual invasion which she later recognized as the basis of her partner's initial ability to coerce her. He had appealed to her for forgiveness for the earlier misuse and desertion: he was a mess, his wife had thrown him out (untrue, as it later transpired), he wanted to restart his life, make something of it. This classically implausible tale disarmed her in several ways. First he wanted to form "a proper family," get to know his daughter, make up for the past. Second, he presented *himself* as needy: he even convinced her that it was her fault that he had deserted her. Thirdly he appeared to be offering to take heavy burdens off her back by sharing responsibilities which she had borne alone since she became pregnant. All that had been fractured would be made whole. His taking things over and making decisions was at first a relief to her after six heavy years as a student/single parent. *Sharing* burdens with him would be qualitatively unlike having to be *dependent* on us.

All her immediate discomfort (and her daughter's resentful resistance) at having to live in a place and a fashion laid down by him she dismissed as the shameful pangs of social snobbery. (He was a casual building laborer: the hoped for career as a rock musician forever remains just round the corner). She must learn to accept his culture and build on the deeper shared values. He had, after all, fully accepted her ideals of equality between the sexes. He wanted her to continue her academic work, to write, to make music, to have a professional career. (Soon after they began to live together she took on a demanding research post, partly at least so that they would have an income when her postgraduate research grant came to an end.) They agreed to share everything. They met each other's friends, she went to his band's gigs, they shared shopping and cooking, she helped with his three younger children who came to stay every weekend.

She recognizes in retrospect that something quite different from mutual exchange was actually happening. He was using her invitation to share her activities, her friends, her (theoretically) feminist ideals, her intellectual and political concerns as justification for never allowing her to be with any other people, except at work, without his being there too. Sharing quickly turned into jealous surveillance. She was not even able to go to the shops by herself. Even in the home his insistence on being a New Man did not mean that he took equal responsibility for domestic chores but that he hovered over her, supervising what *she* did. He did, however, often cook the evening meal and this too was less benevolent than might appear. They lived close to his friends, family, and work so she had a long journey on crowded commuter trains to and from her own job. The journey home was unpredictable but his mealtimes were rigid. After a "hard day on the building site" he needed an early meal, he argued. The effect was to make every journey from work a nightmare in case she was "late" and roused his anger and possessive jealousy. And above all, he never allowed mother and daughter to be alone together. At the same time he gradually left more and more of the weekend care of his other children to Jessica so that this became a regular and very heavy task: he supervised, and might randomly decide to play with the children or set them competitive games but he withdrew from the routine caring while she acquired a heavy sense of responsibility for mothering three more unhappy and demanding children.

Increasingly, especially after moving to be near his work, she found she was no longer seeing her own friends, but was accepting his social world as the proper one for both of them. He also began to prevent her from seeing us and the three brothers to whom she and Stella had been very close, though she fought for Stella's right to visit us. In the name of sharing and commitment she allowed herself to be cut off from her own family and social network, because she saw it as a necessity of his vulnerability, his sense of exclusion. None of us had ever really liked or understood him so she tried to make up to him for that. Indeed, he had never been given unconditional love in his own family, so she must make-up for that too. Thus for every loss that she suffered she responded by redoubling her efforts to care for *him*. Even Stella's misery and resistance she tried to see as something that would pass once father and daughter got to know each other properly: so she expended vast energies to keep the peace between them and to shield Stella from the punishments he inflicted when the child transgressed the often unstated rules, which Stella experienced as arbitrary and humiliating.

Many years ago, Peter Berger and Hansfried Kellner wrote a brilliant essay in which they argued that one of the most vital func-

tions of marriage today (with or without benefit of clergy) is to create
and sustain a shared "nomos" or meaning system by which the two
partners make the same sense of a fragmented world, and present a
common face to it. (Berger and Kellner in Dreitzel 1970, 49-72). They
provide themselves with a "plausibility structure." Typically this
entails the suppression of awkward items which don't quite fit, the
retelling of the separate life histories so that they harmonize, and the
careful management of contexts which might explode the fragile
compromises and near-fictions by which the apparent unity is sustained. What was happening in my daughter's case up to this point
was perhaps no more than a classically difficult case of building a
common nomos from two distant points of the social and personal
spectrum.

It was, however, the point at which she first began to wonder
who precisely she was. She was one self at work, a self continuous
with her Cambridge academic self and with the self that we knew
best, but her work also involved the notorious isolation of the
researcher, which left that self stranded in a social vacuum. At home
she was becoming another self which had some familiar components—a quasi-bohemian element resurrected from the point in ado-
lescence when she had first known her partner and now adapted to
his current music scene; plus a great deal of traditional mothering.
But she also felt she was turning into someone she could not easily
recognize as an *integrated* person. She had always been aware that
she presented to people, particularly boyfriends, the part of her with
which they would be most comfortable, while holding back any
parts which might threaten or alarm them. But the parts presented
had always been *real*—simply not the whole reality. Now she began
to wonder if she had ever had a solid self underneath all these changing faces. Women are specially trained to do this kind of thing
because of that insidious gender imperative to please others and sustain the semi-fictions of harmony and belonging. For Jessica, the
first consciousness of this common process sapped her confidence in
a selfhood she had never before either noticed or doubted.[6]

The problem went deeper than a normal difficulty with
"nomos construction" however. She became aware that his often
repeated claim that he shared her values was a sort of lie. In some
important way he did see himself as a New Man. He talked endlessly of a future in which they would live the life of a successful
professional couple. These were fantasies of material success and of
personal achievement into which all her values "fitted" in his
mind—they were an integral part of the *style* he aspired to. At the

same time however all this was daily, hourly belied by his "building site sexist and racist jokes," his enormous investment into machismo, his "Thatcherite" competitiveness, his materialism, his need to win every argument, dominate every situation. Yet he also, perhaps genuinely, admired all those qualities in her which were farthest removed from "building site culture"—all her educated, middle-class characteristics and her progressive views.

He wanted her to finish her thesis, write, make music, but his behavior was as if calculated to prevent all these things. She came to believe in the end that he had been operating a species of primitive magic. By owning and controlling her he would possess for himself all the things in her and Stella which he coveted. It was a kind of cultural and personal cannibalism. By devouring her he would himself *become* the very things for which he desired her but for which, she began to realize, he also blamed and hated her. But the more he controlled her, the less she was able to display the characteristics he wanted from her, therefore she had to be further punished. He felt cheated. At the very end, what he could not consume he would pollute—her bodily fastidiousness, and her religious beliefs in particular were turned into distorted images of themselves. She stopped going to church and couldn't pray. As self disappeared for her, so did God. Whenever she tried to work on her thesis, write, read a book, play piano or oboe, he sabotaged it. He felt ill, needed her help with the car, wanted a cup of tea, her attention, anything. Eventually an attempt to do any of those things caused wild anger and conflict so she slowly gave up trying. He began to pick fights with her about anything and everything. He wanted to force her to argue with him. It was no achievement to defeat her if she didn't fight him. The worst fights, inevitably, were about those supposedly shared values—sexual equality, socialist ideals—which clearly incensed him, and about the upbringing of children, especially about the kind of person he was trying to turn Stella into. He would keep up these arguments for hours, often whole nights, so she would be too tired to cope with work the following day. He ran up impossible debts, cashing in advance his dream of consumer affluence that he believed was his due and that her "professional" salary, in his fantasy logic, "ought" to have made available. He got violently angry when the unpayable bills came through the door, so she hid them from him and kept the worry to herself, knowing that she was the only reliable breadwinner—his work was intermittent at best.

The violence began ambiguously. He flung her out of bed and punched her "in his sleep"; in the course of wild arguments he "stumbled" and flung her across the room, falling on her and "accidentally" smashing her head on the hearth; he "unintentionally" slammed the door on her in a fury, bruising her from head to toe. This designed "ambiguity" was a kind of game intensifying the threat, challenging her to explode the fiction of "accident," ensuring her collusion in an insidious process of brutalization and humiliation. Eventually it all became fully explicit. She would put up with the endless browbeating just to avoid the violence and shield Stella from these episodes. He never hit Stella seriously (she seemed to intimidate him) but he bullied her and forced her to do things that frightened her. Jessica and Stella quickly learned that the *only* way to protect each other was not to interfere when he was bullying or attacking the other. As many battered women have discovered, children become hostages. Whenever my daughter sees reports of women sent to prison for failing to protect their murdered babies from fathers' and stepfathers' lethal rages she weeps. How do they know she is guilty? Don't they realize it would have been *worse* for the child if she had tried to protect it?

The regime was debilitating. Jessica's academic work lay untouched. She struggled to stay awake at work. She was in permanent fear. She got ill. The excruciating abdominal pain was eventually diagnosed as muscular spasm brought on by stress. She lay in her hospital bed writing delaying letters to creditors, appeals to her bank, and listening to her partner making macho complaints to the authorities about incompetent doctors who didn't know their job. When she was discharged she tried gently to explain the diagnosis to him and was rewarded by a four hour harangue about how there *was* no stress: she was just a hysterical woman.

All her most secure skills slipped away from her. If she ever tried her piano or oboe she stumbled and lost her nerve: he was the musician! She couldn't write, she even forgot how to spell, she could no longer drive a car competently. Every aspect of self in which she had ever taken pride turned to failure and disgrace. He taunted her with her loss of competence but it infuriated him too. She was useless! She felt extinguished, shamed, not worth saving, hopeless. In hospital she hoped she would die.

If all of this sounds implausible be assured that it differs only in its details from the typical process by which abusive men turn the caring program built into women's gender identity against them and convince them that they are indeed worthless and unlovable. The process poisons the roots of self validation on which a woman's identity is founded. My daughter's vulnerability included her academic and musical accomplishments but the sense of worthlessness equally affected her sexual self and her self as mother—the latter most of all perhaps.

What was particularly devastating was the fact that her unrecognized feminine "deep self" was another "heroic mother" just like my mother's overt and my, for long, covert and unrecognized deep self. It was the imperatives of this self, the "traditional" female self, which were used to destroy her second self, the independent, autonomous modern woman. The more she *cared*, in every sense, the more he was able to deflect the energies thus generated, into a destructive manipulation which very nearly destroyed both selves.

Even when there is no "independent" self to be attacked, battered women are typically made to feel they are bad wives, mothers and housekeepers—bad *women*. Most battered women's testimonies include accounts of how they could never get anything right in the home or salvage any proper pride from their domestic responsibilities.

> I was always frightened . . . He screamed at me all the time and the kids. He didn't play with the kids he used to hit them, he'd take it out on them more than on me. He said I neglected things, *it didn't matter what I did it was never good enough* . . . He'd just go berserk till two or three in the morning bawling and shouting, and I'd just sit and hold his legs . . . when I was pregnant many a night I've run out and slept in the passage till the morning. He wanted the place immaculate but he'd never tidy up, he just sat there in his chair from morning till night and got at me all the time about the housework. I had no friends, I felt as if I had nobody. (my emphasis) (Campbell 1984, 86)

Denigration, exhaustion and isolation are very destructive experiences especially when children are used as pawns to coerce the woman. Consider the chronic exhaustion, not unlike my daughter's, entailed for another of Beatrix Campbell's interviewees, who was working as a shop assistant in the daytime.

> After we had the second child we had the rows, he'd not let me go to her when she cried. He'd make me sleep with the kids, then he'd make me come back to bed with him, in and out all night. (Campbell 1984, 90)

The rock bottom condition of all battered women is the same experience of themselves as worthless, unable to get anything right. It is worse, perhaps, when they are financially dependent on the man, but being even the main breadwinner does not in itself protect a woman. These women are not timid, colorless people, constitutionally too feeble to defend themselves: they have been tricked out of their own souls. They are women possessed. Thea Vidale is a tough black Texan stand-up comic whose hard-hitting anti-racist, anti-sexist act was an outrageous success on "the fringe" of the 1992 Edinburgh Festival. The Independent newspaper described her as "large, loud and very, very lewd." In an interview with the newspaper she explained how she came to comedy. She had been a schoolteacher before her children were born, then, when they were little, she was an evening waitress who began to try out her wisecracks in a club act.

> I was a battered wife. If I hadn't started comedy I'd be dead by now. He would've killed me. He was already killing my spirit . . . One time when I was breast feeding my baby he hit me in the head with the lawn chair. He hated me doing something on my own. One time I came in (from work) no later than 12 'cos I know not to do that else he'd kill me. He got ready to kick me and somehow God put a shield around me. I stepped back and he hit the wall and fell down like a cartoon. I stepped over him, said goodnight, went to my bedroom and put the dresser against the door. (emphasis added)

Soon after that she left him and took her act to the road.

> *I'd been so stagnated by my husband, I couldn't remember how to drive a car.* My first tour I couldn't even read a road map—I ain't lyin'. (emphasis added) (Wareham 1992, 13)

This is a woman who can now intimidate and electrify audiences, not just in polite Edinburgh but in places deep in "Klan country" where "they could easily have killed my black ass and you'd have never heard of me again." What must it take to kill a spirit like that? What it takes is precisely what I have described above.

Not everyone is so lucky. There was a recent case in England of a woman who was jailed for the murder of her violent partner whose atrocities had included attacking her every time she used a word he did not understand. By the time she killed him she had become pathologically inarticulate. My daughter forgetting how to spell was a very mild case.

The component processes in these apparently diverse cases are very similar. Consider first *constant surveillance*. This eliminates the woman's private space. She loses control of her body which is permanently available to him. She loses control of her consciousnessness which he fills with himself by sheer presence and persistence. She loses control of her home because he has claimed all the space and property and activities in it. Often she loses the ability to protect her children. Work outside the home may be partially exempt from surveillance but even that can be policed by an ingenious abuser, and undermined in other ways, such as through his making certain that she is permanently exhausted.

Secondly there is the experience of *isolation*, that feeling that she "had nobody" which oppressed one of the women quoted above. Women lose touch with plausibility structures which might root them in an externally validated reality, distinct from that dominated by the abusing man. In my daughter's case she lost touch with all her own networks and was left only the social contacts approved and presided over by her partner. This network played back to her things which reinforced his claims and undermined her sense that the world could be otherwise. All his friends and family (with the one life saving exception of a woman who was already in the process of extricating herself from a similar situation) assumed that it was a woman's duty to take whatever "her man" threw at her. Even her partner's wife who, it transpired, had suffered identical coercion, degradation, and beatings, tried to persuade my daughter that she should stick it out because "if he's like that he *must* love you." When my daughter left, her abuser pursued and hounded her and broke into two consecutive homes. The court considering the requests for a protection order against him, brought by both Jessica and his wife, recommended that he should see a psychiatrist. This psychiatrist also tried to persuade Jessica that he "needed her," that only she could help him, that they should seek *joint* therapy. The police took a similar view when she first reported his breaking in. *Nobody* else wanted responsibility for him. The uniform cultural message was—stand by your man! It was as if *he* were the abused one. It becomes Kafkaesque for a woman trying to protect what remains of her self against such a barrage.

The third component process which follows isolation is *the imposition of the abuser's definitions as the only reality*. Once she has lost effective access to outside plausibility structures his defi-

nitions of the world steadily gain credibility. She has only her own
exhausted will with which to deny them, most crucially of all, his
definitions of her self. My daughter began to believe she was going
mad. Her intellect told her that everything he insisted on was crazy,
sick, terrible but the unremitting energy with which he asserted
his view of reality and controlled the agenda of their lives undermined her confidence in what she had once known as normality. In
The Taming of the Shrew Petruchio forces Kate to greet an old man
as if he is a young maiden, and then reverses the requirement: and
makes her agree that it is morning—no evening! This is often played
for laughs with Kate "humoring" him: if it is not, its real character
as torture becomes too obvious. It is disturbingly similar to what
my daughter endured daily and nightly. Indeed, some researchers
suggest that there is no difference between torture and what happens to battered women: they are identical techniques for bringing
about "the destruction of the integrity of the self" (Hanmer and
Saunders 1984, 88).

The clinching element in these processes is then the addition of
physical violence. All the research on battered women agrees that it
is this which fixes the humiliation and sense of worthlessness in
the victims. Not least, it fuses and confuses physical abuse and sex:
the boundary between play and abuse is, at best, rendered uncertain. Every occasion of even ambiguous, "accidental" violence left
my daughter feeling shamed, not only by the damaged state of her
body, which seemed like the outward demonstration of the state of
her soul, but also because she had not left him then and there. Not
leaving meant she was *colluding* with him. Each repeat reinforced
her sense of having collaborated in her own degradation: each failure
to leave made it progressively harder to summon the resources
needed to confront the violence openly and by the time he explicitly
acknowledged, indeed gloried in the violence, her sense of her own
shame had already bitten too deep to make the break.

Violence was utterly foreign to her previous experience of life.
She was astonished at how normal it was in his culture, where men
just did hit women; that's simply what happens; and then as Sue
Lees, among others, has shown, the women blame each other and
themselves (Lees 1986). Had she but realized, this culture which
surrounded my daughter with its plausibility structures was light
years away from the essentially matriarchal culture of both mine
and her father's working class families. She tried not to reject it for
fear of her own "snobbery," while still sustaining a memory of all
her prior values which condemned it. Much of her smuggled reading

was an attempt to hold on to her old ideas or understand her new context[7] but any open expression of "feminist" criticism was soon interpreted as an act of war and was, anyway, likely to be dismissed by the social network in which they lived as "those hysterical women again." Her worst, and final beating came during International Women's Week. All the ideas she no longer dared to speak of were constantly pushed in his face by his own act of turning on radio or television. By this time more than half of her felt hopelessly unworthy of those distant ideals. In the end it was not her fragile and defeated feminist self that summoned the courage to leave. It was her decision to save her daughter before it was too late which led her to arrange a "safe house" to which to escape. But it was her partner's threat to beat up her gentle and much loved youngest brother which actually precipitated the flight. Her deep impulse to protect—her heroic mother self—retained enough definition and provided enough energy to act even when she was totally paralyzed and without hope in respect of herself. Yet it has also left her with a heavy sense of guilt about "abandoning" his other children and being unable to protect them from him.[8]

I shall conclude with three brief observations. First, I believe that more careful consideration is needed of those processes which cause battered women to blame themselves. I am persuaded that the often unacknowledged but deep acceptance of the female nurturing role as a moral imperative of the female soul is a central component. It may be that Dinnerstein is right to interpret women's guilt and self punishment as a displaced expression of unresolved infantile rage, but the model of displaced rage seems to me to be a more powerful explanation of the actions of male abusers.[9] Only when we have taken full account of the abuse itself do we need to search for such repressed residues of self/mother hate as *primary* reasons for the demoralization of battered women. They have had their selfhood destroyed by men who use women's deepest criteria of self-worth as instruments with which to torture them. No one goes looking for such residues of self-blame to explain the *identical* experiences of the victims of political torture or hostage taking who also find the integrity of the self assaulted.

I have no doubt that Nancy Chodorow was right when she argued recently that even feminist revisions of the Freudian story have a tendency to become new versions of blaming the victim (Chodorow 1989). I fully accept, indeed I know I exemplify, Chodorow's description of the typical Western female whose sense of responsibility for the cosmos is so overdeveloped that she apolo-

women who should change themselves? Is the "caring" prescription the ultimately lethal element in women's ego ideal? And if so what should be done about it this side of the unlikely utopia of shared parenting or genuinely communal child care? Precisely *how* might women more effectively cultivate what John Stuart Mill memorably termed "the self-regarding virtues?" One whole generation of professional women seems to have decided that not having children is their best defence. And even Thea Vidale left her children behind—and continues, uneasily, to justify that hard choice—as the precondition for breaking free from her abuser (Wareham 1992).

I do not have space to explore any of this here except to note that popular culture is full of these themes—an indication that ordinary women are as preoccupied with these problems as are feminist theorists. From Madonna to Sigourney Weaver the popular media bombard us with messages about the possibility of a new female self. In particular, I believe, current science fiction and the genre of quasi-feminist private eye thrillers would repay analysis. Fantasies in which a female hero inhabits a genre which has classically coded individualistic masculine autonomy, tell us a good deal about what a woman can keep and what she must shed of her old female self in order to achieve and sustain a (masculine defined?) "true" autonomy. The ironies are legion. My daughter pointed out to me that a furor arose in the press about the film of one of Sara Paretsky's stories *V. I. Warshawski*, because there was outrage that the female private eye, played by Kathleen Turner, was shown being beaten up by a gang boss *who was not her husband or lover*!

Plus ça change . . .

NOTES

1. If the invitation to write this paper had been couched in terms of the loss not of "soul" but of "self," I might well have chosen to consider the same subject matter but my approach would have been different and probably more distanced, not least because the word would not have triggered the memory of my mother's "saying" and all that followed from it. Leonard Shengold's use of the term "soul murder" to designate the effects of abuse and deprivation on children (Shengold 1989) acted as permission to use a parallel term for the effects of domestic violence on women. The word soul suggests to me the possibility of recognizing—hinting at—a level of discourse which accords some ultimate significance to the person beyond what can be said by the expert social scientific disciplines. The metaphysical and theological connotations of soul suggest a dimension of the integrity of persons,

which is not fully captured by the vocabulary of self and "selfhood." The death of the soul is of greater moment than the death of the self. The poetic language of love and of its corruption says more than, and different from, the scientific analysis of "the self in relationship." Witnessing the pain and fear of my daughter and trying to make sense of it over-taxed the limited resources of my scholarly discipline. That is why an unwritten subtext of my essay is the recognition of the chronic and multifarious need for redemption which is entailed by the human condition. The self for which we each take moral responsibility always stands in need of mercy.

2. What follows is necessarily *my* (partial and selective) version of my daughter's story. Indeed, in many ways it is as much about my relation to my own mother and to my daughter as it is about my daughter's experience of abuse. It involves silences, elisions, and reticences over areas which I feel it would be wrong to intrude upon any further, including the question of how the two central actors became emotionally and sexually involved with each other in the first, and in the second, place. The details given here about my daughter's experience were freely offered by her in over two years of conversations after the main events, but this text does not encompass all that I know of her story and represents only a small fraction of what she knows and understands. This is not her father's story, or her brother's story, it is not her daughter's story or her ex-partner's story; all these would be different in complex and perhaps startling ways. What I have written is essentially my own meditation on motherhood and the way in which a particular, very common, form of traditional mothering leaves the boundaries of the female self vulnerable. It is also perhaps, a not very oblique appeal to mothers and daughters to forgive themselves and each other for the fragilities which they both inherit and pass on. As the poet W. H. Auden wrote in *The Sea and the Mirror*

> "Child? Mother? Either grief will do.
> The need for pardon is the same."
> (Auden 1968, p. 214)

But it is also an argument against women—yet again—merely blaming themselves and each other, however lovingly. There are men in these dramas too, and *they* often play the leading roles.

3. He never admitted the abuse and was not prosecuted for it because the care professionals and the police dealing with the case judged that the children's testimonies were too confused to stand up in court: there was even a suspicion (unprovable in the circumstances) that their extreme confusion was caused by a hallucinogenic substance. It was undisputed that the children were deeply traumatized. They were put on the "At Risk" register of the Social Services department and they and their mother were re-housed by the local authority at an address kept secret from the father. There was also speculation that the father may himself have been the victim

of abuse in childhood. He had also admitted to my daughter and to his wife separately that he had regularly committed incest with his youngest sister from a time when he was a teenager and she was about nine years old—a story confirmed privately, but not to the police, by the sister after the children's ordeal.

So far as Stella is concerned, the social workers and policewoman who interviewed her concluded that there had probably been no sexual abuse. Stella herself says, "Why would he bother with me when he had my mummy to persecute? He never *was* interested in me anyway. He only ever *pretended* to be when he wanted to please mummy." Her denial could, of course, be a way of protecting her mother. There is, however, no sign of any rejection of female identity. (See the discussion of the rejection of the female identity by child victims of sexual abuse in the chapter in this volume by Janet Jacobs.)

4. In her profound and painful account of her mother's life, *Landscape for a Good Woman*, Carolyn Kay Steedman explores the ways in which her mother's stories and glosses on her actions all pointed up the moral that she was a "good woman" who sacrificed herself for her children (Steedman 1986). The grown-up daughter's dissection of the messages, of the silences behind them and the subtexts beneath them—children as burdens, as bargaining counters, as validations or as extensions of self—shows how complex and contradictory the "good mother" label can be, indeed is bound to be when it acts as a mode of "resolving" the structural contradictions in family and society which catch the woman in a pincer movement. I am far from claiming exemption from such processes for my mother or myself. This, however, is not the place to anatomize them.

5. For this reason I have reservations about the ultimate usefulness of a model of "the self," even one so thoughtful as that of O'Keefe (O'Keefe 1982) which does not allow for the differences between male and female selves in Western cultures.

6. I remain somewhat skeptical about attempts to argue the virtues of this female proficiency in shape shifting as a valuable "postmodern" adaptive skill, despite the exhilarating fictons of Angela Carter (Carter 1984, 1992) and the impressive theoretical arguments of Jane Flax (Flax 1989). It must be admitted, however, that both Carter and Flax regard the manipulation of multiple tasks and faces as, at best, paradoxical so far as female identity is concerned.

7. She recalls Beatrix Campbell's book as one of those she read in hospital, trying to understand why men abuse women (Campbell 1984).

8. The children's account of the abuse included a detail which caused particular anguish to my daughter. Their father had prefaced his first sexual approach to them by explaining that he was "sad and lonely" because Jessica

and Stella had left him. Jessica interpreted this as a deliberate (and not entirely unsuccessful) attempt to punish her by laying the responsibility for the unspeakable at her door because she had abandoned both him and his children in her selfish flight. He had already played the "what will it do to the children if you leave me?" card, and the "I can't be responsible for my actions if you go" card in attempts to hold her and then to induce her to return. She had not anticipated his combining the two threats in retrospective blackmail/vengeance in this terrible fashion when she called the bluff, as she had hoped, and left. Fully accepting that the damage to the children was his and in no sense her responsibility was the hardest and perhaps the most important part of her process of recovery.

9. Indeed, it is all too plausible to interpret many of the expressions of masculinity in popular culture as barely disguised legitimations of infantile rage writ large for grown men. Bill Gibson, in his forthcoming analysis of "Warrior Culture" in contemporary American society makes convincing and chilling sense of this aspect of Dinnerstein's argument (Gibson 1994).

REFERENCES

Auden, Wystan Hugh (1968). *Collected Longer Poems.* London: Faber & Faber.

Beechey, Veronica and Elizabeth Whitelegg, eds. 1986. *Women in Britain Today.* Milton Keynes: Open University Press.

Benjamin, Jessica. 1990. *The Bonds of Love.* London: Virago Press.

Campbell, Beatrix. 1984. *Wigan Pier Revisited.* London: Virago Press.

Carter, Angela. 1984. *Nights At the Circus.* London: Picador Books.

————. 1992. *Wise Children.* London: Virago Press.

Chodorow, Nancy. 1978. *The Reproduction of Mothering.* Berkeley: University of California Press.

————. 1989. *Feminism and Psychoanalytic Theory.* Cambridge: Polity Press.

Dinnerstein, Dorothy. 1977. *The Mermaid and the Minotaur.* New York: Harper Row Press.

Dreitzel, Hans Peter, ed. 1970. *Recent Sociology No. 2: Patterns of Communicative Behaviour.* New York & London: Macmillan Press.

Finch, Janet. 1989. *Family Obligations and Social Change.* Cambridge: Polity Press.

Flax, Jane. 1978. "The Conflict between nurturance and autonomy in mother-daughter relationships and within feminism." In *Feminist Studies 2*, pp. 171-89.

———. 1989. *Thinking Fragments*. Berkeley: University of California Press.

Gibson, J. William. 1994, forthcoming. *Warrior Dreams*. New York: Hill & Wang.

Gilligan, Carol. 1982. *In a Different Voice*. Cambridge: Harvard University Press.

Hanmer, Jalna, and Sheila Saunders. 1984. *Well Founded Fear*. London: Hutchinson Press.

Lees, Sue. 1986. *Losing Out*. London: Hutchinson Press.

O'Keefe, Daniel Lawrence. 1982. *Stolen Lightning*. New York: Vintage Books.

Shengold, Leonard. 1989. *Soul Murder*. New Haven and London: Yale University Press.

Stanko, Elizabeth. 1985. *Intimate Intrusions*. London: Routledge Press.

Steedman, Carolyn Kay. 1986. *Landscape for a Good Woman*. London: Virago Press.

Wareham, Mark. 1992. "Gripped by Uncontrollable Thea." In *The Independent*, Wednesday, August 19, 1992.

SUSAN L. NELSON

4

Soul-Loss and Sin: A Dance of Alienation

THE CONDITION OF SIN

In the Christian tradition, we confess that human creatures are not only created in the image of God, that human beings not only are relational, God-dependent, rational, loving and responsible beings, but that they are also sinful. As the new Brief Statement of Faith of the Presbyterian Church (USA) affirms: "But we rebel against God; we hide from our Creator."

The concept of sin has both obvious and complex meanings. The word sin conjures up for us images of disobedience, acts of harm against others and/or the environment, the transgression of boundaries. Sometimes, as in the above statement, it suggests acts of violation against the image of God in others and oneself. Moreover, in the Sermon on the Mount, Jesus is remembered as expanding the understanding of sin to include not only acts (i.e., murder and adultery) but also intentions and attitudes (i.e., hatred and lust).

But the concept of sin means more than a catalogue of one's sins. It also refers to a state of being. To be "in sin" is to be in a state of alienation—alienation from God, from oneself, from others, and from the world. Sin, in this case, describes the state of alienation that results from a rupture in the basic relationality for which human beings were created—a rupture for which humanity (individually and corporately) is responsible. A rupture that means that "natural" relationality has been torn apart, and that human beings, rather than reach outward for God and one another, instead spin around themselves in circles of self-preoccupation, self-protection and, sometimes, self-aggrandizement—as if they alone were responsible for the ordering and controlling of the world.

Our understanding of sin is further complicated because there is a tension that runs down the middle of the classic theological understanding of human responsibility for sin. Following in the steps of Augustine, the tradition has affirmed both that human beings are born into sin—that their state of sin is "original," inherited—and yet that they are also responsible for their sins, their sinful state, and for the sinfulness of the world. On the one hand, to say that their sinful state is original is to mean that it is something given to them over which they have no choice (as Augustine insisted, that they cannot not sin), that it is total in all that their faculties are impaired (e.g., as in the Calvinist notion of total depravity), that it is a state of disorder and bondage from which they cannot save themselves, that in this state of disorder their natural and good desires and needs become out of balance, and that it is a state inherited from their foreparents, Adam and Eve, in whose fall "we sinned all." On the other hand, to say that their sinful state is something for which they are responsible is to say that sin is not essential to human nature. Human beings were created good; their sinful state is the result of their own doings. Classically, the Christian tradition has sought to affirm both insights, and in affirming the paradox that human beings are both born into sin and responsible for their sinfulness, the tradition has risked being understood as contradictory at its heart. Indeed, with the coming of modernity, many theologians have rejected the notion of original sin as it has traditionally been understood—wishing to affirm the human responsibility and possibility of each individual. Yet the intuition that sin is both something that human beings are responsible for and yet also something larger than their realm of responsibility, something into which they are born and that seems to come with being a part of the human race, persists in the theological self-understanding of many strands of contemporary Christianity. Perhaps this is because this understanding of sin both has a well-established biblical base (see, for instance, Romans 7-8) and reflects an accurate intuition into the complexity of the human condition.

Rather than reject the notion of original sin, this paper[1] seeks to explore how we can understand this intuition that humanity "inherits" a state of alienation that means alienation from the ground of their being (God, as some would have it), from others, from the world, and—reflecting the concern of this gathering—from their true way of being a self in the world, and wonders whether alienation as explored in this paper is necessarily sin. Since the Christian tradition has understood "soul" to mean "life," "person," "self," or "the *unity* of personality," (Brown, 1958) I assume that this notion of alienation from a true way of being a self in the world that I would focus upon correlates to our concept of soul-loss. Thus alienation from one's true way of being a self in the world would mean the erosion of one's very soul.

Because the notion of soul/self that undergirds this essay is relational (see next section), the use of soul/self resonates with that of John McDargh, who says that the "becoming real" of the soul/self is "profoundly interpersonal," and focuses on the dynamics of childhood trauma and disappointment. In this paper I will argue that the works of Alice Miller (most particularly *The Drama of the Gifted Child*) and Gershen Kaufman (in *Shame: the Power of Caring*) are speaking about this alienation/soul-loss. Further, I will show how their writings reveal how this alienation/soul-loss is "inherited" in the rupturing or perverting of the human rationality that is basic to human well being. Thus, while affirming that alienation/soul-loss is inherited—an intuition of the Christian doctrine of original sin, I will note that this original alienation has an historical point of origin (meaning, in *this* time, not before history). Furthermore, I will show how this alienation, while inherited, is also a way of being that the alienated individual helps to create. The alienation, in this sense, is not an inherited *state* but a *dance of alienation* in which the alienated one is a creative participant. However, even though this dance of alienation is one for which the alienated one is at least partially responsible, because this dance is often a dance of *survival* and not the willful act of disobedience that the category "sin" as a referent to human alienation traditionally suggests, I will question the appropriateness of the category sin to name this dance of alienation—this soul-loss—and suggest that there may need to be more than one way to speak of human alienation from a theological perspective.

The understanding of the human condition that implicitly underlies the writings of both Miller and Kaufman—as will be amplified further later on—is perhaps best described as deeply relational and painfully vulnerable. Human beings are not born fully formed— like the biblical Adam and Eve. Rather, humans are born as vulnerable infants—needing hands to catch them, arms to hold them, breasts to feed them, and eyes to see them. Human beings need help to grow into the fullness of their human possibility—to learn who they are, what they feel, what they need, and what they can offer the world. They need to be loved and to have others accept and value their love for them.[2]

This is the matrix in which human creatures live, move and have their being—that realm in which who they are is seen and acknowledged and the tension between freedom and finitude finds its meaning. It is the realm where a wound—a rupture in relationality—can mean not being seen and valued as one is, the complementary need to hide one's face so it will not be rejected, the fear of exposure and shame, and the development of a dance of alienation. Thus, human anxiety may not emanate just from the tension between finitude and freedom—between possibilities and limitations as existentialist thinkers such as Søren Kierkegaard have supposed, but also from inter-relationality and the vulnerability their dependence entails.

> In those days they shall no longer say:
> 'The parents have eaten sour grapes,
> and the children's teeth are set on edge.'
> But all shall die for their own sins; the teeth
> of everyone who eats sour grapes shall be set on edge.
> (Jeremiah 31:29-30, NRSV)

THE PRISON

"The fathers have eaten sour grapes and the children's teeth are set on edge." An old proverb known both to Jeremiah and Ezekiel. A proverb that underlines the intrinsic relationship of the child's well-being with that of their parents. In the coming age, Jeremiah promises, the children will *not* be punished for their parents' sins— instead, each one shall be compensated for their own activity. The cycle of generation sin/guilt/punishment will be broken.

What has this to do with a notion of sin and alienation as a state that is both original yet for which human beings are responsible? What is the relationship between the generations and one's experience of oneself as sinful—alienated from God, others, and oneself? How does the relationship between generations effect soul-loss?

Perhaps Paul, in D. H. Lawrence's "The Rocking Horse Winner" provides a bridge to awareness.[3] Paul was a sensitive child—a child who knew the coldness of his mother's heart—even though she showered her children with affection; a child who knew that there was a deep sadness that gripped his mother's soul; a child who felt, somehow, responsible—who hoped that if he listened to the message of the whispering walls he could make his mother happy—make her love him.

But Paul's story did not evolve as he hoped. In response to his mother's worry reflected in the ever present whispering, "There must be more money" Paul took the responsibility to see that there was, in fact, more money. Riding his rocking horse until he knew the name of the winning horse is as anticipated—he could not win his mother's love. Instead of love, he won death as he sacrificed himself to the fruitless task of earning what should have been his birthright as a child: the love and attention of his mother. The sadness of her soul, the hardness of her heart, meant for Paul not life and love but abandonment (did she not see what was happening to him?) and death.

Abandonment, fear of abandonment, responsibility for a parent's happiness, sacrifice of the child's self/soul—all themes of this story—are themes that Alice Miller recognizes as well in the lives of the real human people with whom she works—people who learned at an early age to abandon themselves, to hide their true selves behind a constructed false self, and who continue to be in bondage to the drama of their childhood as they act out their alienation from self and others in their adult lives.

But, why would a child abandon him/herself? And what does self-abandonment mean?

From Miller's perspective, children abandon themselves because they need the love and security of their parents so much that they are not willing to risk that loss. A child is born not fully formed but as an infant who needs love and attention. Children need to be loved and held; they need to be free to express their full range of emotions and have those emotions be accepted and mirrored back; they need to be free and secure enough to pass through stages of narcissistic self-centeredness without being perceived as being selfish. They need to come to know their full range of feelings and emo-

tions and have these feelings affirmed in order to develop a sense of
self-esteem, of self-well-being in order to know who they are, and in
order then to be fully functioning and caring individuals in society.
They need to be respected as separate individuals—allowed to be
the center of their own drama—and given the space/freedom to
explore what that means. A child given the holding, affirmation,
mirroring and respect it needs, Miller argues, will grow to hold,
affirm, mirror and respect others.

> Children who are respected learn respect. Children who are
> cared for learn to care for those weaker than themselves.
> Children who are loved for what they are cannot learn intoler-
> ance. In an environment such as this they will develop their
> **own** ideals, which can be nothing other than humane, since
> they grow out of the experience of love (1984:97).

The problem of self alienation/abandonment/soul-loss which
Miller identifies is that children are born in our present culture into
societies (the macrocosm) or to families (the microcosm) that fail
to hold, affirm, mirror, and respect them or their own developmental
process. The result is what theologian Rita Nakashima Brock has
called woundedness or a brokenheart.[4] Born with heart—with feelings and connections and needs and, thus, with vulnerability—children are often wounded and thus grow themselves around a broken
heart, developing a false self to hide and protect the true, wounded
self.

In her earlier work, *The Drama of the Gifted Child*, Miller
shows how this brokenheartedness—this self-alienation—happens to
a child and how the child participates in the process. Needing to be
born into families that will hold, affirm, mirror, and respect them
and their growth process, the people with whom Miller has worked
instead were born into families where in many ways the dynamics
were reversed. Born to parents who were deprived of the holding,
affirmation, mirroring, and respect they needed as children—to parents who were thus hungry for all the love and affection they did not
receive as infants—Miller's clients were used by their parents to fill
their own needs. Thus, instead of being mirrored, they became the
mirrors for their parents. When they felt a feeling, expressed an emotion, displayed a natural curiosity about their bodies that were not
pleasing to their parents and threatened the parents' own well-being
(perhaps because those feelings and emotions and curiosities had
not been received and affirmed for the parents themselves in their

childhood), the clients as children learned to stifle those troubling desires so as not to displease their parents. So great, it would seem, is a child's need for the affection of the parent in order to survive, that the child will choose to hide parts of him/herself—those crucial parts, Miller argues, to true selfhood—and cover those hidden parts (the hidden self) with a false self that will please the parent. This is the basic drama of abandonment/soul-loss that children continue then to enact in their lives—mustering all their resources in order to stand in the light of their parents' favor.

Ironically, the children in this drama abandon parts of themselves in order to *avoid* the abandonment they fear—but in doing so, they act out the very real abandonment *that has already occurred.* The parent, in showing displeasure over parts of the child's being, abandons those parts; the child, in hiding them, reenacts the drama of abandonment. Thus, the feelings, desires, curiosities of natural human development are tucked away, beyond the recesses of consciousness, neatly bound with cords of fear—the fear of abandonment. To touch—to untie—the cords that bind is to risk a plethora of feelings and agonies that threaten to overwhelm the person. And indeed, Miller notes, a single child, alone in his/her feelings, might well be overwhelmed by such feelings without someone to hold them, share them, appreciate them, and help to make them manageable. Thus, the choice to abandon oneself which children seem to make in order to keep parents from abandoning them is a necessary choice in order to survive. Yet, whether the choice is justifiable or not as an act of survival, the act of hiding oneself to please another is not a benign act. Those hidden feelings rumble around within the person constantly needing to be rejected, and the drama of abandonment is continually acted out—locking the person into a prison of their own making—the prison of their childhood.

Deprived of the attention they so desperately needed in their own childhood, these people then use their own children to fulfill these needs—to be the mirror who can show them what they did not see before, who can love and adore them, and who will not reject them.[5] Thus, these people raise their children to please them, to be "good" reflections of themselves (or of those parts of themselves they want to see)—and reject those parts of their children that they were not allowed to know in themselves. And the drama continues. "The parents taste of sour grapes, and the children's teeth are set on edge."

The tragedy of this drama is manifold. On the one hand, it is the tragedy of the parents who never were given the holding, affirmation, mirroring and respect they needed in childhood and will never get it. On the other hand, the situation is tragic for the child of that parent for it means that the child also never gets to have his/her own childhood—and learns, instead, to abandon itself and its feelings and needs for the good of the parent—learning, in fact, the drama of self-abandonment that has kept its parents, and will keep it, a prisoner of its childhood. And, this drama is tragic for the human community, history, and the well-being of the world as well, for the new generation, which is born with its own possibility which it might give the world is instead robbed of its unique possibility and made to pay the price for the alienation of previous generations.

Thus Miller sketches for us a vision of a human drama of self-alienation that develops into alienation from and for others. She gives us a picture of persons formed in the image of their parents—to be the image of their parents—at great personal expense (the expense of being who they really are). This self-alienation/soul-loss is characterized by loneliness, isolation, and the fear of desertion/abandonment. It entails the loss of feelings (i.e., jealousy, envy, anger, loneliness, impotence, anxiety)—which Miller argues are the key to true human selfhood. It is experienced by many as a feeling of emptiness reflecting the loss of so much of the self. In a sense, this alienation is a state of being (or being partially) dead—of soul loss. But it is a death—a loss of soul—the child would rather suffer than to risk the possibility of losing the parent's love (1982:2-13).

Miller's vision of this human predicament, however, is not confined to the workings of the generations in a family, for she offers us in her two later books *For Your Own Good* and *Thou Shalt Not Be Aware* a view of how society in general perpetuates the alienation of a child from him/herself—through the pedagogical methods in which a child is "schooled" out of him/herself in the former—and through the way in which society, and the psychoanalytic tradition in particular, choose not to see the way in which children are used in abusive and neglectful ways by parents and persons in authority in the latter. Having made the case for the abandonment of the self in her earlier book, in these books, Miller draws on that basic description of self-alienation, but adds to it the dynamics of "poisonous pedagogy" and outright child abuse (and the corresponding proclivity not to see it).[6] Thus, for the purposes of this paper's exploration into the nature of human alienation/soul-loss and the way in which that alienation is original to the human situation, these books add not so much to the sense of the predicament of alienation as they add to our appreciation of the largeness of the situation, of the way in which

children are taught via poisonous pedagogy not to listen to themselves, of the craziness of the child's inner world as s/he is both
abused and taught not to see/feel that abuse, and of the way in which
society creates an environment where the sacrifice of the child is tol-
erated if not even encouraged. All of these elements, however, add
immense weight to the process of self-alienation as we have come to
understand it.

She has also given us a vision of human creatures to whom
being loved is so important that they would blame themselves for
their parents' unhappiness (or even for their parent's abusive behavior) and abandon themselves in order not to lose the bonds of connection. She has shown us how easily people make idols out of those
(their parents) who are meant to be only passing "gods" in their
developmental process. She has shown us how love becomes transformed on the one hand into a duty and on the other into a grasping
formed in the desperate childhood fear of abandonment. And she
has shown how easily humans can and do abandon themselves, losing their very souls in the process; how they blame themselves for
their own alienation; and how they cut themselves off from the very
feelings that might tell them otherwise and point towards their healing. She has thus shown us how the drama of abandonment (the
drama of the gifted child) becomes a dance of alienation—a dance in
which the alienated one is both victim (inheritor of the alienation of
the parents) and participant (one who chooses, for all the reasons
noted above, to live in alienation from self and others). Whether this
dance of alienation, this loss of the soul which is both an inheritance and an act of one's own complicity, is sin or not remains to be
seen.

As we put Miller's work into the context of the question of
sin, alienation, and soul-loss, one aspect of her work needs to be
acknowledged. In her questioning (in her books *Thou Shalt Not Be
Aware* and *Banished Knowledge*) of the way in which the drive theory developed by Freud has been used to keep children and adults
unaware of the actual childhood dramas of abuse that they have
known and repressed, and in her understanding of how the human
person if held, affirmed, mirrored and respected would grow by
nature into a caring individual, she offers a vision of the human person that raises questions for a view of the human predicament that
would name human beings as fallen and thus unable not to sin. If her
challenge to Freudian drive theory developed in these two books is
correct—that human neurosis (might we say perversity/depravity?) is
not so much the result of inherited human drives but originates in

actual childhood traumas which are then reenacted—in a drama of repetition—as people seek to be seen in the dilemma they secretly know, to be helped to consciousness, and to be freed from bondage to the unconscious reenactment—what might that mean for our theories of the fallenness of human nature? For our proclamations of total depravity?

Miller raises the question as to whether human activity is depraved because one inherits a depraved way of being in the world so that one can do no other, or whether the source of human depravity is in actuality deprivation/abuse which then gets internalized as a part of who one is (how one identifies oneself) and is acted out in depraved/abusive ways.

Shame: The Broken Tie that Binds

All of us embrace a common humanity in which we search for meaning in living, for essentially belonging with others, and for valuing of who we are as unique individuals. We need to feel that we are worthwhile in some especial way, as well as whole inside. We yearn to feel that our lives are useful, that what we do and who we are do matter. Yet times come upon us when doubt creeps inside, as if an inner voice whispers despair. Suddenly, we find ourselves questioning our very worth or adequacy. It may come in any number of ways: "I can't relate to people." "I'm a failure." "Nobody could possibly love me." "I'm inadequate as a man or as a mother." When we have begun to doubt ourselves, and in this way to question the very fabric of our lives, secretly we feel to blame; the deficiency lies within ourselves alone. Where once we stood secure in our personhood, now we feel a mounting inner anguish, a sickness of the soul. This is shame." (1980:vii)

It is possible to address the question of shame from many different perspectives. One can consider the ways in which cultures induce shame upon the individual; one can consider the affect of shame; one can consider the way in which shame results from a failure to reach one's ego ideal; and one can consider the ways in which shame is systematically induced in shame-based families. Rather than attempt to assimilate and integrate all the current literature on shame in order to inform our search into contemporary understandings of human alienation, I have chosen for this section of this paper to focus on the work of Gershen Kaufman as detailed in his book *Shame: The Power of Caring*. I believe Kaufman is particularly helpful in our search for understanding human alienation as he outlines the *interpersonal origins* of shame—as he develops the process wherein a person internalizes the shaming process, thereby learning to practice self-alienation, self-shaming—and, as he explains the human defenses against shame and shows how human creatures will act in order to protect themselves from further experiences of shame. Kaufman is certainly not the only expert in this field who touches on these aspects of the experience of shame, but his book makes these concepts most straightforwardly accessible to our work.

To feel shame, Gershen Kaufman notes, is to know oneself as inadequate as a person. It is a feeling of inner anguish that questions who one is, one's meaning in life, one's sense of belonging with others, and one's personal valuableness. To feel shame is to feel oneself "seen in a painfully diminished sense," (1980:vii) to "feel deficient in some vital way as a human being" (1980:viii) and to know "an urgent need to escape or hide [which] may come upon us" (1980:vii).

But shame, according to Kaufman, is more than an experience of being mortified or ashamed. It is not only *this* experience, but also a *process* that builds on repeated and/or severe experiences of shame to fashion an internal shaming process where one no longer needs an "other" in order to feel shamed. It is a process that continually fuels self-doubts concerning one's human worthiness, that undermines a secure and whole self-identity as it replays experiences of being exposed, seen through, and found lacking, and that generates again the awful and paralyzing experience of being shamed. It is a process that cuts one off (or wherein one cuts oneself off) from parts of oneself as one disowns/hides those rejected and exposed parts of oneself. It is a process that binds one's normal human needs, feelings and drives and leaves one confused or ignorant as to what one really feels, needs, or desires. It is an isolating process, as one not only cuts oneself off from parts of oneself, but also from others who, one fears, might repeat the painful shame-inducing experience. It is a process that leads to defensive measures to protect the self—defensive measures that can be used against parts of the self thereby splitting the self—defensive measures that also can cut the self off from others (sometimes in aggressive action toward the other) and from the possible source of comfort that others, in drawing one out of one's isolation, might bring. It is a process that originates between persons but which becomes so firmly lodged within the person that one forgets its source believing instead that the process and the resulting/generating feelings of worthlessness are essential or "given" aspects of who one is. And, it is a process that, in reinforcing one's feeling of worthlessness, enhances one's sense of powerlessness to ever be anything but unacceptable.

And, how does shame come about? To understand Kaufman's description of the process of shame and the alienation it produces in human persons, we must understand the presuppositions about the human condition that inform his perspective.

To be human, Kaufman first assumes (as did Miller), is to be deeply relational. Human persons need others—they need to be wanted and loved—*and* they need to love and to have their love accepted by others. This assumption of the relational nature of human experience informs Kaufman's approach to shame as "the power of caring." Shame might not be such a powerful part of the human experience if one did not care so much—or desire to be cared for. Shame, we might say, is formed in the arms of love. The human condition is one in which one reaches out to others, for affirmation, for connection, in order to love, and build bridges of interconnection—bridges that are the basis for trust and vulnerability—bridges that allow one to reveal oneself to another and to have reasonable expectations for one another. Human beings are bridge builders—and shame is the result of broken bridges.

To be human for Kaufman is not only to build bridges to others, however, it is also to build bridges within oneself. Humans are about the task of forming an identity—a relationship with oneself—a relationship that is built out of experiences, needs, drives and that reflects the way in which one makes meaning out of one's life—a relationship that is shaped out of the experiences one has with others—a relationship that is informed by a process of identification whereby one learns to treat oneself as one is treated by others. Schooled in the experience of respect—where one is treated as a separate individual worthy of love—where one's attempts at loving others are valued and received—one learns self respect. Schooled in the experience of shame, where one is repeatedly shamed and learns that one—or parts of oneself—are shameful, one learns not self-respect but self-alienation.

If to be human is to be relational—to be about the much needed task of building bridges, bridges strong enough to come back and forth upon, then to be human is also to know the reality of broken bridges. No human connection is "perfect"—all relationships must be worked at and given regular maintenance. Given the finitude of the human situation, given the fact that often one's needs conflict and that one's energies give out, given the fact that one cannot always be "present" to others as one would like, crumbled/broken bridges are a regular part of the human situation. Because for Kaufman the source of human shame is interpersonal—resulting from the breaking of the human bridge—shame is, then, a given to the human situation. The difference between shame as a given to the human situation and shame as the debilitating experience outlined above is in how the human persons involved react to shaming incidents.

If to be human is to need others, to work to build bridges with others, to forge one's identity out of one's relationships with others— if to be human is to know broken bridges and the experience of shame when one's expectations for oneself and others are not met and are thus exposed as unworthy/unreasonable—and if to be human is to know the possibility of healing as bridges are mended and one learns to trust others and oneself, to hope, and to know that broken bridges are not the final word—then to be human is also to know the possibility that one's shame might not be healed, that broken bridges might be left unattended, and that one might be left alone in one's feelings of unworthiness. And when these experiences of shame are not attended to, when bridges are not restored, to be human is to live in the danger of greater alienation—as one's sense of oneself as unacceptable and isolated is amplified both by a growing sense of powerlessness to change one's situation, and by an internalization of the shaming process where one can both experience an inner replay of shameful moments while making increasingly greater efforts to keep hidden and separate those parts of oneself that would trigger such pain.

The process of shame, as suggested above, is one that continues onward and inward and outward again from an initial experience of shame when these shaming experiences are internalized—when it is those experiences that predominately come to name one, shape one's expectations for oneself, and inform the ways in which one relates to oneself and to others—when one names parts of oneself as shameful, hides them from sight, becomes vigilant in the watching of oneself, and repeats the drama of shame within oneself, with or without the trigger of an external events, and when one defends against further shaming incidents by aggressively shaming or injuring others. This experience of internalization is one that may begin at an early age, that becomes part of one's unconscious perception of oneself and the way one treats oneself, and (most problematically) that becomes disengaged in one's consciousness from its interpersonal, historical source. It thus becomes a part of one's sense of who one is—cut off from the knowledge that if it is in fact a part of one's identity, it is a part that was learned, that resulted from painful experiences of brokenness, and that is not, then, a given or essential part of one's human nature.

SHAME AND SIN?

Gershen Kaufman's work on shame and the shaming process has given us another glimpse of human alienation. Like Alice Miller, Kaufman reveals to us a sense of human beings as necessarily relational and has shown how great alienation from self and others (soul-loss) can be generated by the rupturing of human relationality. Like Miller, Kaufman's work underscores how vulnerable humans are—in their deep need for relationality/connections—to processes of alienation (in this case, that of shame). He has outlined a process of alienation wherein human beings are hurt by shame, internalize the shame and the process of shaming, and come to know themselves as shameful—choosing to hide themselves (or parts of themselves)—binding those parts off from the whole—living in isolation—in an attempt to be acceptable to others and to themselves. And he has shown how humans defend themselves against possible shaming from themselves and others—defend themselves in ways that are often destructive and alienating to others and themselves.

Between the lines of Kaufman's work, he raises several questions for theologians about the source of some human alienation. He, first of all, has outlined a way in which humans hide themselves from themselves and each other as an expression of their alienation. Secondly, he argues for the interpersonal origin of shame and self-alienation. The state of internalized shame/self-alienation Kaufman describes is not a given to the human situation (although shaming *is inevitable*, given the relational nature of human existence). It is, rather, something that arises from the rupture in human relations and has a historical location. Is it possible that the theological affirmation of the fallenness/depravity of human beings also emanates from a historical location? That this sense of fallenness grows from experiences of shame that are then internalized and become what one then fears to be an essential, given, part of oneself? That the story of the Fall is the story of each human being? Thirdly, the alienation he describes is both something that *happens to* human beings and yet also something that human beings (through identification, internalization, defensiveness, and the binding/hiding of parts of themselves) participate in themselves. Finally, by naming certain defensive tactics as defenses against shame, he raises the question of whether these behaviors (rage, contempt, blaming, power-over others, withdrawal, etc.), which are *survival* mechanisms, yet which are so often named as sinful, *are* sin or whether they are both sinful (leading to further rupturing of relationships—further alienation) *and* symptoms of a deeper problem—that of shame, self-alienation/soul-loss, and the sense of deep unworthiness that separates one from God, self, and others.

SIN AND SOUL-LOSS

The intent of this paper has been to identify two voices in the culture that are speaking of soul-loss/the dance of alienation and to ask in what way the language of sin is appropriate in naming this dance. It has not been an attempt to describe *the* condition of human alienation nor has it meant to suggest that the journeys toward alienation described herein are *the only way* of understanding the genesis of human alienation.[7] It has, however, revealed certain assumptions and raised several questions about the human condition that are, at least from my perspective, worthy of further theological musing.

First, both of the perspectives encountered in this paper work from a presupposition of the relational and developmental nature of the human condition. Unlike Adam and Eve—a traditional source of the Christian view of the human condition—human persons as pictured here are not created fully formed as responsible adults. Rather, they are born as helpless infants—dependent upon caregivers to nurture, hold, mirror, and respect them—to help to teach them who they are—to engender the confidence and respect in themselves that are necessary if they are to become fully responsible, loving adults.

Second, both Miller and Kaufman affirm that this relational nature of human existence makes each human person very vulnerable. The relationality that is the source of human richness and pleasure is also the source of human misery. To be human is to be vulnerable to broken relationships and disappointments, as well as more overt acts of violence. To be human is to be dependent upon others who may not be capable (or may not choose) to give one the love and nurture one needs. To be human is to be subject to the basic finitude of the human condition—a finitude that means that needs and drives conflict, that people die, that disasters happen—that bridges are constantly being broken around and within each person. To remember Brock's metaphor, to be human is to be born with heart—and to know brokenheartedness.

Third, these perspectives have each shown us how humans, in their woundedness, abandon themselves. This abandonment—this dance of alienation—is something that is done to them as relationships are broken, as their significant others fail to nurture them in the way they need, as they learn (as "their eyes are opened" and they see) that parts of themselves are unacceptable. It is also something they do to themselves as in their reenacting of childhood dramas of abandonment and in their hiding and binding of their shameful selves they continue the dance of alienation. Human beings are both encouraged by the woundingness of life to reject themselves, and choose to reject themselves—hiding behind masks of shame, rejection, perfection, etc.

But, fourth, if human persons reject themselves, if they play out the drama of abandonment in continual hiding and self-abandonment—if their lives affect others as they assume defensive postures or demand from others the same abandonment they demand of themselves, then they also do this out of the need to survive—to find some remnant of connection and self-dignity amidst the brokenheartedness of their world. Their sin, their alienation, is part of the human effort towards self-preservation. The irony of this is that, in order not to be abandoned—in order to survive—they become abandoning and abandoned persons. The way of the brokenhearted world then is that one must abandon oneself to survive. The Christian tradition has long valued the notion that one must lose oneself in order to find oneself. The dance of alienation here revealed is that in losing/abandoning parts of oneself, one seeks/finds a false way of being a self in the world. This challenges us to wonder, what is the self, the way of being a self in the world, that the Christian tradition would call one to lose? Are Christians to abandon themselves like these children of abandonment? Or are Christians to abandon the abandoning way of being a self in order to find the vulnerable heart at the center of our being?

Fifth, if the alienation that is uncovered in this paper is in fact an alienation that is learned, that is conditioned by actual historical occasions, and is not something that is inborn in each human person, it is also a state of alienation that is inherited. Augustine has intoned that humans are not born with the possibility not to sin—that the fallenness of the human condition is communicated to humanity through conception and birth. Without challenging Augustine's understanding of the human anguish of alienation and the feeling of powerlessness that alienation engenders within the human soul, the perspectives studied here have shown that humans need not have an inherited defect to experience their lives as ones of alienation,[8] to know both that they are responsible for their situation and that it is yet larger than their personal culpability (that is, that it is inherited), and to know the paralyzing feeling of being unable to remedy the situation.

Because from the moment a person breathes, they breathe in the atmosphere that precedes and surrounds them, because they may learn to know themselves in the eyes of others who cannot/do not give them the attention they need, because bridges of connection are broken and then not attended to, because their parents may demand of them the perfection and self-abandonment that was demanded of them thus perpetuating the cycle of abandonment—because of this, we can speak of this state of alienation as deeply inherited. Human persons, thus, would learn rejection before they could learn that there might be other possibilities.

Yet these two perspectives also show that because human beings are so needful of others and their love that they choose to abandon themselves rather than risk the rejection of themselves, because they blame themselves and think themselves responsible for the rejecting actions (or nonactions) of others, because they persist in reenacting the cycle of abandonment in the way in which they treat not only themselves but others—particularly their own children, because of this, they not only inherit their alienation, but also participate in it. These perspectives thus may be seen as offering theologians a way of understanding the original Augustinian insight into the sinful state of humanity.

Sixth, Paul describes in Romans 7, the drama of bondage to sin. I do not do what I, in my innermost self, would do—and that which I would not do, that I do. In a similar fashion, the dance of alienation and self-abandonment outlined in this paper reveals how human efforts to become acceptable—to become perfect, good, pleasing to others—to work out one's "salvation," one's reconciliation with others and the world—in fact do not increase one's sense of ease and reconciliation with others and self but rather increase one's dis-ease. In a shameful world, the drive to be perfect only leads to greater shame, to a constant preoccupation with oneself, and to the despairing notion that one can never be worthy enough. In the world of imprisonment to childhood dramas of abandonment, the drama of abandonment/giftedness is like a play that never ends—always there is another encore performance demanded—one more time one must be gifted/good/pleasing to earn the attention one so deeply—and understandably—desires.

And finally, we are left with the question whether or not the dance of alienation/soul-loss we have explored here is best named sin. We have seen several reasons to question the appropriateness of such a theological position. Surely, those who inherit the dance of alienation we have explored here are victims of alienating systems and one would wonder whether naming such a dance as sin is not another case of blaming the victim. Secondly, inasmuch as the Christian tradition has linked the state of sin with a prior act of willful disobedience (likened to that of the primal Adam and Eve), one would question whether the choice to abandon oneself which is an act of *survival* could qualify for such a willful act. Such an act is not couched in the desire to make the self the center or to run from one's human responsibility to be the most complete person one could be (traditional renditions of the sins of pride and hiding/flight from self), but in the human need to be seen, heard, and loved and in the desire to stay connected as if one's life depended upon such a connection (as indeed, for a child, it often is). If as a result of this act of survival born in desperation one often does live a life of willful self-preoccupation and the paradoxical abandonment of one's self, one does not start out with such an intention. One might say that the language of sin might be appropriate to describe the dance of alienation and the bondage to alienating ways, but not to name its original source.

Finally, where sin is linked theologically with forgiveness (it being the way to wipe away the guilt that sin engenders), one would question the appropriateness of the name sin for a state wherein one needs healing from alienation more than forgiveness of an original act (and forgiveness may actually be what the *victim* comes in time to grant to those who have been the source of wounding)—and where acts of alienation towards self and others which might indeed call for repentance and forgiveness can mask a deeper alienation/soul-loss that needs the grace of reconciliation. One might wonder, as well, whether the language of sin/guilt/forgiveness might not enhance the feeling of unworthiness that the person bound in shame and destined to repeat their childhood drama of abandonment has learned rather than be the words of good news and assurance they are often claimed to be.

However, we have also seen how the language of sin may well *be* appropriate to name this dance of alienation. First of all, where sin names a state of alienation that is core to one's being, then the dance of alienation we have explored certainly sounds like a state of sin. Moreover, naming this dance of alienation as sin (if the guilt-inducing aspect of the term could be avoided), would affirm both how seriously wounding this dance is and that abandoning activity towards oneself is indeed sinful. Secondly, it might be appropriate to name this dance of alienation as sin since there is an element of complicity entailed—since the "victim" is in some way responsible for the dance. Moreover, since healing from this dance of alienation entails becoming conscious of the dance as one does it and both locating its origin and naming one's participation in it, naming this dance sin might be an effective tactic—calling people to see their alienation, to recognize the seriousness of their plight, to confess their complicity, and to begin the journey to reconciliation. Finally, one could argue that the argument over original intention—that the dance of alienation did not begin with the willful intention of alienation but with the opposite intention of connection—is not an argument against the appropriateness of the name sin for the dance of alienation but accurately reflects the anguish of the human situation where human sin means that one often ends up mired in systems of alienation—dancing joyless steps of bondage—when that had never been one's intent at all. If sin, as Ed Farley suggests in *Good and Evil*, is the human attempt to secure oneself in the face of the tragic condition that human creatures are born into—a condition that means conflict and loss, vulnerability and the desire to be truly and deeply loved in the most fulfilling way—and if the dance of alienation we have described in this paper does in fact reflect an attempt by the person—no matter how young and vulnerable—to secure him/herself, to gain the love they so deeply need, then the name sin would seem to be appropriate.

NOTES

1. Other contemporary theologians who deal with sin and alienation are: Marjorie Suchocki in "The Myth of Presumed Innocence"; Wendy Farley in *Tragic Vision and Divine Compassion* and Ed Farley in *Good and Evil*; Rita Nakashima Brock in *Journeys by Heart*; Mary Potter Engel in "Evil, Sin, and Violation of the Vulnerable" in *Lift Every Voice and Sing*, edited by Engel and Thistlethwaite.

2. There are many works which develop this theme of human vulnerability, dependence, and the centrality of mutuality and relationship in

the development of selfhood. See, for instance, Jessica Benjamin's *The Bonds of Love*, especially chapter 1, for an argument for the importance of mutual relationship/recognition in the formation of the infant.

3. From D. H. Lawrence's "The Rocking Horse Winner," is told and interpreted by Suzanne Short in "Hidden Secrets of Childhood," *Psychological Perspectives*, pp. 109-110.

4. See Rita Nakashima Brock, *Journeys By Heart*, chapter 1, where she draws on Miller's work to develop her metaphors of heart and brokenheartedness.

5. One of the tragic aspects of this predicament is that once these needs are not met, they can never be met. A deprived child is deprived. S/he can learn to give and receive love from others. But, the basic love for the small child, once absent, is forever gone and can only be mourned. However, Miller notes, in the grieving process, the person is set free from the compulsive need to earn their parents' lost affections. Thus, through the mourning of death, comes life.

6. In her later book, *Banished Knowledge*, Miller calls the act of child abuse "mutilating the soul" (1990, 2).

7. And, certainly to argue for a historical event and/or system as a source of human alienation is not a new thought. Karl Marx, for example, saw human alienation rooted in the system of capitalism.

8. Unless, that is, we would wish to name the situation of relationality and vulnerability as such a defect. But that would be to name human finitude as the source of sin—which the tradition has consistently resisted doing.

PART III: PROFESSIONAL DISCOURSE WITHOUT SOUL

5

Soul Recovery through Remystification: Dostoyevski As a Challenger of Modern Psychology

Demystification and deconstruction—a scholarly legitimated "Soul-loss"—has been in focus in the social sciences throughout the last decades. Dostoyevski is in my opinion an important counter figure as a remystificator and reconstructivist. He manages to balance a respect for the ungraspable character of man with an empirical, realistic approach. He labels this position "real realism" (Linnér 1967).

I can still remember the day very well. We sat close to the shore on the island of Rhodes in the Greek archipelago. It was six-thirty in the evening. My wife Agneta and I had rented a scooter and crisscrossed the island during the day. This evening in August

1969 will always stay in my mind. Nothing happened in the outer world. Agneta was talking to the owner of the small restaurant. We planned to stay at the place overnight. She shouted to me to come and have dinner.

But I was so filled with an internal epic world that I did not react. With an uninterrupted intensity my eyes followed the lines of Dostoyevski's *Crime and Punishment* (1866). The axe in the hands of the young student Raskolnikov had just hit the head of the old pantbroker murdering her brutally. Deeply convinced that it was not only possible but necessary to take the law in his own hands—and for a good sake—he had to kill her. In his mind it was pure logic; since injustices were continually committed by the old ugly and evil woman, it was his obligation to kill her. The axe split her head.

I remember that Agneta was quarrelling with me late that evening. But I stayed out on the balcony of the hotel and read the whole night through. A quarter past six in the morning I had finished the book. I went to the taverna and got a cup of coffee together with the fishermen returning from the sea.

What happened to Raskolnikov? "Raskol" means split. Dostoyevski tells us that to kill another is equal to killing oneself. After the murder he became deeply ambivalent and threw away the money. The rest of the book is partly a criminal story, partly a love story but most of all—a narrative that demonstrates deep insight into *la condition humaine.*

I can still feel in my body my excitement and my sorrow for Raskolnikov, his crime, his struggle with his consciousness and finally his confession after having met the humble Sonya, his beloved ("Sonya" or Sofia means wisdom). She became the mediator of his repressed guilt feelings, she helped him to take his responsibility and finally, because of her, he managed to confess. Later she followed him to prison in Siberia.

From that moment on—that afternoon in Greece—Dostoyevski became my multifaced and provocative theologian and psychologist. He has always followed me in clinical and scholarly training, as a psychotherapist, as a hospital chaplain, as a researcher in psychology of religion and as a teacher. He has become an important literary counterfigure to the theoretical and practical perspectives provided by the academic society and the psychiatric clinics I have been working in.

DOSTOYEVSKI'S PARADOX

The memory of Raskolnikov's brutal murder and his psycho-logical reactions has become a crystallization point or a condensed symbol for me. Throughout his novels Dostoyevski constantly reminds his readers that logical rationality is just one side of man. One may never exclude man's ethical awareness or emotional irra-tionality. Morality and spirituality remain as important as the body, the psyche or society in spite of (or, maybe better; due to) its unmea-surable character. The description of man as a rational being, condi-tioned by his societal surroundings and intrapsychological forces, must always be complemented by respect for the mystery of man. The laws of causality must be combined with a finalistic under-standing of man due to the anatomy of the individual. One has to be aware of the burden and dignity of freedom. Because human beings are a mixture or synthesis of spirit and nature, their behavior is a product of both free decisions and various forms of conditioning.

Therefore, the moral and spiritual dimension of man can nei-ther be separated from nor reduced to his psychological and soci-etal conditions. This paradox is the point of departure for Dostoyevski's effort to recover the soul of man. In this respect he can offer contemporary social scientists and psychologists an important contribution as a counterfigure (Kravchenko 1978; Breger 1989).

Let me take my point of departure in my own field; the psy-chology of religion. Of course, we can never abandon the efforts to construct models and theories of man interacting with his religious culture, to collect data, make intense field studies, observe, catego-rize, and operationalize. The scholars have to be aware of difficult logical, hermeneutical, and methodological steps and risktakings in their effort to generate knowledge (whatever that means) in the field.

However, if we are true to our data, there always remains a mystery; the experience of human freedom and responsibility. I think it is of immense importance to always remind oneself of this point of unpredictability in the study of the individual man—not in order to create an unsophisticated and chaotic scientific anarchy but in order to be true to one's observations of man. In that sense, the realm of autonomy in man can be said to represent *one* of our efforts to capture the concept of "soul." This is where Dostoyevski comes in. He tried to be a "real realist."

Working in an academic community on problems of man's reli-giosity I have also found it necessary to complement the scientific endeavor with stories told by the great authors. I often ask my students to read and live inside the different epic universes of the classic novelists. I want them to link psychological theories to those fictional figures that exist as "living persons" in our common cultural heritage, those figures who are struggling with the meaning of life, the absence or presence of a divine reality or man's existential predicaments. To read the classics is another way to recover the soul or to reconstruct the individuality that often professionally is lost due to the (necessary) de-construction of man legitimated in psychology. Thus Strindberg, Hesse, Camus, Proust, and above all Dostoyevski are important writers—especially from the perspectives of psychology of religion.

These writers do not only illustrate religious and psychological themes. They actively contribute important insights that sometimes have been forgotten in ordinary academic psychology. It is the privilege of an author to mirror the general through the individual. In this sense he is a kind of scientist; N=1. That is presumably why his books are still read. We recognize today ourselves in them. Our reading is a kind of validation of Dostoyevski's "theories."

In his novels Dostoyevski manages to combine three dimensions in one. Literary high quality, psychological insights, and philosophical/theological dilemmas are incarnated in his figures. They do not only *think* of the theodicé problem but they feel and act in relation to it, they not only *discuss* the question of the reality of God, but they feel close to, damned or separated from him (Linnér 1975).

Dostoyevski is a soul recoverer in two ways. First, he actively points to the point of mystery where man's autonomy and spirituality are situated and he does it in an empirical manner. Second, he manages to create *gestalts* in his novels where body, psyche, spirituality and morality are closely connected. The split picture of man is kept together and incarnated in his authorship.

Dostoyevski and the Dilemma of De- and Reconstruction

There are many Dostoyevski's. He is both a comforter and an anarchist, he creates fertile and stimulating new connections in his novels. He is a spiritual guide with romantic and idealistic overtones. He is the fifth evangelist. But most of all—he is a Soul recoverer, due to his stressing of man's dual, ir/rational character.

My professional training has been concentrated on different soul loss projects, that is, reducing man in his individuality to abstract but general concepts like "psyche," "ego," "self," "I," "Self-object" (in the intrapsychic schools) or to his "interaction" with his fellow men, internalizing "significant others" or the "generalized Other" (the social psychological schools). The reading of Dostoyevski helps me keep in mind the necessity of emphasis on the mysterious character of every individual man. However, he manages to combine this respect for the integrity of the individual man's soul with a remarkable empirical approach. His soul recovery, due to his effort to "remystify" is paradoxically a result of observations.

As a thoroughgoing late nineteenth century realist writer he was interested in scientific "demystification" of his time. Thus, he very consciously tried to understand man in terms of his political, social psychological or even physiological conditions, and he was well read in contemporary psychiatry, psychology, neurology, criminology, and the like. But, even if he—in terms of Ricoeur—honored the hermeneutics of suspicion, he always returned to the second naiveté. He restored man to his basically infinite, complex nature as carrier of a mystery. This is something Dostoyevski saw in his years of working prison camps in Siberia, in his long struggle with epilepsy and roulette syndromes, and in his countless observations of crime and punishments.

He claims that if the respect for that mystery of man—corresponding to the mystery of God—disappears, something fundamental is lost. If logic, mathematical models, and societal or emotional conditions are the only ways to describe and understand man, man unconsciously will defend his autonomy. Therefore it was important for Dostoyevski—through his figures—to fight against nothing-but-ness. If terms like choice, guilt, and responsibility are disappearing, mankind will eventually kill itself—like Raskolnikov did when he followed his rationality alone. One must remember how Sonya responded after he finally had confessed his crime to her: "What have you done to yourself?!" She did not ask what he had done to the old lady or to her family, even to God. Dostoyevski's main point by letting Sonya ask Raskolnikov this very question is to demonstrate that life is more than rationality and that other people are parts of oneself.

Dostoyevski's underlining of man's ungraspable character was however not a mystification in terms of unclear thinking. But logic and rationality are not sufficient to explain man. If man is only understood as nothing-but or a-function-of something psychological or societal, his essence is lost. Especially there is a risk, claims Dostoyevski, that the sciences dealing with man are raised to an inflated position. *Wissenschaftsaberglaube* is the danger of the medical scientists or the psychologists. They must refer their observations to their own conceptual systems and therefore keep the ungraspable outside. Unconsciously their science can become their total worldview.

Thus Dostoyevski elucidates—but he also manages to keep together—the dilemma every psychological researcher and clinician meets when they are dealing with individuals; to respect the autonomy and identity of a very specific individual (soul) and combine it with the necessary reduction of man in terms of general societal models or psychological theories (*not soul*). Or to turn it to psychology of religion; to both deconstruct a religious phenomenon in terms of its social and psychological genesis and simultaneously claim its sui-generic character (Wikström 1990 and 1993a).

Depression As an Illustrative Case

It has been claimed that every psychology must in higher or lesser degree reduce or ignore the question of man's soul. The main task of psychology is said to generate theories, terms and models and to test them on the basis of empirical or experienced reality. In the efforts to find "variables" to relate to other variables one is pressed to minimize the psychological reality and exclude the question of soul. Or if we turn to psychodynamic traditions: in order to see the emotional or intrapsychological factors one has to limit the perspectives. This is necessary and fruitful.

For example, in my practice as a psychotherapist I have to think in technical terms like "How do I find a *working alliance* with the conscious *ego structure* of the other?" I use theoretical concepts in my thinking in order to be aware of and be able to communicate to other therapists and supervisors what I see and feel. At the same time I must constantly be aware of the unpredictability and ungraspable character of my patient, my fellow man. The mystery of man and the not-mystery of man must be in the conversation and in my mind at the same time. To be a container of this paradox is a heavy task but important for the integrity of the patient and the professional nature of the treatment.

Last week I was sitting in a clinical meeting. We were discussing the treatment of a religious patient; John. He had received the diagnosis "atypic depression" (296.82) according to DSM III, the psychiatric handbook. The family therapist described this symptom in terms of "double bind" and "pathological interactions." The psychoanalyst understood his problems in terms of "cathexes" and grief processes not "worked through." Her colleague, the object relation theorist, talked in terms of reminiscences of "the depressive position." His suffering was described in terms of ego structure, self development or as a sum of early but bad introjects. In our conversation John's religious depression was understood in functional terms—as an interaction between his religious symbolic universe and his intrapsychological makeup. The medical professionals, in their turn understood John's problems as biochemical disturbances. The hospital chaplain formulated John's melancholia as a "dysfunctional cognitive meaning system" and "loss of spiritual support." John's suffering was objectified, but John, the sufferer was professionally ignored.

All professionals were using concepts from their own scientific language games. They described the patient in terms of a general discourse taken from their respective institutional trainings. John was for all of them de-constructed in terms of something else. Or to turn it around, the reified "knowledge" due to their respective social constructions of psychological "reality" was projected on the defenseless patient. But who was right? All perspectives? One specific perspective, a combination of all perspectives or none at all? Maybe the questions of right or wrong are inadequate in this case. Pragmatic criteria are more important. In the supervision room all the professionals dealt with a necessary and scientifically legitimated de-construction or soul loss. But who identified, cared for and cultivated the reconstruction or the restoration of John?

Reconstruction of the Ungraspable

The de-construction of man's soul has now become more and more sophisticated. To demystify is to be scientific. But what is happening when the models of man atomize, reify, and objectify the individual and make man's mystery measurable? Is the question of the proposed ghost in the machine still relevant? I think so. Dostoyevski stressed this opinion. To respect man's autonomy, responsibility and dignity means to restore his inherent value. It is also the basis for democracy.

Of course psychology as a science has to de-construct the multidimensionality of man and generate models that make it possible to understand the unique individual in terms of more general "laws" or dynamics. But I see in modern psychology a risk that the individuality of man can be *reduced* to metanarratives like physical laws, semantic structures, psychodynamic forces or social processes. The necessary *methodological reduction* can—if unobserved by the researcher—be translated into *ontological reductionism.* The consequences are professional loss of soul.

Dostoyevski was searching for realism, but a realism on another level than his contemporary writers. He wanted a realism that took ad notam man's longing for something unseen as a reality, and that legitimated man's moral consciousness as something that could not fully be understood in terms of psychological or biological conditions or a social contract. Of course this is a threat for ordinary science. But maybe this is why he seems to survive many, many forgotten psychologists.

To summarize, when the social sciences' necessary *de*-construction of the human being crosses the borders or passes the barriers, their theories become reality constructors: "Society" exists. "The generalized Other" exists. "Super ego" exists. "Object relations" exist. But the human Soul is lost.

My point is that *re*construction of man or the restoration of man has to be conquered again, without losing what we have learned in the journey through social and behavioral sciences of religion. One part of the second naivete is the remystification. Here Dostoyevski can be of importance. Why? He points to the problem of the risks and advantages with the deconstruction of man but also to the fragility of every construction of the "psychological knowledge" of man.

SOUL LOSS, MODERNITY, AND PSYCHOLOGY

Man was the center of the Age of Enlightenment. The science of psychology was founded on a conception of individual subjects, with internal souls and later internal psychic apparatus. Man became the center of the universe. The idea of the primacy of the individual's rationality, its progressions and development, are part of this very tradition. After Hiroshima and Auschwitz it has become difficult to uphold a belief in general progress solely by means of scientific and technical rationality.

But the latest evolution of psychology seem to have *decentered* the individual subject. Individuality is dissolved into physiology or ensembles of social relations and linguistic structures. The soul is lost.

When the classic scholar Bloom discusses the social sciences in his book "The Closing of the American Mind" (1986) psychology is only credited with a footnote: psychology is mysteriously disappearing from the social sciences. Its unheard of success in the real world may have tempted it to give up its theoretical life. At the Massachusetts Institute of Technology, the Department of Psychology was recently dissolved to become integrated into a new department, "Brain and Cognitive Science."

Except for theoretical contributions of psychoanalysis and the current popularization in the therapeutic market, psychology has little to tell other sciences or the public at large. I think that is due to its professional unawareness of soul loss.

A visit to the psychology shelves of a university bookshop evokes a feeling of boredom. Here are the standard textbooks, the collected works of Freud and Jung, the multitude of therapeutic help-yourself paperbacks, and some hard cognitive science books. The new provocative insights about man in current culture are more likely to be found in the shelves for literature, art and anthropology.

After the great personality theories were developed, nothing seems to have happened. The development of humanistic psychology was caught in its opposition to behaviorism, and cognitive psychology has taken over the hegemony of behaviorism, replacing the white rat with the computer and substituting the grand theories by eclectic models. Let me describe some traits in the professional "soul-loss" project (Kvale 1990).

A crisis concerning the search for *legitimation in external contexts* of metanarratives was prominent in classical psychology. Analogies to physics guaranteed psychology status as a science. Also in recent humanistic psychology there is a quest for respectability by appealing to external frames of reference, like phenomenology, hermeneutics, existentialism, and so forth. Such metanarratives that made it possible to de-construct—in terms of something that was "true" or at least provisory true—are questioned.

Commensurability was the main theme of psychology, science sometimes being equated with quantification. The credo of natural science invaded psychology; "go forth and make all mankind measurable—and commensurable." The antithesis became a retreat to the uniqueness of the individual self rather than focusing on the complete contextual rootedness of man's activity in his specific language and culture.

The joint basis for the many controversies between behaviorism and humanism has been the *abstraction of man from his context*. Both the behavioral laws of nature as well as of humanistic self-actualization have rested on up-rooting man from his local and lived world, from his social interaction and network. A de-contextualization of man from his specific culture plus the study of behavior or consciousness abstracted from its cultural roots was in one way an effort to keep the individual person together. This very decontextualized person was the subject matter of the psychologist.

Thus, the self seems no longer to be the absolute point of departure, a self-contained entity, but a network or ensemble of relations. The individual is spread out; I am a part of the greater societal Self.

Modernity designates any science that legitimates itself with references to a *metadiscourse*, making an explicit or implicit appeal to some grand narrative, such as the dialectics of the Spirit, the hermeneutics of meaning or the creation of social or psychological laws. In contrast to these metadiscourses one now can observe a *corrosion of legitimations*. Postmodernity indicates a condition after the utopias are dead.

When the rationality presupposed by the psychologists seldom is found in the given reality then another "deeper," more essential reality is constructed to account for the disorder we observe in the world around us. This overstressed conception of rationality has in its turn fostered a skeptical counterreaction in the form of romanticism and irrationalist movements.

But still *rationality is expanding.* Thinking goes beyond the cognitive and scientific domain nowatimes. It also includes the ethical and esthetical domains of life. Classical modernity held a restricted concept of rationality. It was limited to formal or technical rationality. It was a concentration of methods, programs, plans, predictions and control. Respect for the esthetical or the ethical dimensions of man was maintained.

The Kantian split between science and morality is now questioned and there is an attempt to rehabilitate the ethical dimensions in the understanding of man. The professional split between facts and values can no longer be sustained. One claims for example that art is not only a cultural activity. It is a form of "knowing" the world. Just a few years ago rationalists claimed that the nonlinear did not exist. Yet today even mathematics can describe fractals as "beautiful."

Action may never be what it appears to be: it was always understood in terms of something under the surface; a deeper reality or laws, a symptom of basic sexual instincts, or economic forces, and so on. There is an ongoing pursuit of the underlying plan or rationale to explain what manifestly appears.

A postmodern attitude relates to what is given, rather than what has been or what *could be*. The fervent critical attitude of the sixties and seventies—as antiauthoritarian and anticapitalistic—has dissolved. An attitude of tolerant indifference has replaced the involvement in and commitment to the social movement and inner journeys. What is left is living, here and now. Fascination may take the place of reflection, seduction may replace argumentation.

To the existentialist the discovery of a world without meaning was tragic; today's loss of unitary meaning is merely accepted: "that is just the way the world is." Man has stopped waiting for Godot. The absurd is not met with despair; there is rather a living with what is, making the best out of it, a happy nihilism. With the death of the utopias, the local and personal responsibility for actions here and now, becomes important. The autonomy of the individual returns, the soul is partly recovered but only in the local arena not at the universal level.

The classical *dichotomy* between the universal and the individual, between society and the unique person is more and more abandoned. Man is a self stretched out between what it is and what it ought to be. Both universal laws or the unique self are seen as abstractions from one's being-in-the-world. Instead of talking of general laws as something objectively given and the individual as a subject and something relative, pragmatic criteria and contextual relativism have evolved. The legitimation is rather done through action or linguistic praxis.

When the grand metanarratives collapsed, the *local* came into focus. Small, heterogeneous and changing language games replaced the global meaning systems. But stressing the local is not only a withdrawal of global meaning structures. From our perspective it is something that goes beyond the old polarity between the universal and the individual, the objective and the subjective.

Finally when the *human language* is said to be neither universal nor individual but rooted in a specific culture as dialects, philosophy more and more must deal with language acts, linguistic analyses. Consequently the basic ontological questions are nonsensical for no metalanguages, whatsoever, can exist. Nothing can be true or morally good in an absolute way. Language is not copying or mirroring reality. Rather language constitutes reality or better—each language constructs specific aspects of reality in its own way.

This is precisely where the risks of the language of psychology come in—Dostoyevski would have claimed. The reality of psychology is namely a social construction. No one has ever *seen* "transference," a "projection" or a super ego. They are all concepts used in small segments of subcultures of the society. But there is so to speak an ongoing ontologizing of these terms and therefore a reification of man among psychologists.

Now, altogether there is a turning point both for psychology as a science and for the soul. The very esse in psychology, the I, is disappearing. The main focus of language or man's interaction implies a *decentralization* of the subject. I am not using the language; instead the language is speaking through me. The individual is just a medium for his language and culture.

This very Soul-loss—legitimated in terms of postmodernism and extreme contextualism—is partly questioned by ego psychologists, humanists, and the cognitive scientists but also by Dostoyevski. His questions are more modern than ever. Maybe we can call him a post-post-modernist-psychologist. Man's experienced and observed responsibility must be in the center of our understanding of man and built into a general anthropology. The mysterious autonomy is the base for a democratic society. Man's longing for the unseen must also be taken at face value. The moral consciousness and the spiritual realms of man ask for a center in man—and why not call this his Soul?

DOSTOYEVSKI AS A "REAL REALIST" AND SOUL RECOVERER

The Russian Orthodox church, which strongly influenced Dostoyevski stresses man in his totality in contrast to the churches in the West. The concept of the heart is central. Russian theology is, for example, more concentrated on the symbols in the liturgy than on systematic dogmatic thinking. Faith is generated through participation in the ceremonies more than by a commitment or a conversion.

If we prefer psychoanalytic concepts, Russian Orthodox piety is far more concerned with primary than secondary processes, more with regression in the service of ego than strengthening the defense mechanisms.

The Church, the sacred music, the icons, the smell of incense and the gestures in the divine liturgy activate dimensions of man's capacity other than the intellect.

Therefore there is a link between the mystery of man and the mystery of God both in theological god-talk and in the ritual language game and semiotic. God is only possible to grasp through symbols. The symbols used are evocative. Through the symbol the symbolized is channeled, but there always remains a hidden part, something unseen. This fact must be respected. And as even man is a symbol, an icon, something in him belongs to the ungraspable.

Knowledge, therefore, is not something exclusively for *ratio* but belongs to the whole man. Truth, Goodness and Beauty have the same genesis; God. They are witnesses in man's psyche of the Absolute from which he has come and to which he will return.

Dostoyevski's psychological thinking is thus colored by his Christian faith. Therefore his psychology is ontological. It takes its departure in man's being in the world but it is supported by his empirical observations that make him sure of man's mystery.

In theological concepts—one consequence of the fall is man's freedom. Man has the capacity and need to act from his own decision. The specific character of man is not that he is material or that he belongs to the cosmos. The unique is instead what separates him from the creation and links him to his creator. The mixture of explicable causality and responsible finality is seen in the classical symbol of Gen. 2:7. Man is both chained in causal laws and free to raise himself above them. This is the paradox of man; man's soul.

This theological paradox is mirrored in the two concepts often used in Dostoyevski's time, "personalism" and "individuality." The *individual* is a member of a given society, it is man in his biological and social existence. But the *person* exists in the individual, it is original and his spiritual and unexplicable center. The person is qualitatively something else than all the parts of which individuality is built.

The term person is in its turn linked to morals and values. Man's capacity to feel responsibility and guilt cannot be understood only in terms of upbringing or socialization. The not inviolable is instead a gift. Maximus Confessor calls man's basic consciousness a "cosmic drive," a longing back to man's original birth. Life emanates from God. The entrance of faith into man is located on an elementary, vital level—even below moral and intellectual distinctions.

All these theological and philosophical considerations exist of course as a background to Dostoyevski's way of telling us that man is something "more" than his conditions. However, he came to this conclusion through observations rather than by just imposing idealistic thinking to his fictive figures. He was a real realist. He searched for a realism that included the possibility (but not necessity) of man's spirituality.

Real Realism

The psycho-physiological or the social context does not fully explain, and cannot fully explain man. There is a mediating structure between stimuli and response in men that is not understandable in terms of biology or cultural surroundings. Always there is a zone of autonomy, a space of integrity. Without it man only exists as a link in a chain of causality, a cog in the machinery or an evolutionary artifact.

In the 1840s, romantic idealism lost its grip on the Russian writers. The French social realism of Balzac, Hugo and George Sand created more and more physiological scenarios—society became more important.

Both Gogol and Dostoyevski wrote about the real society. But Gogol was first and foremost a social realist writer where Dostoyevski is a psychologist. For Gogol the individual is a representative of a particular society or subworld. For Dostoyevski society is interesting only insofar as it has influence on the individual's psyche (Fanger 1965). Society is, so to speak, always filtered through an individual psyche—where other determinants are found—man's autonomy—or Soul.

Realistic truth and moral authority were in Dostoyevski's way of thinking intimately related. He considered himself therefore to be a better realist—or in our terms a better scholar or scientist—than those of his contemporaries. A letter written in 1869 is applicable to the whole of his production. "I have my own view of reality, and what most people call almost fantastic and exceptional, is for me sometimes the very essence of the real. Everyday trivialities and a conventional view of them, in my opinion, are not only short of realism, but even contrary to it" (Linnér 1967, 92). Moral and existential extremes like the saint-like Furst Mysjkin in *The Idiot* or Ivan Karamazov, the atheist, must therefore not be reduced to manifestations of peculiar mental dispositions.

"Classical realism" recognized only one level of reality, that which deals with this world. To describe the Inferno or the Paradise meant to them to step outside its bounds. When Dostoyevski made realism his genre, he therefore placed himself in a paradoxical situation. His realism was neither romantic nor idealistic but "real" in another—inclusive—way. His picture of the world and men after all, obviously contained possibilities for other than earthly realities. These were built in in his anthropology and epistemology.

But he never offered his readers his own opinion. Nowhere in the novels does he himself declare that a God exists and that man is immortal; instead he inserts for example the pious monk Zosima's teaching or the godly Sonya's example into his histories. These passages are in the context completely natural, in line with the character and previous history of the person in question. In other words, Dostoyevski *opens doors* to the supra-real, but he himself does not take the step out over realism's threshold into that world. This made it all the more important for him to make his saintly portraits convincing. They must possess the same credibility as other figures.

Dostoyevski never takes steps *outside* realism. The pious monk Zosima's remarks about eternal life, and so forth, can therefore be accepted both for a Christian or an atheist reader. The ambiguity of this perspective resembles Dostoyevski's treatment of the demonic. His description of the devil's appearance to Ivan Karamazov can be interpreted as an hallucination. Dostoyevski himself pointed out those psychiatric aspects (Rice 1985). But it can *also* be understood as a real devil. The conversation between the eldest brother Ivan Karamazov and the devil demonstrates such a dual perspective. He leaves it to the reader to decide. His cast of characters is *not* divided into idealistic or real people. The idea of the "other world" is as true as not true. He respects the integrity of his own figures.

Life Rather Than Logic

No statistics are needed to show that "sudden" and unexpected behavior is a trait of Dostoyevski's characters. His figures' psychological and moral impulsiveness startles both others and themselves—not to mention the reader. One hears occasionally that their behavior is unmotivated. Proust says that the writer does not show us the reasons for his character's actions. He merely states that the causes are eclipsed by the behavior they explain. There is a splendid unpredictability. But Dostoyevski himself once made a little comment on psychological causality. "Let us not forget," he writes in *The Idiot*, "that the causes of human actions are infinitely more subtle and varied than we—always in retrospect—explain them and they can rarely be clearly outlined. The best thing a writer can do is sometimes to limit himself to a simple presentation of the events" (6:547). This is not an expression of chaotic indeterminism. All Dostoyevski is asserting is that the close connection beneath even apparently simple actions may be enormously complex. And especially that sometimes the mysterious life is more important to just accept than to understand its meaning.

Dostoyevski argues in his meandering way "perhaps the goal on earth towards which mankind is striving consists merely of this incessant process of trying to arrive, in other words, in life itself and not really in the goal that must be formulated as a rule; two plus two is four. But that two plus two equal four is not life but the beginning of death" (4:160). A few pages earlier he speaks of the limits of our reason, which satisfies only our intellectual faculty. Reason represents but a twentieth part of our total capacity for living and that is insufficient. "Man's nature functions as a whole, together with everything conscious or unconscious that is found within it, and it lives even if it lies" (4:155). As a moral guidepost the Underground Man is admittedly problematic, but here he has the full support of the author. *If we fail to recognize the irrational needs within us, we lose our identity, our humanity.* We are reduced to piano keys or organ pipes, when what men need is to be human beings. Life had taken the place of dialectics, Dostoyevski says. In the end we lose sight of the hero Raskolnikov (5.573). We read that Raskolnikov was unable to concentrate on any single thought that evening when he murdered and he could no longer make any conscious decisions; "he could only feel." This breakthrough implies that reflection has been dethroned in the psychological hierarchy and replaced by mysterious emotions. In other words: life instead of dialectics.

To summarize. If we transfer Dostoyevski's world to the contemporary psychologist's soul-loss his message will be: "Go and look for a psychology that mirrors the real reality where questions of transcendence are not automatically included or excluded but respected." The "principles of exclusion of the transcendent" has been the rule in the psychology of religion since the days of Theodore Flournoy. In recent years Wulff seems to support a psychology where transcendence is included a priori (Wulff 1991, 639). I think both are reductionistic, the one towards a pure functionalism and the other towards essentialism.

Of course psychology or sociology of religion cannot claim that there exists something hidden in the machine. But they can at least *try* to reconstruct man after the scientifically legitimated deconstruction. And in this restorative process the psychologist may use tools where the ungraspable character of man is not filtered away, so—why not read Dostoyevski?

———————

This afternoon I have been sitting in two different rooms. For two hours I was sitting in the hospital together with a young patient of mine, Fred, who sometimes is hallucinating. Fred is now deeply convinced that he met two angels the last time he visited the hamburger restaurant McDonalds. They were whispering messages to him from God and now he is so sad that he cannot remember what they told him. Fred is totally reality-oriented and he functions very well with his family and his job. His problem is that he has fallen into a trap. It is partly due to the incapacity of the psychiatrist to allow or legitimate his "mystical" (?) experiences in their own right. The same can be said about his pastor. Fred's experiences are challenging his authority—grace must be channelled through the Bible and/or the Sacraments. Neither of them legitimates a double perspective: that his experiences of the angel must stand on their own feet rather than immediately being enlarged or reduced to a theological or psychiatric metadiscourse. I was thinking of Dostoyevski's real realism.

Later the same evening the doctoral seminarians and I were discussing the concept of "truth," "truth claimings," and "illusion and reality" in Freud's writings and Winnicott's concept of "the transitional space." One of my students said, "Well professor, aren't concepts like 'transitional space,' or 'reconstruction towards second naiveté' merely provisional and only mirror the very, very old insight that has always existed and always must exist; man is more than his conditions?" I agreed.

REFERENCES

Bloom, A. 1986. *The Closing of the American Mind*. New York: Schuster.

Breger, Lewis. 1989. *Dostoyevski. The Author as Psychoanalyst*. New York: New York University Press.

Dostoyevski, Fjodor. 1972. *The Brothers Karamazov*. Trans. D. Magarshack. London: Penguin.

Fanger, Don. 1965. *Dostoyevski and romantic Realism*. Cambridge, Mass.

Kravchenko, Maria. 1978. *Dostoyevski and the Psychologists*. Amsterdam: Adolf M. Hakkert.

Kvale, Steinar. 1990. Postmodernism and Psychology. *The Humanist Psychologist*. Vol. 18:35-54.

Linnér, Sven. 1967. *Dostoyevski on Realism*. Uppsala: Almqvist & Wiksell.

———. 1975. *Starets Zosima in the Brothers Karamazov. A study in the mimesis of virtue*. Acta Universitatis Upsaliensis, Stockholm Studies i Russian literature 4.

Rice, James L. 1985. *Dostoyevski and the Healing art: An essay in Literary and Medical History*. Ann Arbor: Ardis Publishers.

Wikström, Owe. 1990. Ritual studies in the History of religions; a Challenge for the Psychology of Religion. In *Current Studies on Rituals. Perspective for the Psychology of Religion*. International Series in the Psychology of Religion in Amsterdam. Atlanta: Rodopi, 57-71.

———. 1993a. God as "acting Agent" in Psychotherapy. Theoretical remarks. In *Clinical Psychology of Religion. Proceedings from a Colloquium in Krakow*, Poland. Dec. 1990. Amsterdam: Rodopi.

———. 1993b. Psychology in the Phenomenology of Religion. A critical essay. In *Religion and Mental Health*, ed. L. Brown. New York: Springer.

6

Enrapt Spirits and the Melancholy Soul: The Locus of Division in the Christian Self and American Society

If, as Erik Erikson suggests, the word "self" refers to our sense of "I" or "I-awareness" (1968, 216-221; 1981), the word "soul" concerns our being itself, and, more specifically, our experience of ourselves as living, vital beings, beings who have been given the breath of life. If self-language applies to soul, it is in the sense that Erikson uses it when he says that before birth, and before we are shaped by parental face and voice, we are a "pure self," confirmed by what the German mystic Angelus Silesius calls the God of "pure nothing" (1958, 264). To speak of soul-loss, then, is to say that we have lost touch with the source or well-spring of our very being. We are cut off from our origins as though orphaned.

In this essay, I will be engaging in an exercise of "soul-retrieval" (Ingerman 1991). The method I will be using for this retrieval of the soul will draw heavily on the institutions of our early ancestors who located the soul somewhere in the human body. As Morris Jastrow, Jr., points out:

The earliest philosophy of mankind is necessarily materialistic. In man's first endeavors to find a solution for the two most striking mysteries of which he is conscious, the world of phenomena about him and the fact of his own existence, it is natural that he should, on the one hand, trace the origin of the world to some single substance as the starting-point of the evolution of matter, and that on the other, he should be led to localize in himself an element that would appear to him to constitute the essence of his own life. (1912, 143)

Jastrow suggests that we should not be reluctant to engage in "experiments" to "weigh the human soul," experiments "which rest essentially on the same crudely materialistic conceptions that led simple folk and even philosophers in antiquity to locate the soul somewhere in the human body" (p. 143).

The first part of this essay focuses on our current situation of soul-loss. Here I draw on the writings of contemporary psychologists to explain why we have come to this point in human civilization where the soul is said to be lost. The second part of my essay centers on the earliest efforts of humankind to locate the soul in the human body. In this discussion, I consider the merits of locating the soul in the liver, and explore the connections between the soul's location in the liver and the fact that, throughout Christian history, melancholy has been the quintessential form of soul-sickness. The third part of my essay focuses on soul-loss in contemporary American society. Here, I explore the tendency of Americans to counteract their personal and societal melancholia with the experiences of the sublime, which is decreasingly associated with the natural world and its wonders and increasingly associated with the technology of destruction. Throughout the essay, I draw on James Hillman's distinction between spirit and soul (1975; 1979). I make no corresponding effort to explore the relation between self and soul in any systematic way, but there are intimations throughout of my belief that the endangerment of the self (Capps 1992a) and the loss of the soul are related phenomena.

THE SOUL'S REDUCTIONISTS

In *Freud and Man's Soul* (1984), Bruno Bettelheim complains that English translations of Freud's writings have created serious misunderstandings of Freud's work, and, in his view, the mistranslation that has most hampered our understanding of Freud is "the elimination of his references to the soul (die Seele)" (p. 70). While Freud evoked the image of the soul quite frequently, especially in crucial passages where he was attempting to provide a broad view of his system, his reflections on "the structure of the soul" and "the organization of the soul" are almost always translated "mental apparatus" or "mental organization," thus giving the impression that Freud was only concerned with the "mind." Given our concern in this essay with the location of the soul in the body, this mistranslation is especially unfortunate as it gives the false impression that Freud supported some sort of mind-body split.

Bettelheim also points out that Freud used the word soul to refer to the therapeutic process itself, and claimed that the soul is the very object of psychoanalytic treatment. It is the soul that is sick, the soul that requires treatment. In effect, psychoanalysis is truly about the care of the soul. On the other hand, Freud also insisted that the soul effects its own treatment, and the analyst is only a midwife in a process that the soul itself originates and carries through. Thus, in the opening passage of the article titled "Psychical Treatment (Treatment of the Soul)," he writes:

> Psyche is a Greek word and its German translation is "soul."
> Psychical treatment hence means "treatment of the soul." One could thus think that what is meant is: treatment of the morbid phenomena in the life of the soul. But this is not the meaning of this term. Psychical treatment wishes to signify, rather, treatment originating in the soul, treatment—of psychic or bodily disorders—by measures which influence above all and immediately the soul of man. (cf. Bettelheim 1984, 73-74)

Freud's point here is that "treatment" does not mean what is done to the soul from without, but the treatment the soul offers itself.

This idea of the soul as the locus and source of healing is completely lost when the *Standard Edition of the Complete Psychological Works of Sigmund Freud* translates the word soul (Seele) as "mental" and when "psychical treatment" is said to "take its start in the mind." This translation misses Freud's point that treatment concerns the very core of one's being, and that the "pathology" being addressed is the loss of one's soul. What Freud wanted precisely to challenge was the "medicalization" of the language of treatment, where emphasis is placed on "psychiatric" or "personality" disorders, and to restore its original Greek sense of soul-sickness. Instead, the translations of his work give the impression that he was an advocate of the very position from which he had tried to dissociate himself.

Thus, Bettelheim draws our attention to the fact that poor translations have been responsible for the loss of "soul language" in psychoanalytic thought and practice. As the impulse behind such translations was to make Freud's writings sound more scientific, the culprit in this case is science, which, in its desire to demystify and objectify, found it necessary to reduce the language of the soul to what were considered by Freud's translators to be its scientific equivalents.

THE SPIRIT'S INFLATERS

A different explanation for the loss of soul language is presented by James Hillman in *Re-Visioning Psychology* (1975) and his essay, "Peaks and Vales" (1979). For Hillman, this loss is partly due to the reductionism pointed to by Bettelheim, and he shares Freud's view that the medical understanding of treatment produces a failure to realize that the disease is in the innermost soul (1975, 73-74). But he also notes that, if we decrease "signs of medical sickness," we also "inflate their value by considering them as signs of spiritual suffering" (p. 75). Thus, he distinguishes between soul and "spirit," and suggests that even as the medical model "deflates" the soul by inflating the mind, so the spiritual perspective inflates the spirit, and, in so doing, obscures the soul's depths of sufferings.

Hillman discusses this "spiritualization" of the soul in a section of *Re-Visioning Psychology* concerned with humanistic psychology, and he takes Abraham Maslow, with his notion of the "peak experience," as representative. What humanistic psychology does is to deny the soul the depths of its affliction:

> Yes, there is pathology, it would agree. But psychopathology indicates an existence hindered and a consciousness focused upon its hindrances. As human nature is basically a consciousness-developing organism of increased information . . . the larger wholeness of each personality can integrate the smaller disturbances of its functions. In actualizing and realizing higher needs, lower ones become integrated. (p. 65)

When these disturbances are no longer frustrated but given sympathetic acceptance, "they transform into good green, growing energies, returning chastened and matured to the garden of our wholeness" (pp. 65-66). The model for this "positive transcendence of our pathologies" is the peak experience.

According to Hillman, this program of transcending the soul's afflictions has two fundamental flaws. One is that

> its idea of the psyche is naive if not delusional. For where is sin, and where are viciousness, failure, and the crippling vicissitudes that fate brings through pathologizing? When we turn to its literature we find scarce mention of such saturnine and sobering ideas as necessity, limitation, ancestry, or fundamental lacks or wants—the basic lacunae of each personality. It is out of touch with the stoic, tragic view of existential, irrational, pathological man. (p. 65)

The other flaw is that "highs and peaks say nothing about the worth of the person undergoing them, for they can occur also in psychopaths and criminals, having nothing to do either with creativity or maturity, Maslow's goals" (p. 66). Pathologizing itself can produce peaks: kleptomanic stealing, pyromanic barn-burning, sadism, grave desecrations—these too provide ecstatic joys. Also, transcendence by means of a "high" easily turns into a manic denial of depression.

Hillman is also critical of Westernized forms of Oriental solutions to psychopathology as these, too, deny the soul the depths of its afflictions. In these systems, the soul's pathologies are acknowledged to be real, but they are seen from another, finer perspective:

> Pathological events are evidence of the lower, unactualized rungs of the ladder. Our way shall be around them. Meditate, contemplate, exercise through them and away from them, but do not dwell there for insight. . . . Psychopathology in and for itself is not an authentic expression of the soul's divinity. Divinity is up at the peaks, not in the swamp of our funk, not in the sludge of depression and anxiety, the depths to which actual life regularly returns. (p. 66)

This Westernized form of oriental solutions to psychopathology ignores the context out of which Eastern spirituality derives: "In the East this spirit is rooted in the thick yellow loam of richly pathologized imagery—demons, monsters, grotesque Goddesses, tortures, and obscenities. It rises within a pathologized world of want and despair, chained by obligations, agonized" (p. 67). All this is missing from Eastern spirituality when uprooted and imported to the West.

Hillman admits to disparaging the transcendental approaches of humanistic and Oriental psychology, but he does so because they disparage the actual soul. By turning away from its pathologizings they turn away from its full richness. By going upward towards spiritual betterment they leave its afflictions, giving them less validity and less reality than spiritual goals. In the name of the higher spirit, the soul is betrayed (p. 67).

SPIRIT AND SOUL

In *Re-Visioning Psychology*, Hillman appends to his discussion of the transcendental denial of the soul and its afflictions a brief excursus on the differences between spirit and soul. Soul and spirit need to be differentiated because in Christianity, soul has become identified with spirit to the soul's own detriment: "Already in the early vocabulary used by Paul, pneuma or spirit had begun to replace psyche or soul. The New Testament scarcely mentions soul phenomena such as dreams, but stresses spirit phenomena such as miracles, speaking in tongues, prophecy, and visions" (p. 68).

The images ascribed to spirit blaze with light: "Spirit is fast, and it quickens what it touches. Its direction is vertical, and ascending." While there are many spirits, and many kinds of spirit, the notion of spirit has come to be associated with "the sublimations of higher and abstract disciplines, the intellectual mind, refinements, and purifications." Thus, the philosophers have tended to view spirit as their province, and have kept soul out of their works or assigned it to a lower place:

> Descartes confined soul to the pineal gland, a little enclave between the opposing powers of internal mind and external space. More recently, Santayana has put soul down in the realm of matter and considered it an antimetaphysical principle. Collingwood equated soul with feeling and considered that psychology had no business invading the realm of thought and ideas. The spiritual point of view always posits itself as superior, and operates particularly well in a fantasy of transcendence among ultimates and absolutes. (p. 68)

In contrast to images of spirit, soul images are connected with the night world, the realm of the dead, and the moon: "We still catch our soul's most essential nature in death experiences, in dreams of the night, and in the images of 'lunacy'" (p. 68). Unlike spirit, which extracts meanings (insights) and puts them into action, soul sticks to the realm of experience and to reflections within experience:

> It moves indirectly in circular reasonings, where retreats are as important as advances, prefering labyrinths and corners, giving a metaphorical sense to life through such words as *close, near, slow,* and *deep.* Soul involves us in the pack and welter of phenomena and the flow of impressions. It is the "patient" part of us. Soul is vulnerable and suffers; it is passive and remembers. (p. 69)

Whereas spirit says look up, gain distance, attend to the beyond and above, and travels by means of a *via negativa*—"not this, not that"—for "strait is the gate and only first or last things will do," soul replies, "But this too may have a place—who knows?" So, "the cooking vessel of the soul takes in everything, everything can become soul; and by taking into its imagination any and all events, psychic space grows" (p. 69).

THE VALE OF SOUL-MAKING

Hillman elaborates these differences between spirit and soul in his article, "Peaks and Vales" (1979). Here, again, he traces the loss of soul to early Christianity, which, beginning with Paul, substituted spirit for soul. He notes that at the Council of Constantinople in 869, "the soul lost its dominion. At this council, the idea of human nature as devolving from a tripartite cosmos of spirit, soul, and body was reduced to a dualism of spirit (or mind) and body (or matter)." Yet, this council only made official "a long process beginning with Paul, the Saint, of substituting and disguising, and forever after confusing, soul with spirit" (p. 54).

A key figure in this development was Tertullian who contended that the soul may be identified with a kind of "natural" Christianity, or Christianity in its most unreflective and least elevated form. Christians who aspire to a higher level of faith and commitment to God will cultivate the spiritual life, and not be satis-

fied with soul-religion. As the Council of Nicea in 787 deprived
images of their inherent authenticity, soul was also associated with
images and image worship, with an unreflective, natural Christianity
that spiritual Christians might tolerate in others, and even themselves have recourse to in moments of fear and dread, but recognize
as base and immature.

In this essay, Hillman continues his critique of Maslow's
notion of the peak experience. He commends Maslow for reintroducing pneuma into psychology, but points out that Maslow, in
doing so, also reintroduced the old confusion of pneuma with psyche
(or soul). "Peak" experiences concern the spirit and its elevation,
and "the peak experience is a way of describing pneumatic experience." The one who seeks the peak experience "is in search of
spirit." But the peak experience has nothing to do with the psyche,
or soul, for soul is identified, metaphorically, with the vales of life;
and in the usual religious language of our culture, the vale is a
depressed emotional place—the vale of tears, the lonesome valley,
and the valley of the shadow of death. As Hillman points out, the
first definition of "valley" in the *Oxford English Dictionary* is "a
long depression or hollow." Other meanings of the words "vale"
and valley refer to "such sad things as the decline of years and old
age, the world regarded as the scene of the mortal, the earthly, the
lowly" (p. 58). Hillman quotes John Keats' proposal, "Call the world,
if you please, the vale of soul-making." Hillman also notes that in
mythology the valleys are the places where the nymphs hold sway,
and nymphs are personifications of the wisps of clouds of mist clinging to valleys, mountains, and water sources. Thus, "nymphs veil
our vision, keep us shortsighted, myopic, caught—no long range dis-
tancing, no projections or prophecies as from a peak" (p. 58).

Hillman recognizes that the desire for spiritual transcendence is
strong in us, especially when, in the vigor of youth, we leave behind
the low and mundane valleys of our childhood and aspire to transcend the limitations of our lives, and to breathe the spirit of limitlessness. We seek to become universal men and women. But he cau-
tions that the valley world of the soul is steeped in history, whereas
in the peak experience of the spirit, history is that which is to be
overcome, the debris over which we climb in our ascent, and must
therefore be denied:

> Thus, from the spirit point of view, it can make no difference if
> our teacher be a Zaddik from a Polish *shtetl*, an Indian from
> under a Mexican cactus, or a Japanese master in a garden of

stones; these differences are but conditionings of history, personalistic hangups. The spirit is impersonal, rooted not in local soul, but timeless. (p. 62)[1]

Spirit ascends the mountain, thinking that it can leave soul behind, and believing that it will not pay a price for having done so. But,

> from the viewpoint of soul and life in the vale, going up the mountain feels like a desertion. . . . Its viewpoint appears in the long hollow depression of the valley, the inner and closed dejection that accompanies the exaltation of ascension. The soul feels left behind, and we see this soul reacting with resentments. Spiritual teachings warn the initiate so often about introspective broodings, about jealousy, spite, and pettiness, about attachments to sensations and memories. These cautions present an accurate phenomenology of how the soul feels when the spirit bids farewell. (p. 62)

So the soul develops its pathologies. There are the depressions and dejections that come with spirit's rejections, and the resentments created by spirit's attempt to run roughshod over the soul's local history, resentments which emerge in what psychotherapy terms our "complexes." In mythological terms, the Appolonian spirit, with its desire to make us feel free and open, and responsive to our higher self, has to come to terms with old Saturn, who is imprisoned "in paranoid systems of judgment, defensive maneuvers, and melancholic conclusions" (p. 72). If, as the name implies, the spiritual disciplines are disciplines of the transcendent spirit, then it is the task of psychotherapy, as *its* name implies (psyche-therapy), to concern itself with the residues of the spiritual ascent: with soul's depressions, resentments, paranoias, and melancholias.

On the other hand, if soul is associated with pathologies arising from its localism, it also has its localistic cures as well. For Hillman, humor is particularly important in this regard, for, whereas spirit assumes a position of humility as it confronts the inevitable limits of self and life, soul goes in for the humorous:

> Humility and humor are two ways of coming down to *humus*, to the human condition. Humility would have us bow down to the world and pay our dues to its reality. Render unto Caesar. Humor brings us down with a pratfall. Heavy meaningful reality becomes suspect, seen through, the world laughable—paranoia dissolved. (p. 64)

To illustrate the soul's preference for the humorous, Hillman cites a letter written by the fourteenth Dalai Lama of Tibet. This venerable master of the spirit uses the peaks and valleys metaphor to distinguish spirit and soul, and describes soul as "communal," as loving to hum in unison. But, says the Dalai Lama, soul is not enough, for "the creative soul craves spirit," and so, "the most beautiful monks one day bid farewell to their comrades and go to make their solitary journey toward the peaks, there to mate with the cosmos" (p. 59). Meanwhile, the less "creative" souls are content to pass the day sustained by the common, ordinary amusements of daily life. Western visitors to Tibet have noted that these folks may spend the better part of the day recounting an amusing event, such as an accidental pratfall by one of their number, who failed to notice a stone that lay—or was placed?—in the path where he was walking. This is soul, and it manifests itself not in songs of ascent, but in laughter emanating from the belly. As the title of a book by Paul Watzlawick puts it, "The situation is hopeless, but not serious" (1983).

THE SOUL AND HUMAN ANATOMY

The Locus of the Soul in the Body

Employing Hillman's distinction between spirit and soul, and his use of spatial imagery—peaks and vales—to express it, I now want to consider how this spirit/soul split is represented, metaphorically, in the body. I suggest that Hillman's spatial imagery for spirit and soul—peaks and vales—externalizes a conflict that we actually experience, internally, in our bodies. Moreover, we resort to such external imagery because internal imagery no longer seems to work once we inflate the pathologies of the soul by considering them signs of spiritual suffering. Thus, I propose that to recover the soul, to make it mean something once again, we need to "remedicalize" it, not, however, by translating soul into the psychiatric language of "mental process," but by relocating soul in the body and its processes, thus transposing Hillman's spatial imagery into the inner landscape of the human body—in a word, to "anatomize" it. What is needed, in other words, is the reaffirmation of the ancient tradition that the soul is "located," as it were, in the digestive system—the lower body—and, more precisely, in the central organ of the digestive system, the liver; and the corollary affirmation that the spirit has its "location" in the higher blood-vascular system and, more specifically, in the central organ of that system, the heart (Gray 1974). In proposing this anatomical approach to soul and spirit, I am agreeing with the philosophical tradition that assigns soul a lower place—in the realm of matter—but I suggest that this assignment does not mean that the soul is inferior to the spirit. Rather, my purpose here is to "elevate" the soul in our minds by "lowering" it, so to speak, in our bodies.

In our previous conference on "the endangered self," John McDargh (1992) drew our attention to Eugene Gendlin's idea that we experience ourselves through our bodies (our "felt bodily sense") and Troels Norager (1992) discussed the demise of religious "heart" language, asking whether such language has any future in our modern scientific age. These two essays stand in the background of my concern to view the soul as a profoundly visceral phenomenon. Specifically, I am suggesting that Hillman's differentiation between spirit/peak and soul/vale has been replicated in Western (and thus Christian) reflections on the vital organs.

Throughout human history, our premodern predecessors have been vexed and perplexed by the question of the soul's location in our bodies: If you and I have a soul, where is it located? While it is characteristic of moderns to consider this a meaningless question, perhaps it is safe for us, in what is now being called a postmodern age, not to dismiss this question quite so facilely. In any case, this is a vital question for us to ask if we agree that, while the "reduction" of the soul to "mental states" is bad enough, the "inflation" of the spirit at the expense of the soul is even worse. If I agree with this argument, this is only partly because it is my personal fate to be a seminary professor who is confronted almost daily with those who believe that what Christians most need in our day and time is a kind of "spiritual renewal" reflected in greater attention to matters of "spirituality." More crucial for me is the fact that it is also my fate to be an American, and to be living in an era in American history when our political leaders associate spiritual renewal with the deployment of awesome military technology. I will have more to say about this later in the chapter.

According to Jastrow (1912) and Selzer (1974), our ancient predecessors believed the soul is located in the liver. The liver was regarded as the center of vitality, the source of all mental and emotional activity, "nay, the seat of the soul itself" (Selzer, 64). The liver was also considered to be the organ through which the gods spoke, a belief that supported divination practices, as priests would slit open the belly of a sheep or goat and read the markings on the

animal's liver. Selzer points out, however, that with "the separation of medicine from the apron strings of religion and the rise of
anatomy as a study in itself, the liver was toppled from its central
role and the heart was elevated" (p. 65). Evidently, anatomical
research demonstrated that it was not the size or markings of an
organ but its essential function that counted, and, on this measure,
the heart came to be viewed as the true center of human vitality.
After all, the heart is the organ that pumps blood—that lifegiving
force—throughout the body.

Christianity, in Selzer's view, became a religion of the heart,
and, moreover, it transformed earlier barbaric heart rituals into a
more spiritualized form. If the ancient warrior cut out the heart of
his enemy and ate it with gusto, believing that to devour the slain
enemy's heart was to take upon oneself the strength, valor, and skill
of the vanquished, the early Christians engaged in the more civilized, and spiritualized, practice of *adoring* the heart of a saint: "It
was not the livers or brains or entrails of saints that were lifted from
the body in sublimest autopsy, it was the heart, thus snipped and
cradled into worshipful palms, then soaked in wine and herbs and set
into silver reliquaries for the veneration" (p. 63). This veneration of
the heart was also supported by the Greek philosophical tradition,
for, as Selzer notes, it was Plato who

> placed the higher emotions, such as courage, squarely above
> the diaphragm, and situated the baser appetites below, espe-
> cially in the liver, where they squat like furry beasts even
> today, as is indicated in the term "lily-livered," or "choleric,"
> or worse, "bilious." (pp. 65-66)

While Selzer's history of the triumph of the heart at the
expense of the liver as the seat of human vitality is rather sketchy, it
supports Hillman's distinction between spirit and soul. If
Christianity became the religion of spirit (pneuma), it did so in part
by giving special prominence to the heart, displacing the liver as
the locus of divine messages. Also, as previously noted, Selzer's
account of the triumph of the heart over the liver supports Hillman's
spatial images. Heart becomes associated with the peaks, while liver
has its place in the vales below. As Hillman himself points out,
"Sometimes going up the mountain one seeks escape from the
underworld, and so the Gods appear from below bringing all sorts of
physiological disorders. They will be heard, if only through intestinal
rumblings and their fire burning in the bladder" (1979, 71).

Selzer's account of the triumph of the heart may also explain why Christians did not have much use for soul-language. If, as Hillman argues, Christianity quickly became a religion of spirit, we may assume that, for Christians, the soul continued to be identified with the liver, and for this reason alone the soul would necessarily be devalued.[2]

Melancholy: The Symptom of Soul-Sickness

The most distressing and vexing psychological disorder throughout the course of Christian history—melancholia—has seldom been associated with the heart and the blood-vascular system, but has almost always been linked to the liver and the digestive system. In *Melancholia and Depression: From Hippocratic Times to Modern Times* (1986), Stanley Jackson sheds additional light on the plight of the soul by surveying the history of explanations for melancholia and depression. He notes that the term *melancholia*

> had its origins in terms that meant black bile and itself was used to mean the black bile as well as to name a disease. The black bile was a concept embedded in the context of humoral theory, which for approximately two thousand years was a central explanatory scheme for dealing with diseases. The black bile was considered to be the essential element in the pathogenesis of melancholia. (p. 7)

Writing in the fifth century B.C.E., Hippocrates was the first to include black bile among the four humours (the others being blood, yellow bile, and phlegm), and throughout the fifth century, black bile was held to be responsible for a great variety of diseases ranging from the headache, vertigo, paralysis, spasms, epilepsy, mental disturbances, and diseases of the kidney, liver, and spleen (p. 8). While black bile, unlike the other three humours, is difficult to reconcile with any known substances today, Jackson cites Henry E. Sigerist's suggestion that

> In this as in other cases the Greeks based their theories on observations. We know that the stool of patients suffering from bleeding gastric ulcers is black, as sometimes are the substances vomited by patients with carcinoma of the stomach. A form of malaria is still known as "black water fever" because the urine as a result of acute intravascular hemolysis suddenly

becomes very dark, if not black at least mahogany-colored. Similar observations may have led to the assumption that ordinary yellow bile through corruption could become black and that this black bile caused diseases, notably the "black bile disease" named melancholy. (p. 8)

Plato, a younger contemporary of Hippocrates, and who knew his views, employed a version of the humoral theory in *Timaeus*. According to Jackson, Plato conceived of a form of black bile as among the causes of many diseases, the formation of such black bile being the outcome of flesh decomposing and finding its way back into the blood. Plato noted that this decomposed matter grew black from "long burning" and became bitter, and that sometimes when the "bitter element was refined away . . . the black part assumes an acidity which takes the place of the bitterness." He also indicated that the pathogenic forms of the humours have the potential to wander about the body, and, finding no exit or escape, they become "pent up within and mingle their own vapours with the motions of the soul," and thus create an "infinite variety" of emotional distress and mental disorders (pp. 8-9).

Besides the black bile theory, another important feature of humoral theory and its explanation for the disease of melancholia was the spleen, as this organ was thought to have an especially important connection with the black bile. While Erasistratus considered the spleen an organ of little consequence, Galen thought it important, as it served to filter out "the thick earthy atrabilious humors that formed in the liver" (pp. 9-10). Because "black bile" was not among the three basic humors, but a "corruption" of one of the humours (yellow bile), it is easy to see how it came to be viewed as the cause of many diseases, both physical and emotional. Yet, because it was associated with bitterness and acidity, black bile had especially to do with the disease of melancholia, which was reflected in attitudes of bitterness, dejection, resentment, and, in more recent times, with depression. Thus, among the Greeks, melancholia came to be viewed as the quintessential disease or pathology of the soul.

In early Christianity, beginning with the writings of Evagrius of Pontus, a fourth century Egyptian monk, melancholia came to be viewed as one of the deadly sins and penance was considered the appropriate "medicine" for its healing. Melancholia was also assimilated into Christian views of demonic spirits, as Evagrius suggested that melancholy is itself an evil spirit, and is the effect of the "noonday demon" who attacks ascetics with particular vengeance (pp. 67-

68). On the other hand, many Scholastic writers "considered some instances of acedia (or melancholy) to be derived from an imbalance of the humors, thus making it a disease or the outcome of a disease. . . . The presence of such a natural cause tended to lessen the sinfulness of the vice in the eyes of these authors; it resulted more from disease than moral failing" (p. 71). Instead of advocating penance for melancholia attributable to an imbalance of the humors, these authors suggested that the afflicted could be helped by listening to music.

However, the long-term effect of the Christian ascetic movement, was to "spiritualize" melancholia, separating it from the humoral theory in which it had originally been situated. By the late middle ages, two competing theories regarding melancholia were well established, the original Greek idea that it is attributable to a bilious condition, rooted essentially in the digestive system, and the Christian ascetic view that it has more to do with the passions, and is therefore associated with the human heart. Robert Burton's monumental *The Anatomy of Melancholy* (1979), which first appeared in 1621 and went through several expansions during Burton's lifetime, the final version appearing posthumously in 1651, accepts the humoral views propounded by Galen and Hippocrates, but gives far less attention to its somatic than to its emotional causes, such as sorrow, fear, envy, and malice, as well as to such social and environmental influences as poverty and air pollution. This evolution is precisely what Hillman's excursus on the spirit and soul would have predicted: Melancholy is slowly but irrevocably dissociated from the digestive system—the locus of the soul—and this also results in a dissociation of the emotional dimensions of melancholy from their somatic roots. Melancholy becomes a "spiritual condition," the digestive system is no longer the seat of emotions like sorrow, fear, envy and malice, and, as a result, the soul becomes a vacuous concept, as it no longer has anything to do with human emotions and passions. The final indignity to the soul comes when even those who continued to subscribe to the humoral theory treated melancholy as a medical matter only, and no longer viewed its physical causes as having anything to do with the soul.

When the melancholic condition is thus spiritualized, the result is a failure to take any real account of the price that accompanies any spiritual ascent: the bitterness of a soul that has been left behind to nurture its resentments, paranoia, and other pathological defenses. When the soul was believed to have its locus in the liver, the fact that the soul could exact a price for our efforts to live as disembodied spirits—as "hearts lifted from the body in the sublimest autopsy"—could not be ignored. Now the soul is an empty and vacuous notion, and digestive disorders are merely of medical interest. They are not, as they were in original theories of melancholy, symptoms of a sick or pathologizing soul. The spirit need no longer answer to the soul, as the soul itself has been rendered inocuous. It either ceases to exist at all or, if it does, it has no power to hurt, or to take its revenge on the spirit that has abandoned it. As for melancholy or depression, it is no longer a sickness of the soul. Instead, it becomes a mental disorder.

The Liver-Soul As Self-Regenerative

What we also lose when the soul is lost, rendered vacuous, is the sense that the soul is beneficent. Through its association with the liver, the soul was understood to be the regenerative agent within the human self. Through direct observation, the ancient Greeks recognized that the liver is self-regenerative, the only organ of the body which has this capacity to regenerate itself. As Selzer describes its self-regenerative capacities, citing the case of Prometheus:

> Remember Prometheus? That poor devil who was chained to a rock, and had his liver pecked out each day by a vulture? Well, he was a classical example of the regeneration of tissue, for every night his liver grew back to the ready for the dreaded diurnal feast. And so will yours grow back, regenerate, reappear, regain all of its old efficiency and know-how. All it requires is quitting the booze, now and then. The evergrateful, forgiving liver will respond joyously with a multitude of mitoses and cell divisions that will replace the sick tissues with spanking new nodules and lobules of functioning cells. This rejuvenation is carried on with the speed and alacrity of a starfish growing a new ray from the stump of the old. . . . How unlike the lofty brain which has no power of regeneration at all. Once a brain cell dies, you are forever one shy. (pp. 76-77)

When the self-regenerative nature of the liver is associated with the soul, the soul's beneficent nature is readily appreciated: The self-regenerative nature of the liver does not call attention to the soul's bitterness, but to its capacity to forgive, especially to forgive the spirit its grandiosity, its visions of limitlessness, its callous denial of the debris over which it climbs in its dreams of transcendence. Thus, we might say that soul-loss need not be permanent or final, as the soul is a self-regenerating organ that sees to its own recovery. Unlike spirit, which seems to need an external "director" (see Foucault, 1988), soul, as Freud argued, is able to treat itself.

A dramatic example of the liver's capacity for self-regeneration is the recent liver transplant from a baboon to a human. At a news conference following the recipient's death seventy-one days after the transplant operation, the medical team acknowledged that their "almost pathological fear of [organ] rejection" may have contributed to the patient's death, as this fear of rejection which "had been seen in a virulent form in every other case [of organ transplant] ever done," led the team to order far more diagnostic testing than was needed in this case, and one such test precipitated a serious reaction that may have contributed to the patient's death. As it turned out, the medical team need not have worried, for the liver adapted itself to the recipient's body: "Within a month of the transplant operation, the baboon liver had tripled in size on its own to meet the metabolic needs of the recipient." According to the pathologist who performed the autopsy, "It adjusted nicely for a man of his size and weight" noting that "the liver is an unusual organ because it has the capacity to regenerate, the pathologist observed, "No one knows why the liver grew and why it stopped when it did" (*New York Times*, September 9, 1992, sec. A, p. 13).

If we moderns can no longer believe that the soul is actually located in the liver, then surely the fact that the liver is self-regenerative is enough to support belief that the liver is at the very least an apt metaphor for the soul. (The postmoderns among us may be able to believe what the ancients did, i.e., that the liver is in fact the temple of the soul). In either case, what the liver "tells" us—what its markings, as it were, show—is that, yes, one can try to kill the soul, yet the soul always has a way of coming back, or renewing itself. For the one who has tried to kill it—whether the host or external enemies—this is an ambiguous prospect at best, as the soul may forgive, but it may also avenge itself. As the pathologist suggests, the liver is a mysterious organ, and so is the soul.

The Digestive System and Soul-Recovery

Shortly after its publication in 1958, Erik Erikson's *Young Man Luther* (1958) provoked a great deal of controversy and received not a little outright ridicule in theological circles, mainly for its claim that Luther's great "theological breakthrough" happened when he was sitting in the "sweat chamber" (or toilet). For Erikson, it was of considerable significance that Luther's experience of divine grace occurred when he was sitting on the toilet. He takes the psychiatrist, Dr. Paul J. Reiter, to task for stating that the location really doesn't matter. On the contrary, "This whole geographic issue . . . deserves special mention exactly because it *does* point up certain psychiatric relevances. First of all, the location mentioned serves a particular physical need which hides its emotional relevance as long as it happens to function smoothly" (p. 204). As Erikson notes, Luther suffered from lifelong constipation and urine retention. Thus, "in this creative moment the tension of nights and days of meditation found release throughout his being—and nobody who has read Luther's private remarks can doubt that his total being always included his bowels" (p. 205). Thus, for Erikson there is something profoundly physiological in Luther's new understanding of God as one who is "no longer lurking in the periphery of space and time," but is rather "moving from inside" of us, and is thus, in a very real sense, "what works in us" (pp. 213-214).

This analysis of Luther's theological breakthrough, of his experience of the grace of God, suggests that the digestive system may be implicated in the recovery of one's soul. Yet, Erikson's analysis was ridiculed by the theological community, as it could not imagine that God and the digestive system have anything to do with one another. This is not surprising, of course, as it is consistent with the history we have just reviewed, namely, of soul denial motivated by a commitment to some higher spirituality.

Nor could the theological community recognize, as Luther (and Erikson) surely did, the obvious humor in this odd collusion of divine grace and the digestive system. As Erikson shows throughout *Young Man Luther*, Luther's own ribald humor often centered upon the vicissitudes of the digestive process, even as this same process figured in Luther's melancholic moods as well. As Erikson points out, "In melancholy moods, [Luther] expressed his depressive self-repudication also in anal terms: 'I am like ripe shit,' he said once at the dinner table during a fit of depression (and the boys eagerly wrote it down), 'and the world is a gigantic ass-hole. We probably will let go of each other soon'" (p. 206). This is soul-talk. This is not the spiritual Luther of whom Erikson could say, "I will state, as a clinican's judgment, that nobody could speak and sing as Luther later did if his mother's voice had not sung to him of some heaven" (p. 72). Rather, this is the soulful, gut-rumbling Luther, who assuaged his melancholia by means of self-deprecating humor.

It is worth noting that the reaction of the theological community to *Young Man Luther* was similar to its reaction to the melancholic Luther in his own time. As Burton observes in *The Anatomy of Melancholia*, it was Luther's follower, Philip Melancthon, who added spirit to the four humours, and who held "the fountain of these spirits to be the heart," as spirit, the "instrument of the soul, is expressed from the blood" (pp. 38-39). In effect, Melancthon "spiritualized" Luther's understanding of God, lifting God from vale to peak, from liver to heart, and, in so doing, rendering Luther's theology soul-less. Ever since, Lutheranism has honored a sanitized Luther, and has viewed his preoccupation with his digestive system as merely a "medical" matter or as merely a function of his sociocultural background, and therefore as integral neither to his own religious experience nor to anyone else's.[3]

The Passing of the Stone As Experience of Divine Grace

If constipation and urine retention were the physiological occasion for Luther's experience of divine grace, consider the potential for experience of divine grace afforded by the passing or the surgical removal of stones. Selzer describes the cessation of pain following the loosening of a kidney stone as "no less than being touched by the hand of God" (p. 85). He cites Samuel Pepys' diary entry four days after the surgical removal of a kidney stone the size of a tennis ball: "Up early, this being by God's great blessing the fourth solemn day of my cutting for the stone" (p. 87). Selzer emphasizes the fact that, where stones are concerned, "Nothing one does can relieve it or make it worse. Play, run, ride, debauch. It will affect you neither for good nor ill. Say as much, if you can, for the pox, the gout, the bursten belly" (p. 86). One could conclude, as Luther surely did, that soul-recovery is not a matter of human agency or volition, that it depends on a divine act of grace. Furthermore, Selzer makes the point that, "Unlike other illnesses that are years in recovery, and leave residual distempers aplenty, the passed stone carries itself clean off" (p. 86). Which is to say, with Luther, that when salvation arrives, it is complete and thorough. The change is total, and nothing is as it was. Our former condition is but a memory having no residual effects. As one cannot do anything to relieve the pain, and as there is no behavior one need avoid for fear of making matters worse, so the stone, when it passes, leaves the soul as healthy as it ever was. No residual effects. Salvation is not, as religion of the spirit assumes, an arduous ascent. Rather, it is the sudden and total cessation of psychic pain (as when a depressive episode unaccountably lifts for no discernible reason).[4]

Soul-Loss in Contemporary America

When we come to study the phenomenon of conversion or religious regeneration, we shall see that a not infrequent consequence of the change operated in the subject is a transfiguration of the face of nature in his eyes. A new heaven seems to shine upon a new earth. In melancholiacs there is usually a similar change, only it is in the reverse direction. The world now looks remote, strange, sinister, uncanny. Its color is gone, its breath is cold, there is no speculation in the eyes it glares with. (William James)

Melancholy: The American Form of Soul-Sickness

Following Hillman, I have emphasized the role played by Christianity, almost from its beginnings, in contributing to the loss of soul. However, our conference theme invites us to consider soul-loss in modern societies, which implies that the soul—so much a constituent feature of the everyday life of primitive and premodern societies—has been a casualty of modern societies. In his conference paper last year, Richard K. Fenn (1992) made a very persuasive argument that it is the "open" society that most threatens the "unconditioned nature of the self" (or soul). I want to take this point seriously, as it does not really contradict Hillman's contention that Christianity has sowed the seeds of soul-loss, for it is now taken as axiomatic by sociologists and historians of religion that Christianity is not an enemy but an ally of modernity.

The modern society that especially interests me is America, as it well illustrates the irony to which Hillman draws our attention, namely, that the major enemy of the soul is not scientific rationality (as seems more to have been the case in Europe; cf. Norager 1992), but our tendency in America to degrade the soul in the name of spirituality. In addressing this irony, it would be easy to scapegoat the "new age movement," or to participate in the current debunking of "expressive individualism" (Bellah et al. 1985; cf. Capps and Fenn 1992). Such efforts to identify convenient scapegoats are much too facile, as the elevation of spirit at the expense of soul is American to the core. As I intend to show, it is a central theme in the political rhetoric of our times.

A related reason for my wanting to focus on soul-loss in America is that we Americans are especially susceptible to the soul-pathology identified as melancholy (and what is commonly termed depression in the psychotherapeutic literature). This was the position that William James developed in his chapter on the "sick-soul" in *The Varieties of Religious Experience* (1958). While he included many non-American testimonials of melancholia in this chapter, including such historically diverse figures as Luther, Father Gatray, John Bunyan and Leo Tolstoy, the most moving and compelling such testimony is his own, written when he was in his late twenties (Erikson 1968, 150-155), but represented in *The Varieties* as the testimony of a Frenchman (James 1958, 135-136). James cites it as an example of "the worst kind of melancholy . . . which takes the form of panic fear." Portions of the account follow:

> Whilst in this state of philosophic pessimism and general depression of spirits about my prospects, I went one evening into a dressing-room in the twilight to procure some article that was there; when suddenly there fell upon me without any warning, just as if it came out of the darkness, a horrible fear of my own existence. Simultaneously there arose in my mind the image of an epileptic patient whom I had seen in the asylum, a black-haired youth with greenish skin, entirely idiotic, who used to sit all day on one of the benches, or rather shelves against the wall, with his knees drawn up against his chin, and the coarse gray undershirt, which was his only garment, drawn over them enclosing his entire figure. . . . *That shape am I*, I felt, potentially. Nothing that I possess can defend me against that fate, if the hour for it should strike for me as it struck for him. There was such a horror of him, and such a perception of my own merely momentary discrepancy from him, that it was as if something hitherto solid within my breast gave way entirely, and I became a mass of quivering fear. After this the universe was changed for me altogether. I awoke morning after morning with a horrible dread at the pit of my stomach, and with a sense of the insecurity of life that I never knew before, and that I have never felt since. (pp. 136-137)

Note especially his references to the physiological features of this experience: "Something hitherto solid within my breast gave way entirely" and was replaced by "a horrible dread at the pit of my stomach." In a very real, literal sense, his spirit sagged, and he was left vulnerable to the emotions of soul; in this instance, the emotions of fear, dread, and a never before experienced sense of the insecurity of life.

Continuing, he says that this experience "was like a revelation," and that, while the immediate feelings passed away," "the experience has made me sympathetic with the morbid feelings of others ever since." For several months, he was unable to go out in the dark alone, and

> In general I dreaded to be left alone. I remember wondering how other people could live, how I myself had ever lived, so unconscious of that pit of insecurity beneath the surface of life. My mother in particular, a very cheerful person, seemed to me a perfect paradox in her unconsciousness of danger, which you may well believe I was very careful not to disturb by revelations of my own state of mind. I have always thought that this experience of melancholia of mine had a religious bearing. (p. 136)

When his "French correspondent" was asked to explain more fully what he meant by his statement that the experience had "a religious bearing," this was his reply:

> I mean that the fear was so invasive and powerful that if I had not clung to scripture-texts like "The eternal God is my refuge," etc., "Come unto me, all ye that labor and are heavy-laden," etc., "I am the resurrection and the life," etc., I think I should have grown really insane. (p. 136)

James adds two footnotes to this account. The first is a quote from John Bunyan's *Grace Abounding to the Chief of Sinners*, in which Bunyan describes a similar personal experience in strongly physiological language. Bunyan writes that he felt his "very body . . . to shake and totter" and "felt also such clogging and heat at my stomach, by reason of this my terror, that I was, especially at some times, as if my breastbone would have split asunder." He continues: "Thus did I wind, and twine, and shrink, under the burden that was upon me; which burden also did so oppress me that I could neither stand, nor go, nor lie, either at rest or quiet" (p. 136).

The second is a reference to "another case of fear equally sudden," and cites an article written by James' father, Henry James, Sr. The elder James' account, too, describes the episode in intense physical tones:

> One day . . . towards the close of May, having eaten a comfortable dinner, I remained sitting at the table after the family had disappeared, idly gazing at the embers in the grate, thinking of nothing, and feeling only the exhilaration incident to a good digestion, when suddenly—in a lightning flash as it were—fear came upon me and trembling, which made all my bones to shake. (quoted in Matthiessen 1948, 161; see Erikson 1968, 153)

The momentary exhilaration which accompanied "a good digestion" quickly faded, as fear came upon him, causing his whole body to tremble. Spirit again gave way to soul. His commentary on this sudden surge of panic fear attested that this experience was that of melancholy:

> Time and again while living at this dismal water-cure, and listening to its endless "strife of tongues" about diet, and regimen, and disease . . . I have said to myself, the curse of mankind, that which keeps our manhood so little and so depraved, is its sense of self-hood, and the absurd, abominable opinionativeness it engenders. How sweet it would be to find oneself no longer man, but one of those innocent and ignorant sheep pasturing upon that placid hillside, and drinking in eternal dew and freshness from nature's lavish bosom. (Matthiessen, 162)

Among the sheep, there is no "strife of tongues" about diet, regimen, and disease, and no effort to insure a good digestion by means of some sort of water-cure. Nor, for that matter, do the sheep experience the alternation of peaks and vales that humans do, as they are always to be found on a placid hillside, drinking the eternal dew and freshness from nature's generous bosom. For humans, it is very different. Our "sense of self-hood" *is* related to the vicissitudes of our bodies, and we are therefore constantly arguing and contending over strategies for staying fit and combatting disease.

Thus, the fate of the body is a powerful theme in melancholia, and William James in *The Varieties* makes much of the fact that melancholia is experienced in and through the body. He warns against the non-sufferer's tendency to talk about melancholia in intellectualized language:

> Not the conception or intellectual perception of evil, but the grisly blood-freezing heart-palsying sensation of it close upon

one, and no other conception or sensation able to live for a moment in its presence. How irrelevantly removed seem all our usual refined optimisms and intellectual and moral consolations in presence of a need of help like this! (pp. 136-137)

The fact that James devotes the entire chapter on the sick-soul to the phenomenon of melancholy indicates how sensitive he was to the deep fear of melancholia (or depression) in the American psyche. I found corroborating evidence of this fear in my recent surveys of laity and clergy attitudes regarding the deadly sins (Capps 1989, 1992). Laity and clergy both ranked melancholy (described as "a personal bitterness toward life; hatred and disgust for the world and the people with whom one associates") as the deadliest of sins (36% of the laity and 26% of the clergy ranked it so). Since only 2% of the clergy and 5% of the laity indicated that they were personally struggling with melancholy at the time of the survey, melancholy would seem to be an experience or condition which Americans do not suffer from now but nonetheless dread happening to them sometime in the future. It is an experience they can imagine happening to themselves involuntarily and over which they will have little or no control.

If melancholy is the vale of American religious experience, what is the peak, and how are they related to one another? I suggest that the "sublime" is at the heart of Americans' quest for peak religious experience, and that, in contrast to melancholy, the sublime is strongly associated in Americans' minds and rhetoric with the blood-vascular system (whose primary organ is the heart). Recall Selzer's depiction of the removal of the heart from the body of the saint so that it might be adored by Christian devotees as an act of "sublimest autopsy." This use of the language of "sublimity" to describe a symbolic act of releasing the spirit from the body is most appropriate, as it not only captures the moral seriousness of the act but also its intense emotional pitch: As the heart of the saint is upraised, so the heart of the adoring one is lifted higher and higher until it experiences almost unbearable rapture.

In *American Sublime: The Genealogy of a Poetic Genre* (1991), Rob Wilson considers what he calls the Americanization of the sublime:

Crossing the Atlantic, the sublime underwent an ideological seachange. If the Enlightenment sublime had represented the unrepresentable, confronted privation, and pushed language to

the limits of imagining the vastness of natural and stellar infini-
tude as the subjects' innermost ground, the Americanization of
this sublime rhetoric represented, in effect, the interiorization
of national claims as this Americanized self's inalienable
ground. . . . The genre of the sublime helped to consolidate an
American identity founded in representing a landscape of
immensity and wildness ("power") open to multiple identifications ("use"). (pp. 4-5)

Wilson argues that the American sublime is grounded in this paradox: While "the sublime experience of huge natural forces may dwarf
and empty the self . . . it no less underwrites the ongoing appropriation of nature-writ-large within a giddying sense of self-empowerment that Emerson declared to be enacted as 'an instantaneous in-
streaming causing power'" (p. 13). So, while Americans have written
eloquently about the "strange states of self-dispossession" and "ego-
dwarfing before Niagara-like powers" which are beyond human domination and control, still, on a more primary level of selfhood, the
American sublime has been a "self-enabling and communally adhesive 'supreme fiction,'" an "'overbelief' in power and grandeur that
enables further production of power and grandeur" (p. 13).

    As Wilson is concerned with the sublime as a poetic genre, he
explores the early American precursors of the sublime in Anne
Bradstreet's and William Livingston's reflections on landscape as
the vehicles of "emotional transport" (what Bradstreet called the
"enrapt spirit"); nineteenth century representations of the sublime in
the poetry of William Cullen Bryant and Walt Whitman; Wallace
Stevens' modernist attempt to reconfigure the American sublime
through "decreation" of false notions of the sublime; and the postmodern sublime in the poetry of John Ashbery, Louis Simpson and
Galway Kinnell.

    In the final chapter, titled "Towards the Nuclear Sublime,"
Wilson focuses on the shift from "the *natural* sublime that made
Niagara Falls and Lake Ontario function as collective symbols of
material force and liberal empowerment in Emerson's America"
(p. 232) to the *nuclear* sublime reflected in the first atomic explosion
at Alamogordo, New Mexico, on July 16, 1945, a cataclysmic event
described in the official government report as having "the beauty
the great poets dream about but describe most poorly and inadequately" (p. 229). Following Kenneth Burke's distinction between
the *beautiful* as that which we love because we are able fictively to
dominate it, and the sublime as that which we admire because it

subjugates us, Wilson asks whether the same self-empowerment ascribed to the natural sublime, in which the "very superior force of nature can inspire a force of resistance that releases inner resources of self-preservation," is imaginable in the case of the nuclear sublime? Moreover, "Can Los Alamos displace Niagara as a figure of national empowerment?" (p. 236).

As far as *self*-empowerment is concerned, Wilson argues that the *nuclear sublime* has largely been represented by American poets of the latter half of the twentieth century as the very antithesis of self-empowerment. Allen Ginsberg's "Plutonian Ode" begins on this ironic note: "Father Whitman I celebrate a matter that renders Self oblivion." Yet, Wilson also notes that in recent years we have witnessed the emergence of an American sublime in which the poem itself assumes the role formerly ascribed to nature. Thus, certain poems by Galway Kinnell, Gary Snyder and Robert Bly reflect a kind of nostalgic retreat into "a mystique of images served up from unconscious depths and animistic states of mineral/animal being" designed to "counter technological anxiety by experiencing a flow of ecstasies before libidinous objects of desire" (p. 255). Here, the sublime poem itself works as

> a structure which produces/reproduces the desire for another unifying experience, another uplift into rapture, the transport of the "body without organs." The poem moves to produce an ecstasy of language ("jouissance"), an excess, by multiplying surface or depth images intended to heal the daily dose of self-division. (p. 255)

For Wilson, however, this places too much burden on poetry itelf to heal our self-division. Moreover, it assumes that the healing of our spirit/soul division occurs through a spiritual peak experience rather than the reconciliation of spirit and soul.

But, as our concern here is with soul-loss in "modern societies," it is the question of the nuclear sublime's effect on *national* empowerment that warrants particular attention. Here, I would suggest that if Los Alamos was not an adequate figure of national empowerment in the nuclear age, Desert Storm—with its awesome display of what Wilson calls "technological vastness"—surely aspired to be. When the first air attacks on the city of Baghdad broke the stillness of that January night, many Americans felt within themselves the "sublime elevation" which Walt Whitman once described as "that condition [in which] the whole body is elevated to a state by others unknown—inwardly and out-wardly illuminated, purified, made solid, strong, yet bouyant" (Wilson 1991, 161). Moreover, as President Bush declared during and after the war, Desert Storm bouyed the spirits of Americans after the debacle of Vietnam, and thus provided what Wilson calls a "communally adhesive 'supreme fiction,' and 'overbelief' in power and grandeur that enables further production of power and grandeur." Desert Storm was the peak experience of national empowerment.

What, then, went wrong? Is it merely that the sublime is not sustainable indefinitely? Or is it rather that the soul exacts a price for each of our spiritual elevations, our rapturous uplifts? I suggest that the soul of America is now reacting to its degradation of a year ago with characteristic, and predictable vengeance. In the aftermath of this spiritual excess named "Desert Storm," the nation is experiencing something like black bile disease, which, as Plato pointed out, is the outcome of the flesh decomposing and returning back into the blood stream. There is a deep bitterness flowing through the land, its name is melancholy, and it is a sickness deep within the American soul.[5] As Joseph Lowery, one of the founders of the 1960s civil rights movement, recently told a Methodist congregation in Atlanta:

> It is not our economy we need to be worried about. What's imperiled today in America is her soul. We can deal with the economy. If we lose our souls, what, then, is there for us? There is no sanctuary for the soul from the sorrow of the society in which we live.

What can we, as a nation, do about our addiction to the sub-lime? I confess that I do not know the answer, for, apparently, our revulsion against the destructiveness of war, and knowledge that atrocities will surely be committed, has not been enough to dis-suade us from participating periodically in these sublime autopsies.

So I will conclude on a modest—yet hopeful—note, taking a leaf from William James' recollection that, when he was in the throes of melancholy, it was his clinging to scripture-texts that saved him from going really insane: Since neither the soul, nor the spirit, can find an escape or exit from the body, the solution is surely not an inflated spirituality at the expense of the soul, but recognition and acceptance of their common fate. In an earlier essay (Capps 1990), I cited Psalm 131 as a prescription against the tyranny of narcissism, especially its grandiose forms (where there is, in effect, an excess of spirit). I now cite the same Psalm as an antidote against the seductions of the sublime:[6]

> O Lord, my heart is not lifted up,
> my eyes are not raised too high;
> I do not occupy myself with things
> too great and marvelous for me.
>
> But I have calmed and quieted my soul,
> like a child quieted at its mother's breast;
> like a child that is quieted is my soul.
>
> O Israel [read: America], hope in the Lord
> from this time forth and evermore.

A heart that is *not* lifted high—removed from the body in sublimest autopsy—and a soul that is at peace with itself and its surroundings: This is not the language of an inflated spirit and a degraded soul. It is the language of spirit and soul reconciled to one another. It says that for spirit to be authentic, this cannot be at the expense of soul, but arise from the soul, as when the mourners gathered around the gravesite—knowing their soul-loss—are yet able to raise their voices in mournful yet resonantly heartfelt singing.

National days of repentance and remorse—when our spiritual excesses are confessed and our souls are bared and lifted—are evidently a thing of the past. So perhaps the best resource individual citizens possess today is the deflating power of humor: soul's refusal to accord spirit the seriousness it demands. Such deflation of spirit is implied in Wallace Stevens' "The American Sublime" (1972, 114), which poses this presumably urgent question (one that visitors to Niagara Falls are often heard to ask): What is one supposed to eat and to drink when one stands beholding the sublime? Thus does the soul, resident in the digestive system, mock the pretensions of spirit. And thus does the soul initiate its own treatment.

NOTES

1. Hillman's suggestion that ethnicity is central to the soul is echoed in Michael M. J. Fischer's (1986) observation that autobiographical works that take ethnicity seriously reflect "the paradoxical sense that ethnicity is something reinvented and reinterpreted in each generation by each individ-

ual and that it is often something quite puzzling to the individual, something over which he or she lacks control. Ethnicity is not something that is simply passed on from generation to generation, taught and learned; it is something dynamic, often unsuccessfully repressed or avoided" (p. 195). Expanding on the idea that we often experience ethnicity as the return of the repressed, as having "the compulsion of an 'id-like' force," Fischer points out that "The *id*, as Freud originally used the term, was merely *das Es*, the itness of experience, made particularly potent for the German-speaking child, who is referred to in the neuter—*das Kind*—and who only gradually develops an acknowledged, engendered, individuated self. The recognition of something about one's essential being thus seems to stem from outside one's immediate consciousness and control, and yet requires an effort of self-definition. Ethnicity in its contemporary form is thus neither, as the sociological literature would have it, simply a matter of group process (support systems), nor a matter of transition (assimilation), nor a matter of straightforward transmission from generation to generation (socialization)" (pp. 196-197). This sounds much like the "soul" as Hillman views it, and, indeed, Fischer goes on to talk about the Pythagorean notion that the recognition of something about one's essential being is the work of the soul as it engages in exercises of memory (or introspection similar to that of the contemporary autobiographer).

2. Jastrow (1912) also notes that ancient India privileged the heart: "In Sanskrit literature the heart is the seat of thought, and since thought is the most significant and most direct manifestation of the soul, the heart is identified with the soul, and, as such, becomes also the source of all emotions and the general symbol of vitality" (p. 144). In contrast, the ancient Hebrews held that the liver is the seat of the soul, and Jastrow cites various verses to support this (Lamentations 2:11; Job 16:13; Proverbs 7:23; Psalms 7:6; and Psalms 30:13). Also, the Talmud refers to medical remedies that employ the liver of a dog or the gall of a fish: "Both remedies are clearly based on the supposition that the liver as the seat of life or of the soul is capable of restoring the intellect and sight, which are manifestations of soul life" (p. 15).

3. Steven Kepnes has shared with me the following Jewish prayer which is said after using the toilet: "Blessed art thou, Lord our God, King of the universe, who hast formed man in wisdom, and created in him a system of ducts and tubes. It is well known before thy glorious throne that if but one of these be opened, or if one of those be closed, it would be impossible to exist in thy presence. Blessed are thou, O Lord, who healest all creatures and doest wonders."

4. In my discussion of the soulful nature of the digestive system, the persons whose experiences have been recounted are male. This prompts me to note another of Erik Erikson's controversial writings, his "Womanhood and the Inner Space" (1968, 261-282), for in this essay he suggests that the

woman's "inner" life is especially related to the reproductive system, and that it is this "inner space" which is "at the center of despair even as it is the very center of potential fulfillment" (p. 278; see also Erikson 1975). Women surely have a unique understanding of "that which moves inside for appropriate body metaphors of divine grace. Some of the women at our conference noted that the imagery employed in my discussion of the digestive system and divine grace emphasizes the relief that occurs when a "blockage" is overcome, when the material that was pent up and held back is again allowed passage. This, they suggested, is a uniquely male way of speaking about the inner space and therefore of the ways that God is understood to move in us.

I fully agree with this observation. Viewing divine grace from the perspective of the reproductive system would surely make greater use of relational images and metaphors. But I would also note that what I have been arguing here does have relevance to women who suffer from the eating disorders, anorexia and bulimea, and the fact that women who have given birth to several children are prime candidates for gall stones is an indication that the fates of the digestive and reproductive systems are interrelated. Also, in my survey of laity and clergy attitudes toward the deadly sins (Capps 1989, 1992), twice as many women than men (24% to 12%) indicated that they were currently struggling personally with the sin of gluttony (described in the survey as "addictive habits, like excessive or erratic eating and drinking, which cause oneself and others untold misery"). This suggests that women are actually *more* likely than men to share Luther's view that the digestive system plays a significant role in the religious experience of an individual.

5. William Safire suggests that President Bush himself suffered from melancholia after the euphoria of Desert Storm died down: "The self-assured Bush served the nation well through the Persian Gulf crisis; nobody can ever take his hundred hours of greatness away from him. . . . Then Bush the winner was replaced by Bush the loser. For the first half of 1992, he seemed dispirited; many thought he was ill. . . . [He] seemed to slide into melancholia." ("Bush's Gamble," *The New York Times Magazine*, October 18, 1992, p. 32). Safire attributes Bush's melancholia to the erosion of his approval rating and the economy's failure to respond to the Federal Reserve's dramatic interest rate cut of December. I would not question this, but I would also suggest that President Bush's melancholia was partly a *direct* consequence of Desert Storm, even as it seems to have been so for the American public in general. I would also note that the "low point" for Mr. Bush was his public vomiting episode in Japan in December, a certain indication that, unbeknownst to him, his soul was troubling him.

6. Patrick D. Miller, an expert on the Psalms, is persuaded that Psalm 131 was written by a woman (personal conversation). He bases this view on the fact that in the Hebrew text the word "mother" is self-referential. This

is the only psalm that may with confidence be said to have been written by a woman, though others quite likely were. It is significant to me that I have chosen the words of an ancient Jewish woman as an antidote to the problem of spiritual excess and soul-loss in American public life.

REFERENCES

Bellah, Robert N. et al. 1985. *Habits of the Heart: Individualism and Commitment in American Life.* Berkeley: University of California Press.

Bettelheim, Bruno. 1984. *Freud and Man's Soul.* New York: Vintage Books.

Burton, Robert. 1979. *The Anatomy of Melancholy.* Joan K. Peters, ed. New York: Frederick Unger Publishing Company.

Capps, Donald. 1989. "The deadly sins and saving virtues: How they are viewed by laity." *Pastoral Psychology* 37:229-253.

———. 1990. "Sin, narcissism, and the changing face of conversion." *Journal of Religion and Health* 29:233-253.

———. 1992a. "The desire to be another man's son: The child Jesus as an endangered self." In Richard K. Fenn and Donald Capps, *The Endangered Self*, 21-35. Princeton, New Jersey: Center for Religion, Self and Society, Monograph Series, no. 2.

Capps, Donald and Richard K. Fenn, eds. 1992. *Individualism Reconsidered: Readings Bearing on the Endangered Self in Modern Society.* Princeton, New Jersey: Center for Religion, Self and Society, Monograph Series, no. 1.

Erikson, Erik H. 1958. *Young Man Luther: A Study in Psychoanalysis and History.* New York: W. W. Norton and Company.

———. 1968. "Womanhood and the inner space." In *Identity: Youth and Crisis*, 261-282. New York: W. W. Norton and Company.

———. 1975. "Once more the inner space." In *Life History and the Historical Moment*, 225-247. New York: W. W. Norton and Company.

———. 1981. "The Galilean sayings and the sense of 'I'." *The Yale Review* (Spring) 1981:321-362.

Fenn, Richard K. 1992. "The endangered self: The threat of soul-loss in American society." In Richard K. Fenn and Donald Capps, eds., *The Endangered Self*, 143-152. Princeton, New Jersey: Center for Religion, Self and Society, Monograph Series, no. 2.

Fischer, Michael M. J. 1986. "Ethnicity and the post-modern arts of memory." In James Clifford and George E. Marcus, eds., *Writing Culture: The Poetics and Politics of Ethnography*, 194-233. Berkeley: University of California Press.

Foucault, Michel. 1988. "Technologies of the self." In Luther H. Martin, Huck Gutman, and Patrick H. Hutton, eds., *Technologies of the Self: A Seminar with Michel Foucault*, 16-49. Amherst: University of Massachusetts Press.

Gray, Henry. 1974. *Anatomy: Descriptive and Surgical*. T. Pickering Pick and Robert Howden, eds. Philadelphia: Running Press.

Hillman, James. 1975. *Re-Visioning Psychology*. New York: Harper and Row, Publishers.

———. 1979. "Peaks and vales: The soul/spirit distinction as basis for the differences between psychotherapy and spiritual discipline." In James Hillman et al., *Puer Papers*, 54-74. Irving, Texas: Spring Publications, Inc.

Ingerman, Sandra. 1991. *Soul Retrieval: Mending the Fragmented Self*. San Francisco: HarperSanFrancisco.

Jackson, Stanley W. 1986. *Melancholia and Depression: From Hippocratic Times to Modern Times*. New Haven: Yale University Press.

James, William. 1958. *The Varieties of Religious Experience*. New York: Mentor Books.

Jastrow, Morris, Jr. 1912. "The liver as the seat of the soul." In David Gordon Lyon and George Foot Moore, eds., *Studies in the History of Religions*, 143-168. New York: The Macmillan Company.

Mattheissen, F. O. 1948. *The James Family*. New York: Alfred A. Knopf.

McDargh, John. 1992. "Emerson and the life of the self: A psychoanalytic conversation." In Richard K. Fenn and Donald Capps, eds., *The Endangered Self*, 7-20. Princeton, New Jersey: Center for Religion, Self and Society, Monograph Series, no. 2.

Norager, Troels. 1992. "The eclipse of the heart: The shift from pre-scientific to scientific metapsychology, and its implications for the theme of the endangered self." In Richard K. Fenn and Donald Capps, eds., *The Endangered Self*, 47-57. Princeton, New Jersey: Center for Religion, Self and Society, Monograph Series, no. 2.

Selzer, Richard. 1974. *Mortal Lessons: Notes on the Art of Surgery*. New York: A Touchstone Book.

Stevens, Wallace. 1972. *The Palm at the End of the Mind: Selected Poems and a Play.* Holly Stevens, ed. New York: Vintage Books.

Watzlawick, Paul. 1983. *The Situation is Hopeless, But Not Serious: The Pursuit of Unhappiness.* New York: W. W. Norton and Company.

Wilson, Rob. 1991. *American Sublime: The Genealogy of a Poetic Genre.* Madison: The University of Wisconsin Press.

7

Soul-Loss and Religious Consolation in Two Lives

SCROOGE ON "SOUL-LOSS"

"Soul" and its cross-cultural equivalents generally identify a vital, subtle component of the individual expressed in health, mood, moral conduct, altered states of consciousness, and other personal phenomena. In traditional cultures around the world, belief in one or more souls dictated procedure and explained outcome in a variety of personal undertakings—romance, reproduction, combat, breadwinning, devotion.

In the modern West, the cultural setting of this conference, we invoke the soul at gravesides and from pulpits. However, in virtually every other context in which we need to understand or manipulate an individual, we rely not on the idea of the soul but on scientific constructs such as defense mechanisms, cognitive structures, the ego, the unconscious, DNA, and neurotransmitters. In the treatment of aberrant behavior, flagging vitality, infertility, marital discord, and career failure, the ritual diagnostics of soul sickness have been replaced by brain maps, personality inventories, and blood-work.

If soul appears at all in scientific treatments of the person, it serves usually as a metaphor for a component framed more precisely or literally in modern secular language. Its function is evocative rather than analytic. Thus Freud used *"Seele"* not to identify a dis-crete element of the person but to refer figuratively to the totality of id, ego, and superego (Bettelheim 1982, 86f.).

Just so, in each of the papers presented at the conference, soul and soul-loss were psychologized, that is, used metaphorically for mental phenomena ordinarily described in humanistic or scientific terms (sexual abuse, bulimia, sadomasochism, addiction, moral anomie, etc.). In most papers, I think soul imagery only obfuscated the discussion of a relatively familiar social-psychological syndrome. To make matters worse, usage was idiosyncratic. In its native set-tings, soul-loss designated quite specific symptoms and causes; how-ever, no two conference writers used the term alike.

In all, it seemed to me dishonest—not to mention pointless—to apply a primitive diagnosis to conditions originally and adequately framed by modern science. Contemporary physicists might just as well reintroduce "ether" into their deliberations; physicians, "humors."

Let me emphasize, this is not a wholesale endorsement of sci-entific over traditional concepts of the self. There are no perfect the-ories; scientific models of the person, like soul constructs, may be relatively sophisticated or crude, functional or inoperative. Rather, I am protesting the artificial and gratuitous introduction of ancient terminology into a discussion that, given the training of discussants, is ineluctably scientific. Although entertaining, this exercise in nomenclatural cross-breeding, in my view, only distracted conferees from genuine puzzles of selfhood.

My paper attempts to explain scientifically the differential capacity of religion, in two lives, to alleviate mental pain. In this investigation, soul terminology has no organic place. Psychological concepts (such as cognitive style and defense mech-anisms) sufficiently frame the subjects' despair and healing. The conditions I halfheartedly designate as soul-loss are more effi-ciently labeled "hysteria" in one case and "clinical depression" in the other. Indeed, Wikstrom might argue that my analysis pro-motes soul-loss by failing to recognize an unclassifiable, unpre-dictable personal core.

I confess insensitivity, a temperamental matter-of-factness that numbs me to the subtle essences of people or the rarified sources of their distress. Unable to expose a human soul, I make a more humble offering to the conference: two personal histories of everyday, concrete pain and relief. I find these lives worthy of serious attention precisely as embodiments of an imperfectly conceived, but at times highly illuminating psychological order.

CLASSICAL VIEWS OF RELIGIOUS CONSOLATION

In groundbreaking psychological studies of religion, James (1961) and Freud (1961) both emphasized its coping function. Indeed, behind their nearly opposite appraisals of religion lies a common recognition of its palliative powers.

Through the lives of celebrities and ordinary folk—Tolstoy, Bunyan, Augustine, Colonel Gardiner, Henry Alline—James (1961) showed how religion can unify and invigorate divided, troubled selves. "Easily, permanently, and successfully, it often transforms the most intolerable misery into the profoundest and most enduring happiness" (p. 150). Despite theological differences, religions around the world offered "a certain uniform deliverance"—a solution to "uneasiness" through connection with higher powers (p. 393).

Skeptical, like Freud, of the truth of religious doctrines, James (1961, 393-394) called attention to the "real effects," nevertheless, of belief in them. "Spiritual strength really increases in the subject when he has [religious experiences], a new life opens for him." "When we commune with [the unseen], work is actually done upon our finite personality, for we are turned into new men, and consequences in the way of conduct follow in the natural world upon our regenerative change." Its tonic effect, its capacity to access vital subconscious energy, assured the survival of religion "with or without intellectual content . . . true or false."

Freud (1961) portrayed religion as wish-fulfillment—reassuring, unverifiable beliefs based on childhood longings: "Over each one of us there watches a benevolent Providence . . . which will not suffer us to become a plaything of the overmighty and pitiless forces of nature . . . all the terrors, the sufferings and the hardships of life are destined to be obliterated. Life after death . . . brings us all the perfection that we may perhaps have missed here" (p. 19).

While Freud recognized the usefulness of religion in establishing civilization, he could not overlook the falseness, as he thought, of its claims. Because religion derived from desire rather than inspection of "what exists outside us and independently of us," finally, no matter how soothing, "Its consolations deserve no trust" (Freud 1965, 148-150). Our "mental apparatus," he (1961, 55) claimed, "has been developed precisely in the attempt to explore the external world" and it was "possible for scientific work to gain some knowledge about the reality of the world, by means of which we can increase our power." Insusceptible to experimental correction, religion obstructed material progress in the fight against suffering.

Religion, James and Freud agreed, imparts courage through imaginative alliance with elusive, incorporeal powers. But under siege, is this our best shot? Of different intellectual temperaments, the two thinkers favored different remedies for human vulnerability—subjectively-generated confidence versus accurate empirical knowledge. James observed that, somehow, belief in friendly supernaturals unleashed vital subliminal energy; Freud, that it obstructed real problem solving.

Against this conceptual background, I present two lives which dramatize conditions, benefits, and liabilities of religious consolation. The subjects were chosen for high contrast, not representativeness. Gladys is a black, rural Southerner—the unlearned pastor of a small pentecostal congregation; Joe, a white, northeastern urbanite—an erudite Catholic priest and author. In common they have clerical vocation and the experience of mental distress I will metaphorically call soul-loss—roughly, impaired ego-functioning associated with traumatic and/or chronic rejection by others.

Specifically, childhood abuse from his alcoholic father contributed to Joe's ongoing struggle against severe depression. Gladys reports lifelong persecution by family and peers accompanied by disabling psychosomatic symptoms. Both subjects recounted episodes in which, like the primitive victim of soul loss, they were paralyzed by despair. Gladys survived through faith; Joe, through psychotherapy.

Contrasting religious and secular styles of coping, as I do later, requires a restrictive, substantive definition of religion. I will understand religion as, essentially, devotion to, preoccupation with, the supernatural (intangible, mysterious forces or beings thought to control human destiny). How, if at all, did supernaturalism help each subject overcome damaging rejection?

Gladys Day (1925-

Gladys Day is currently pastor of Signs and Wonders Tabernacle in Ferriston, Georgia,[1] one of a dozen or so pentecostal congregations founded by Bishop Theodore T. Wells of Macon. His followers credit Bishop Wells with extraordinary powers of healing and clairvoyance. Under his tutelage, Gladys wields supernatural defenses that, according to sect teachings, symbolize divine anointing.

In the interviews, Gladys seldom answered questions directly but preferred to dramatize stories, which were sometimes irrelevant to what had been asked. The life history she presented was riddled with contradictions. For example, in one or two contexts, Gladys portrayed her mother as "a lady," a church-goer, and her father as her antagonist, "a sinner man" inclined to "hurt you if you crossed him." Yet, in other stories, she presented her father as her ally, and her mother as the villain. In her youth, she had been obedient and well-behaved, Gladys claimed; yet, she went on to tell how, in her teens, she had two babies out of wedlock by different fathers. Of course, the alternate pictures could both be factual. What I wish to underscore in Gladys' failure to work the pieces into a complex, coherent whole—the fragmented or unintegrated quality of her perceptions and memories.

She strikingly displayed what Shapiro (1965, 108-133) calls an "hysterical style of cognition," a global, diffuse way of perceiving and remembering. Hysterics, according to Shapiro (p. 112-115), are "highly susceptible to what is immediately impressive, striking, or merely obvious" and uninclined to record "sharply defined, technical data." Indeed, they suffer an "incapacity for persistent or intense intellectual concentration," a "distractibility" which deprives them of a resolute sense of "plain hard fact." Thus the hysteric is unable to analyze motives or anticipate the consequences of actions effectively. The cognitive processes that transform impressions and passing emotions into self-conscious judgments and clear ideas "are, in the hysterical person, markedly attenuated" (p. 130).

This perceptual style provides a key for understanding both Gladys' soul-loss and its relief by the wonder-working Bishop Wells. In one story after another, she portrayed herself as attacked or ridiculed by others—her mother, father, sisters, husband, daughters, pastor, neighbor, and so forth. While Gladys has undoubtedly been victimized, it is clear, even from her side of the story, that sometimes she provokes conflicts with aggressive behavior, needlessly isolating herself and inviting attack. Her unmonitored expressions of rage, along with her general imperceptiveness, seem to incite and, in the minds of perpetrators, excuse cruel and contemptuous treatment.

Likewise, two personal qualities that are extensions of the hysterical cognitive style have shaped her spiritual career. One is suggestibility, exhibited in a strong susceptibility to faith-healing. The other is a tendency to dissociation, demonstrated in the (sometimes tormenting) inner voices she hears, and her repeated possession by "death spirits" who threaten to kill her. Thus, thanks to a fragmented ego, Gladys could know firsthand the Bishop's healing powers, and the reality of indwelling supernaturals. Whatever its causes, Gladys' hysterical perceptual style simultaneously perpetuates soul-loss and nurtures the faith that palliates it. I tell her story in three biographical periods.

Youth persecution. Gladys grew up on a farm, the first of three daughters born to Jack and Carrie Barber. She characterized herself as "different" from other children. "I never played much . . . I just sit and look. But," she added candidly, "I was mean about fighting"— mainly her sisters, who, she explained, "would try to whoop me" and "tell stories on me and make me get a whoopin'." Not to be trifled with, Gladys had the last word: "When Mama'd go, I would just butt they heads together!" She demonstrated with a vigorous clap.

Her mother occasionally deserted the family, and when present, overtly favored the younger girls. "I felt like I was the least one," Gladys complained. "Look like the others could get away with something and they would have more than I had. I've laid down a plenty nights and cried." Why was her mother so unfair? "I really don't know," Gladys insisted.

Her father could also be cruel, as, for example, when he scoffed at her adolescent conversion. Testing what would become a major defense tactic—the supernatural humiliation of her enemies— Gladys asked God to "trouble" her father's food, which she was in charge of preparing. Three days later, she reports, her father, having mysteriously lost his appetite, promised never again to doubt her.

"All my life the Lord been dealin' with me," Gladys drew the moral of the story. As further evidence, she cited youthful precognitions of disaster. "I could see things happening but I couldn't do nothin' about it. See visions [of] people dying," which, she added, sometimes came to pass.

In 1948, Gladys married Ozell Day, a uneducated laborer. Between 1948 and 1954, Gladys gave birth to four of their thirteen children, lost a premature infant, and had two miscarriages. She began to suffer from severe hemorrhaging as well as symptoms which may have been psychological in origin. For example, she experienced "black-outs" in which she remained conscious but "would be just like a person in a trance where they just do nothing, just sit and look." Sunlight temporarily blinded her. If she went outdoors during the day, Gladys said, "It would get night. I couldn't see a thing, don't care how bright the sun was shining." Doctors were baffled; neighbors considered her insane.

Ozell quickly tired of coming home to an invalid and a brood of hungry children. When he began drinking and seeing other women, their marriage became a dog-fight. If Ozell tried to strike her, Gladys (who is half again his size) hit him back. "When I got a little mad with him," she confessed, "I would [provoke him]. He'd have to run. Or try to shoot him." "I cut his hands up so bad one time," Gladys chortled at the memory, "he couldn't work. Trying to cut his throat."

During that first decade of marriage, Gladys faithfully attended a neighborhood Methodist Church. Yet she could not keep herself from using foul language, dipping snuff, and cheating on Ozell. In short, she concluded, "I just had a formal godliness." "I didn't have no power over no kind of spirits. I didn't have no power over nothing."

The Quest for Holiness. In January 1957, Bishop Wells came to Ferriston on a tent crusade. For a week, Gladys heard him preach the healing power of God and the need for sanctification. After receiving prayer one night, the very next morning, she reported, "all whatever was wrong with me—it fell right off." When Ozell came home and found the wash hanging out to dry, "he had to sit on the porch, he was so amazed." Nevertheless, he remains skeptical of the Bishop's powers, contending that Gladys was "brainwashed." Gladys' own faith in the healer has never wavered.

From 1957 until 1972, she saw Bishop Wells only once. Even after 1972, when he had established a Ferriston congregation, her contact with him was limited since his headquarters is over one hundred miles away. Perhaps distance facilitates Gladys' one enduring relationship of trust. Certainly in her immediate circle, her pursuit of holiness after 1957 created rather than resolved tension.

Having seen God's healing power, Gladys began investigating the Bishop's claim that salvation required spiritual baptism. After chiding her Methodist pastor for neglecting holiness, she sensed hostility in his congregation and sought spiritual baptism at the Church of God in Christ. Again, she felt unwanted. Walking two miles to services, it was galling to be passed on the road by fellow-worshipers in automobiles.

At least she learned to use the name "Jesus." "You can call that word and that just like having a gun if you be sincere," Gladys explained. For example, late one night when she was walking home from church, "a big dog" lunged towards her. "I hollered, 'Jesus!'" she reenacted the scene. As if she had wielded a stick, "That dog put on brakes!"

The murder of Letitia's four year old son in late 1971 intensified Gladys' religious search. Several weeks in advance, a voice had warned her, "'Something's gon happen. Something's gon happen'." Moreover, in a dream she saw Letitia weeping beside an open casket but could not determine who was inside.

On the day of the murder, Gladys was keeping Letitia's son, as usual, while Letitia attended nursing classes. Gladys remembers calling the boy inside when the temperature began to drop. Later, when Letitia arrived, she found her firstborn dead on her mother's doorstep. An autopsy revealed his windpipe had been crushed. "We really don't know what happened," said Gladys, weeping as she told the story.

Since, at his birth, the family had heavily insured the boy's life, and under the circumstances, were entitled to double indemnity, local and state officials investigated. Gladys was repeatedly summoned downtown to answer questions, and although she desperately needed Ozell's support, he refused to accompany her. The authorities even tapped her wires. "Oh, sugar, I had a time!" she summarized.

One Sunday at a languid Baptist service, she reached the end of her rope. Worshipers seemed to be "nodding on the preacher," and the Spirit commanded her to leave. "It was in me to be loud," Gladys said. "I went down the streets, holding up my hands, talking to the Lord." Confessing the need for spiritual baptism, she begged aloud, "Lord, you got to send somebody to do something about it. What I got worked up in me now, I need somebody." The following summer, the Bishop returned for another crusade.

Anointing. Shortly after his arrival, Gladys received spiritual baptism, signified by tongues. If she lived "holy," the Bishop taught, the indwelling Spirit would provide moral direction, strength against temptation, healing powers, and peace of mind—the spiritual armor she needed. At once, she stopped cursing and dipping snuff, and was able to "accept" her grandson's death. This was only the beginning.

Not long after her spiritual baptism, Gladys had a dream in which a woman with no legs—"nothin' but her arms and her Bible"—came in the back door and preached to her. For some time, Gladys reported, she had been receiving divine interpretations of scripture. "Look like sometime I would read, and inside it would just go on and on . . . and I couldn't stop it from talking." Likewise, just before she fell asleep after reading the Bible in bed, "look like the people in the Old Testament, the prophets, would come and tell what was the meaning of lot of stuff." The Lord was calling her to the ministry, she concluded, and despite her husband's objections, she applied to the Bishop for a preaching license.

Ozell, by then an alcoholic, responded to his wife's deepening religious preoccupation with commensurate cruelty and violence. In the fall of 1987, Gladys contemplated divorce. However, when the Spirit warned against it, she acquiesced, reminding the Lord, "You got to make it passable for me." A few months later, drunk one Sunday, Ozell had a seizure that frightened him into permanent sobriety—in Gladys' view, an answer to her prayer.

However, Ozell was only the first of many who would oppose her ministry. Of the endless betrayals Gladys says she has endured in the service of God, perhaps the most traumatic was her deception and public humiliation by her own daughter and the married itinerant pastor of Ferriston Signs and Wonders.

Janelle was "just a child," according to Gladys, when, under her mother's watchful eye, she received "a little glance" from the fortyish Elder Daniels. Trusting the pastor, Gladys set aside her suspicions for a time; but around 1986, she said, "the Lord began to deal with me about it." She accused Daniels of an illicit attraction revealed to her, she claimed, by God. The following Sunday morning, he corrected her from the pulpit: "'You need to fast and pray about that spirit you got.'"

Incensed at the public rebuke, Gladys prayed instead to catch the lovers together. After witnessing a rendezvous near her home, she confronted both Daniels (giving notice, "God gon strike you down") and Janelle, who continued to deny the affair. Later the couple left town together and eventually married.

Fortunately, Gladys was saved at the time. Otherwise, "I'da killed Elder [Daniels] about my child," she swore. "Cause that was my baby! No experience! I'da killed him!" In the meantime, Ozell and the congregation accused her, of all people, of "cloakin'" for the lovers. "I just cried—oooooh! I had a plenty a sleepless night," Gladys moaned. "You see me, honey? I been pierced!"

Under the circumstances, Gladys succumbed for the second time to what she called a "death spirit." Several years earlier, she had been singing a hymn in church when, suddenly, a voice told her, "'You better sing, 'cause you ain't comin' back here no more'." For three days, she was bedridden, and something in her throat prevented her from eating. Symptoms disappeared when, by telephone, the Bishop prayed for her.

Similarly, at the height of the scandal in 1986, the death spirit returned, this time ordering her to look at herself in the bathroom mirror. Before her eyes, Gladys said, she saw her skin "shrink up just like wasn't no life in it. . . . I stood there and looked, I stood there and looked." A few hours later, "Look like a little wind slapped me side the head. I didn't have a bit of strength in my body." Again, for several days, she could not eat or walk. Again, she recovered when the Bishop prayed for her.

It did not take long for Gladys to clash with Elder Daniels' successor. In another grueling battle, Gladys was pitted against the pastor and other women in the congregation, including a daughter. Around 1989, Bishop Wells appointed Gladys pastor, but it was a Pyrrhic victory. By mid-1990, membership had dwindled to a few women and their children. Along with prejudice against a female preacher, Gladys attributed the decline to several incidents of inexplicable treachery. "I don't know why people fight me, but they do," she said. "Mens and womens. . . . I don't know what it is."

From childhood, it seems, Gladys' relationships have followed an unhappy pattern of escalating hostility: rejected for reasons she cannot comprehend, she expresses righteous indignation in intimidating, aggressive behavior; this, in turn, elicits further (for her, still inexplicable) rejection, which heightens her aggression, and so on. Inadequate monitoring of her own conduct and a poor grasp of the motivations of others have repeatedly alienated Gladys from those who otherwise might be allies.

Religion, particularly after her spiritual baptism, brought Gladys new self-confidence, self-awareness, and self-control. But did it alleviate destructive interpersonal behavior? For the most part, faith merely translated the rejection-aggression pattern into a supernatural idiom, making Gladys a martyr and her persecutors enemies of God. Indeed, by transforming squabbles into moral crusades, religion probably heightened her belligerence. Twenty years after her spiritual baptism, Gladys still trusts mainly the Bishop, whom she seldom sees, and the intangible, inscrutable Yahweh.

Nevertheless, these trusting relationships represent breaks in the rejection-aggression cycle. "I am a witness," Gladys declared, "if you do something to me now—and I don't care who you is—if I can hold my peace and not talk back, God gon work on you!" Although making a threat, Gladys assumed mutual obligations between herself and God: God would protect her if she controlled herself. Honoring this bond, she has occasionally tried to mend breaches, as, indeed, she finally did with Elder Daniels. In the midst of her anguish, Gladys said, "This is what tore me up: I knowed I had to forgive him." Through the intervention of a third party, eventually, she found herself on her son-in-law's front porch. "I greeted him." she reported, "and told him I loved him." The reconciliation endures—one of the "real effects," in James' (1961, 400) phrase, of Gladys' far-fetched supernaturalism.

Joe Gallagher (1929-   )

Joe's[2] cognitive style is the antithesis of Gladys'. His IQ tested at over 140 (Gallagher 1983, 198). The winner of scholastic prizes in school; a philosophy major in college; an archivist, translator, and journalist for the Catholic Church; and the author of books of poetry and literary criticism—Joe has cultivated his intellectual gifts. His analytic mindset goes hand in hand with hyper-selfconsciousness, a tendency to over-monitor his feelings and actions.

Alert to possible repercussions and highly susceptible to guilt, Joe was unable to discharge openly the anger that accompanies rejection. Childhood trauma exacerbated an inherited tendency to mental illness (uncles and siblings have been hospitalized for schizophrenia and manic depression). Thus, Joe has suffered, in his words, "a series of nervous collapses connected with depression, anxiety (cosmic dread/the horror of existence), self-doubt, and various personal, family, philosophic and religious confusions" (Gallagher 1989, 8).

Early Disaster. A native of Baltimore, where he has spent most of his life, Joe was the second child born to Frank and Ellen Gallagher, both of Irish-Catholic descent. Shortly after Joe's birth, as the Depression began, Frank lost his job and began drinking heavily. At times, the family had to rely on public assistance. "I can't recall ever owning a bat or a ball or a bike or skates," Joe wrote, "nor can I remember any adult male who was interested in showing us boys how to use such things" (Gallagher 1989, 5,3).

Frank was often absent. His presence, according to Joe, meant "arguments and drunken stumbling and maybe physical violence."

Once, for trying to choke his wife, Frank was sentenced to jail. Although he did not physically assault his offspring, he was callous and cruel to them. Joe describes the time the Good Humor truck came by and his father bought some ice cream for himself but none for the children, claiming, "'You've already had your fun.'" Likewise, to teach Joe's brother a lesson, Frank allowed the child to burn his hand on a hot light bulb (Gallagher 1983, 196-197).

In 1944, Frank died of pneumonia. "'Every man's life is a search for a father,'" Joe quoted Thomas Wolfe. "If he dies when you're fourteen, he's even harder to find" (Gallagher 1983, 86). In the years ahead, Joe would seek a father—vainly, for the most part—in teachers, clerical superiors, and therapists.

His childhood dilemma, as Joe reconstructed it, led to an enduring struggle with anger:

> the fear [of being hurt by his father] makes me angry, but I dare not add my anger to an already intolerably explosive situation. If I did I would hurt my hurting mother and make myself feel guiltier, or else I might get hurt even more in return. . . . And I am afraid to be afraid lest I unleash within myself an anger which might prove murderous.

Indeed, a therapist reckoned Joe's inner rage sufficient "to blow up Baltimore city" (Gallagher 1983, 197-198).

Without strenuous religious indoctrination, at age nine, Joe chose his vocation. "[T]he beauty and the mysteriousness of church, and maybe the orderliness" had attracted him. "People were respectful there." "It wasn't that God was calling me," he summarized, "it was that there was an opening."

On the whole, however, belief in the Catholic deity seems to have disheartened more than comforted Joe. "I took the issues of sin, guilt and eternal rejection very seriously," he wrote, "and could much more feelingly believe in God's severe judgment and severe demands than I could in his mercy and understanding" (Gallagher 1989, 8).

Vocational Crisis. At age twenty, Joe experienced his first severe depression during "a lonely and quite unhappy" year at Catholic University, where he had accepted a scholarship. Transferring to a Baltimore seminary attended by many of his high school classmates boosted his spirits. However, just before ordination, Joe recalled, "Once again theological gloom and confusion had produced a paralyzing depression in me." He informed the rector of his plans to leave; however, doing his "farewell laundry," he experienced "a surge of energy and rededication." At this time, he observed, "Aspects of my personality such as wrath and sexuality were so well repressed that I didn't realize they were repressed" (Gallagher 1989, 7-8; 1983, 152).

With the cultural upheaval of the 1960s, Joe vented fury in criticism of the political and ecclesiastical establishment. Expressing anger, however, even in the name of higher values, was anxiety-provoking.

As writer and editor for the Baltimore archdiocesan newspaper, the *Catholic Review*, Joe enjoyed a relationship of mutual respect with his superior, Archbishop Lawrence Shehan. In 1965, following his appointment as cardinal, Shehan named Joe monsignor. In 1966, however, Shehan wanted to suppress an editorial Joe had written against the American use of napalm in Vietnam. Controversy erupted again when, in an editorial, Joe criticized the racism of a Catholic gubernatorial candidate. In late 1966, Joe offered his resignation and Shehan accepted.

"I should perhaps stress what a blow to my ideals and to my pride this whole affair was," Joe wrote. "I cared very passionately about the manifold sufferings of human beings, and I very much wanted to embody the belief that my church cared about such things too." Moreover, just when fellow journalists were giving him positive feedback, Joe lamented, "my ecclesiastical superior, my 'father in God,' came to judge me an expendable obstacle. . . . Once again, a father both failed me and rejected me" (Gallagher 1983, 321-323).

In 1967, Joe joined the faculty at a Baltimore seminary. The following year, he responded to a national pastoral letter he felt inadequately addressed the Vietnam War and the civil rights struggle. In "An Open Letter to the U.S. Catholic Bishops" (published in the *National Catholic Register*), he called the hierarchy insensitive to "Gospel values," "hopelessly remote . . . bourgeois, defensive, legalistic, real-estated, cigared, Cadillacked, mansioned" (Gallagher 1983, 374, 372).

Likewise, Joe took offense at *Humanae Vitae*, the 1968 anti-contraception encyclical, which, he thought, would contribute to "over-population, children that can't be cared for, pain and suffering and starvation." He registered his distress in his journal: "More than ever, I do not see how I can function as a priest . . . since my whole being (intellect and emotions) revolts against the harshness and inhumanity of this position." In the Baltimore *Sunday Sun* (August 11, 1968), he called the encyclical "tragic and disastrous" and resigned the title monsignor, since it implied "some special allegiance to the Holy Father" he could "no longer extend" (Gallagher 1983, 230, 241-243).

Rather than glorying in his defiance, however, Joe anticipated repercussions and succumbed to anxiety and despair. "Spiritually and psychologically," he wrote, "I was pulling from my face an oxygen mask I had been born with. Could I survive without it? The very question caused palpitations that sounded as though the answer was no." In the end, a compromise was struck with his superiors in which, to rejoin the seminary faculty, he had only to promise, in future, not to attack publicly the papal position on birth control (Gallagher 1983, 239, 280).

In the early 1970s, a psychiatrist told Joe that the priesthood was so "destructive" for him, he should leave it (Gallagher 1983, 224). Later Joe completed but never mailed papers requesting laicization. Family obligations—for example, helping raise his deceased brother's children—took precedence over building a new life for himself. "I didn't have the leisure," he explained, "to make a personal life decision that maybe any other sensible person would have done in my particular situation."

Insight. Powerful, insensitive, rejecting—the Catholic God and hierarchy had become Frank's stand-ins. Joe's vocation was perpetuating the painful cycle of his childhood—rejection by a pitiless tyrant, which led to righteous indignation, which stimulated guilt and anxiety.

Psychotherapy helped him recognize and break the pattern. In 1967, he began treatment with a counselor who taught him "how to float emotionally" (Gallagher 1983, 297). "[T]hanks to good therapists," he said, he now allowed himself "to feel a lot of these negative emotions," he said, such as anger. "I have been more and more in touch with what I really feel."

Thus, in *The Christian Under Stress* (published in 1970 and reissued in 1988 as *How to Survive Being Human*), Joe preached self-acceptace, recommending the "key affirmation" (p. 23):

> It is alright to be human. . . . to have feelings and to have human limitations. . . . It is alright to have negative feelings—to be angry, confused, frustrated . . . whether these feelings are directed toward God, the Church, or life in general.

In the final chapter, he summarized his advice in three steps: "Know yourself, accept yourself, involve yourself" (p. 132).

Had he, through therapy, resolved his feelings towards his father? "Reasonably well," Joe thought. "Or what I've resolved is maybe the necessity of thinking that I had to resolve it." "I feel in a sense that I don't have to cure my neuroses any more." To knowing, accepting, and involving yourself, he had added "forget yourself." "I think I'm on [this] fourth step," he said in the interview. Having learned to "sort of float on existence and to take a day at a [time]," he had known "periods of real, real calm and real serenity and real enjoyment in latter years."

He struggled less with theological dilemmas. "I think I sense in everything either God or the absence of God," Joe reflected. However, this had always amounted to perplexity: "I can't [understand] him, and who he is, and who I am, and how all this fits together, and what are you supposed to do, and why is it you don't know what you're supposed to do."

Early experience made naive trust in God impossible. "I saw so much disaster around me," Joe explained. "I've been always sort of thinking all the time about how does all this fit together. I never could just say, well, I'm just gonna believe and don't bring up any objections." Some days he found "the goodness of things and the mystery of the most simple thing . . . overwhelming." Other days, he was "overwhelmed by the negative and the dark." "[E]verything has a negative side. And negative things have positive sides," he summarized. "That almost is worthy of being on my tombstone." After puzzling for years over paradoxes like this, he had finally learned, Joe said, to "just kind of go along with it. You know, float, enjoy."

While therapy helped Joe accept rather than struggle against anger and existential ambiguities, it did not dramatically improve his capacity for intimacy with God or people. The more mysterious God became, the more irrelevant he was even to Joe's most painful dilemmas. Had God mandated his opposition to *Humanae Vitae*? I queried. "Well, because God is so mysterious to me," Joe replied, "I'm very reluctant to be sure." Certainly God had not consoled him in the ensuing storm. "I guess in some senses," he reckoned, "I haven't felt for a long time what you might call the comfort of God's presence. Because I think the presence of mystery can be as terrifying as it can be comforting." In *How to Survive Being Human*, references to God are rare and incidental.

In December of 1979, Joe had a heart attack which necessitated surgery and extensive drug therapy. "I have pretty much disappeared from the official church scene," he wrote a few years later (1983, 276). In 1985, he entered early medical retirement. Today he still feels alienated from the Church. "I just can't care about it," he said. "And I don't." He enjoys pursing the projects and friendships he chooses. Although serene, it was in all, as Joe put it, "a strange life. It's kind of a free-floating existence."

RELIGION AND "SOUL-LOSS" IN THE LIVES

Why did religion assuage soul-loss in Gladys' case but exacerbate it in Joe's? What were the advantages and shortcomings of their alternate paths to recovery?

From childhood, each subject's image of God reflected the experience of rejection, but in different ways. For Gladys, God was the supernatural antidote to a hostile social environment; for Joe, an amplification of the one who betrayed him. Like most Christian groups, Bishop Wells' sect and the Catholic Church present God as both loving and stern. Why would Joe find one image of the supernatural compelling, and Gladys another?

According to psychoanalysts, early object relations supply the raw materials for adult theism. The mental representation of God "is used by children to modulate the unavoidable failures of their parents," according to Rizzuto (1979, 204)—perhaps as a "painful divine enlargement" of "displaced rage and terror" or as "a God who has more and better love to offer" than the parent. Again, why did Joe's God-image mirror, and Gladys' idealize, rejecting parents?

Perhaps there is a clue in the way each handled anger. Poor integration allowed Gladys to externalize aggression with little guilt or anxiety. There was no need to displace it onto God. However, for the hyper-introspective Joe, the task of repressing rage, as he himself maintains, was overwhelming, and I think he enlisted religious symbols first and foremost to that end. In childhood, belief in a terrifying, omnipotent version of his father aided repression; later, during the 1960s, the same uncaring deity served as a safety valve—a target against which some aggression could be released in the name of reform. As therapy helped him uncover and accept his anger, God became increasingly ambivalent (both good and terrifying)—in the end, a cipher.[3]

Adult religion, however, is always more than the playing-out of early object relations. Believers make conscious theological judgments that affect the consoling function of faith. In the cases at hand, again, cognitive style (analytic vs. hysterical) was decisive. "The problem of evil," Joe said—not suffering in itself, but the intellectual attempt to square it with the existence of a benevolent deity—robbed him of religious consolation. By contrast, cognitive diffuseness allowed Gladys, despite the unmitigated shabbiness of her life, to imagine herself the darling of the creator of the universe.

In different ways, the cases teach, religious and psychotherapeutic treatments of soul-loss succeed and fail. As Shengold explains, psychotherapy heals through "insight" (1989, 284-300). Ideally, the therapist helps the victim of abuse, first, recover memory of the trauma and, second, integrate it into a coherent, functional identity. Insight is essentially inward journeying—usually stressful—through the past.

As an aid to besieged selves, psychotherapy taps the human capacity for realism, for living in full consciousness of unalterable, unpleasant past events and existential conditions. Endurance in itself is victory, and the sadder-but-wiser survivor understands the tragedy of the past well enough to avoid future replays. Certainly Joe found relief through unflinching self-exploration and the acceptance of unveiled wounds and impulses.

Yet Joe's case also exposes the limitations of insight. While therapy yields a working knowledge of personal history, it cannot justify human endurance in general. Joe learned to survive by "floating," but not how to negotiate confidently and purposefully the beauty and terror of the external world. As Becker observes: "Psychology narrows the cause for personal unhappiness down to the person himself, and then he is stuck with himself. . . . All the analysis in the world doesn't allow the person to find out *who he is* and why he is here on earth, why he has to die, and how he can make his life a triumph" (1973, 193).

In this respect, religion is more therapeutic. Tapping imagination, it imparts, to borrow James' (1961, 391) phrase, "a zest, or a meaning, or an enchantment and glory to the common objects of life" unattainable through realism. Faith made Gladys not a wiser victim, but a victorious champion of cosmic order. The abuse she suffered represented not some inexorable law of the jungle, but the mysterious preliminary to eternal beatitude. While Joe crept warily, step by step, up the steep stairway to serenity, Gladys shot off the ground on the rocket of imagination.

Of course, that rocket can be difficult to steer. Disregarding empirical circumstances is as dangerous as it is glorious. No one would dream of riding in an automobile, Freud (1965, 150) offered a metaphor for religious consolation, "If its driver announced that he drove, unperturbed by traffic regulations, in accordance with the impulses of his soaring imagination." In many respects, Gladys is a therapist's nightmare. To the extent that she is aware of her own pain and rage, it is through an elaborate religious subterfuge. Unable to perceive realistically the needs and weaknesses of others and herself, she seems doomed to repeat endlessly, albeit disguised as holy war, a destructive rejection-aggression cycle.

Conclusion

James (1961, 391) described the religious viewpoint as "enchantment and glory"; Freud (1961, 31), as "incompatible with everything we have laboriously discovered about the reality of the world." Both epithets are appropriate to Glady's faith. Paradoxically, the supernaturalism that psychically strengthened and physically healed her, also disguised and perpetuated destructive interpersonal behavior. Religion made her simultaneously a champion of righteousness in a brutal world *and* a dupe. Both Freud and James were correct as far as they went; but neither, in my view, fully appreciated the peculiar combination of heroism and idiocy that religion entails.

Indeed, the cases suggest that Freud and James otherwise oversimplified the relationship between religion and suffering. We saw several very intricate interconnections between distress and religion. In what might be called "coincidental wish-fulfillment," religious means to an end were employed; when the goal somehow materialized, supernatural sources were credited—for example, in Gladys' healing, or her use of Jesus for protection. Sometimes, the supernatural explanation detracted attention from a reliable naturalistic solution, as when Gladys assumed that the mystical vibrations of Jesus, rather than her yelling, stopped the dog.

Joe's appropriation of the punishing Catholic deity illustrates a more "unconscious defensive" connection between pain and religion. Religion reinforced an entrenched defense mechanism. Symmetry between the specific psychic conflict and available religious symbols was crucial. The Catholic image of an intolerant, omnipotent deity—an enlargement of Joe's own fearful father—was well-suited to assist the repression of anger. Of course, eventually, the defense mechanism itself, with its religious sanction, became the source of anguish.

We might continue reviewing the convoluted connections in each life between empirical causes of pain and religious assuagements. Enough has been said, I think, to point out the haphazardness and inefficiency of religious trouble-shooting. Freud called religion wish-fulfillment; James identified deliverance from uneasiness as the common essence of religions. Both assumed a tight, direct link between faith and human suffering. Recent research, however, underscores that people differentially rely on religion when facing disaster, and when they do, its effectiveness varies (e.g., Fichter 1981; Kroll-Smith & Couch 1987; Pargament 1990; Pargament et al. 1990). Granted that for some people, such as Gladys, religious commitment is broadly rooted in need, a more refined view of the coping potential of religion is in order (Pargament 1990; Pargament et al. 1990).

It should begin, I think, with the recognition that religious traditions translate all of life—triumph and tragedy—into supernatural drama. In this light, the indifference of faith to fact stressed by Freud seems to reflect not a structured coping device, blindness for the purpose of defense, but simply the nature of religion—which, for many reasons or for no reason, renders everything supernaturally. Some images of the supernatural, as Freud pointed out, inspire confidence against overwhelming forces, assure ultimate justice. Others, however, do not; for example, in the Book of Job, a central Judeo-Christian treatment of suffering, the Almighty whimsically gambles with the fate of a righteous man.

As part of a larger worldview, religious assuagements assume specific definitions of good and evil, of the purpose of existence, and invariably carry restrictions and costs for the long-term user. When people turn to religion for comfort, in other words, they are tapping a larger ideology which construes personal pain according to its own internal logic. Moreover, sufferers bring their own processing equipment and prerequisites. As Joe's case shows, even accessible and apparently fitting spiritual consolations—a fatherless boy enters the priesthood of a deity addressed as "merciful Father"—may not work.

Yet in other cases, religious solutions precisely fit the victim's circumstances—as in the meeting, in 1957, between Gladys, suggestible and psychogenically ill, and the charismatic Bishop, prophet of a healing God. This sort of "perfect match" between, on the one hand, the sufferer's needs and sensibilities, and, on the other, the promises and techniques of a tradition, perhaps underlies the relatively rare, dramatic kind of religious revitalization James portrayed.

James repeatedly recognized that not everyone was temperamentally receptive to religion (1961, 120, 150, 171). Yet, in explaining the remarkable transformations of individuals who were, he resorted, finally, to a generic rejuvenation process in which basic religious gestures, such as prayer, accessed a vague subliminal energy (p. 394ff.). Today we have the psychological tools for a more precise explanation. We should search, I think, not for a single, universal process of religious restoration, but for diverse (sometimes idiosyncratic) interactions between a particular sort of personal deficiency or chaos and a specific religious idea or practice that somehow answers or controls it.

For example, as indicated, Gladys' hysterical mentality is the key to understanding her spiritual healing. At least some of the symptoms the Bishop cured (temporary blindness and immobilization) seem to have been, in the first place, dissociative reactions. The successful religious technique (a healer's ritual pronouncement, or suggestion) depended, like the illness itself, on a diffuse style of awareness. Likewise, after spiritual baptism, Gladys achieved a measure of self-control when inner voices advising restraint took on the authority of the indwelling Spirit and thereby dominated a chorus of vocalized impulses. In all, religion did not integrate Gladys' personality but rather manipulated its fractured condition for healing and regularity.

For better or for worse, the cases suggest, people do not choose to take comfort in religion any more than they dictate with whom they will fall in love. Supernatural consolations fizzle or perform in a life according to a shifting, unpredictable combination of cultural opportunities and personal sensibilities. Inevitably, some who seek solace in religion will not find it.

NOTES

1. In rural southwest Georgia, Ferriston is a county seat of about five thousand people. Gladys kindly consented to interviews in 1983, 1990, and 1991. I interviewed her eldest daughter Letitia in 1983 and 1990; and, in 1983, Letitia's husband and other members of Ferriston Signs and Wonders. Subjects were promised anonymity. To preserve it, I use pseudonyms for persons, towns, and sects.

2. I met Joe, my husband's friend, in 1986. Here I draw heavily upon his own lucid and entertaining writings, particularly a journal for 1979 (Gallagher 1983), which tells the story of his life; and an unpublished "Life Review" prepared in 1989. I interviewed him by telephone in early 1992. He has generously consented to the use of his name and writings.

3. I thank Kenneth Pargament for reading a draft of this paper and providing useful suggestions for improvement. From clinical experience, he

offered an alternative to my "safety valve" hypothesis of why Joe fashioned a God in the unpleasant image of his father, viz., that doing so provided a further opportunity to salvage the relationship. Likewise, Jones (1991) describes clients who, in both transference and theism, recreated and amended disastrous primary relations.

REFERENCES

Becker, Ernest. 1973. The Denial of Death. New York: The Free Press.

Bettelheim, Bruno. 1982. "Freud and the Soul." The New Yorker, March 1:52-93.

Fichter, Joseph H. 1981. Religion and Pain: The Spiritual Dimensions of Health Care. New York: Crossroads.

Freud, Sigmund. 1961. The Future of an Illusion. Trans. & ed. James Strachey. New York: W. W. Norton. Originally published, 1927.

――――. 1965. New Introductory Lectures on Psychoanalysis. Trans. & ed. James Strachey. New York: W. W. Norton. Originally published, 1933.

Gallagher, Joseph. 1983. The Pain and the Privilege: Diary of a City Priest. Garden City, NY: Image Books.

――――. 1988. How to Survive Being Human. Westminster, MD: Christian Classics. Originally published as The Christian Under Pressure, 1970.

――――. 1989. Joseph Gallagher: Life Review. Unpublished manuscript.

James, William. 1961. The Varieties of Religious Experience. New York: Collier Books. Originally published, 1902.

Jones, James W. 1991. Contemporary Psychoanalysis and Religion: Transference and Transcendence. New Haven: Yale University Press.

Kroll-Smith, J. Stephen, and Stephen R. Couch. 1987. "A Chronic Technical Disaster and the Irrelevance of Religious Meaning: The Case of Centralia, Pennsylvania." Journal for the Scientific Study of Religion 26:25-37.

Pargament, Kenneth I. et al. 1990. "God Help Me: (I): Religious Coping Efforts as Predictors of the Outcomes to Significant Negative Life Events." American Journal of Community Psychology 18:793-824.

Pargament, Kenneth I. 1990. "God Help Me: Toward a Theoretical Framework of Coping for the Psychology of Religion." Research in the Social-Scientific Study of Religion 2:195-224.

Rizzuto, Ana-Maria. 1979. The Birth of the Living God: A Psychoanalytic Study. Chicago: University of Chicago Press.

Shapiro, David. 1965. Neurotic Styles. New York: Basic Books.

Shengold, Leonard. 1989. Soul Murder: The Effects of Childhood Abuse and Deprivation. New Haven: Yale University Press.

PART IV: SOUL-LOSS, THE DECADENCE OF RITUAL, AND PLAY

ROGER A. JOHNSON[1]

8

Soul-Loss, Sex Magic, and Taboos in Contemporary America: The Death of Rabbit Angstrom

Obituary Notice, The Standard, *Brewer, PA, 1990*

Harold C. Angstrom died of heart failure while vacationing at his winter residence in Deleon, Florida. He was 56 at the time of his death. Mr. Angstrom had been the Chief Sales Representative of the Springer Motor Company, one of Brewer's two Toyota dealers. He recently portrayed Uncle Sam in the Brewer Fourth of July Parade, and was cheered by many local residents who remembered him as a high school basketball hero. Mr. Angstrom is sur-vived by his wife, Janice, presently with Pearson and Schrack Realty, his son Nelson, manager of Springer Motor Company, and two grandchildren, Judy and Roy.

John Updike brought his four-volume saga of Rabbit to a close with the 1990 publication of *Rabbit at Rest*.[2] In this volume, as in its predecessors—*Run Rabbit* (1960), *Rabbit Redux* (1971), and *Rabbit is Rich* (1981)—Updike ensconced his fictional hero in the facts and mores of American social history.[3] Rabbit is Updike's version of a late twentieth century American Everyman (the gender is intentionally specific): a minimal self, devoid of resources beyond the immediate, diminished by a superficial and impersonal culture, and demolished by the relentless attacks of family, his only hope for survival. Morality and mystery appear to this Everyman only by their absence.

As the title of Updike's last Rabbit volume suggests, it recounts Rabbit's movement towards his own death—the Big Rest. Like the Gospel of Mark, Updike announces early in his text that this will be the story of a hero's death. Sentence one of the first page of text reads:

> Standing amid the tan, excited post-Christmas crowd at the Southwest Florida Regional Airport, Rabbit Angstrom has a sudden feeling that what he has come to meet, what's floating in unseen about to land, is not his son Nelson and daughter-in-law Pru and their two children but something more ominous and intimately his: his own death shaped vaguely like an airplane. (p. 3)

Five hundred ten pages later, the promised end comes—or, comes as close as it can in a text narrated by a hero scheduled to die. In between page one and page 512, Updike recounts his vision of a social pathology that drove its victim to his death.

Rabbit's death, at age fifty-six, is not the product of a naturally frail body. His height, physical strength, and agility have been his most prominent characteristics in all four volumes, including this last one. In his mid-fifties, Rabbit is still regarded by his peers as "a jock," one of those natural athletes who can drive the longest ball of his foursome; even in the last days of his life, he can still sink a basket from twenty feet out, with the ball in a perfect arc, never touching the rim: "He knows as it leaves his hands it will drop" (pp. 505-506). As in the case of "Voodoo deaths" described by Daniel O'Keefe, the multiple causes of Rabbit's demise belong mostly to his social world, not his biology.[4]

Updike's vision of contemporary America, and its threats to human life, is not consistent with the standard brand ideologies prominent in our politics or culture. For example, Rabbit does not experience African-Americans as a threat to his safety, even when he is the only White in a Black neighborhood. He never learned the lesson of Willie Horton and the politics of race, even though one of his golf partners explains the Reagan-Bush victories to him in just these terms:

> Face it: the bulk of this country is scared to death of the blacks. That's the one gut issue we've got. (p. 61)

Instead, when Rabbit began taking long walks on the advice of his doctor, he accidentally discovered a Black neighborhood to which he repeatedly returned. In this lower-class neighborhood, much like the one he knew in childhood, he felt more "at home" than in his own middle-class, all-white condominium.

While Rabbit may have been more comfortable in an all-Black neighborhood than his stereotypical white counterpart, his discomfort with women increases with the years of his life. While an American male, Rabbit is most definitely not a patriarch, politically correct ideologies notwithstanding. His family structure is unambiguously matrilineal: property and other economic assets are inherited from mother (Ma Springer) to daughter (Janice), without the smallest portion going to the son-in-law/husband (Rabbit). With inherited property comes power and authority; hence, the matriarchal character of Rabbit's familial and economic life. While Rabbit worked most of his adult life selling Toyota cars, including a period of time when he managed Springer Motors, his wife now owns "the lot," makes all decisions, and refuses to take seriously his counsel, even as the business plunges to its ruin. His wife's money allowed them to buy a condominium in Florida ["the mass-produced paradise where Janice's money has taken him" (p. 44)]; her money made possible the purchase of Penn Park, the only home Rabbit really loved, which, by the end of the novel, his wife intends to sell in order to cover business debts.

Because Updike's version of race and gender relations in contemporary America deviates from the more dominant ideological patterns of our society, he has been, and will continue to be, challenged by a variety of critics. In this brief essay, I will not pursue that project. Updike's version of kinky sex and oppressed men have been constants in his writing for the past three decades, and both are prominent in *Rabbit at Rest*. Both will appear in this paper, as perceived through Rabbit's eyes.[5]

Instead of a social critique of Updike, I intend to use this last Rabbit text as if it were a body of social data, as if Updike were a field anthropologist, collecting information on the connections between social transactions, soul-loss, sex, and death. In reporting this data from *Rabbit at Rest*, I will also be using some categories provided by Daniel O'Keefe and borrowed by him from field anthropologists.

The essay unfolds in four sections. The first describes Updike's picture of the social and cultural environment of contemporary America. It is a land of freedom, to be sure, but one so bereft of self-forming connections as to leave any soul in an impoverished condition. The second section focuses on "family values," those intimate bonds which supposedly sustain human life, but which Updike perceives to be a battlefield of genders and generations. In the third section, I report Rabbit's experience of sex, its meaning and consequences. While I will not attempt to emulate the grandeur of Updike's prose, or even his explicit and repeated use of the f___ word, I will present Rabbit's confidence in the magic of sex as the only source of healing for his wounded self. However, even a culture as infatuated with freedom as ours still has some taboos governing sexual activities. Rabbit breaks one of them and suffers the consequences. The essay concludes with an account of Rabbit's death, as he "chooses" to die by doing what he did best.

THE ENVIRONMENT OF AN IMPOVERISHED SOUL:
FREEDOM WITHOUT CONNECTION

It's good for the soul, [Rabbit] says, about as religious a remark as he dares put forth, since his "it" refers not to God or the disciplines of any religious community, but merely to a standard bar bowl of mixed nuts and chips (p. 71). While Rabbit is not a man who often spoke of the soul, his one comment on this subject, quoted above, offers an inadvertent insight into the spiritual poverty of his social world.[6] Living out the American dream of limitless freedom, Rabbit's life lacks those social bonds which not only shape the self, but enable it to survive and change in the midst of an often hostile environment.

The deficiencies of Rabbit's social world are already apparent in my version of his obituary: it lacks any reference to the "mediating institutions" so prominent in death notices and self-formation. Rabbit was a generic American—not a member of a religious congregation (though "baptized and confirmed at Mt. Judge Lutheran Church"), community organization (though a life-long resident of "greater Brewer, PA"), ethnic club (though a Swedish-American), or even a professional association (though a Toyota car salesman and manager). He had been an active member of the Valley Country Club in Brewer, but after some friends left, he lost interest in his one civic organization and rarely played golf there.

In addition, Rabbit does not have a circle of friends whose ties extend through significant periods of time and who continue to carry on a lively exchange by phone, if not in person. When left to himself, apart from his wife and her contacts, Rabbit's phone does not ring; its silence oppresses him. Nor does he identify himself with any neighborhood group, whether in his Florida condominium or Penn Park subdivision. The social resources that build a strong sense of self, capable of withstanding the onslaughts of the hostile environment in which he lived, are not provided by the daily dose of television and local newsprint (in Florida or Pennsylvania) available to Rabbit.

After his semi-retirement from the car business, he found his sense of self confirmed only through his intimate relationships with family and former or present sexual partners. The latter disappoint him by either dying, betraying his intimacy with them, or both. National political campaigns or issues rarely surfaced within the horizon of his experience; when such subjects do come up, they provide yet another occasion for his humiliation. For example, when his golf partners voice their objections to Reagan and Bush, Rabbit is too embarrassed to admit that he voted Republican in all three elections. Such are the limited resources of his social world.

Rabbit's relations with others, different from himself, are even more limited than his links with homogenous groups. What Rabbit recognizes only dimly, the reader cannot miss. The only world he understood was sharply restricted: by social class, race, gender, and sexual orientation. Specifically, it is a world of middle-class white Gentile straight males. To be sure, Rabbit encountered many women, some Jewish men, and a few Blacks and gay men, but he is the first to admit his total inability to understand these people. He may envy them—for example, "he treasures the perspective [of his Jewish golfing partners]; it seems more manly than his, sadder and wiser and less shaky" (p. 57)—but he has no sense of how they came to be the way they are, or the communities which formed the particular identities he admired. On the one hand, he is not gifted with a large capacity for understanding those different from himself; on the other hand, his direct contact with groups of people significantly different from himself—except for women—is extremely limited.

God is still another void in Rabbit's world, though it had not always been so.

When God hadn't a friend in the world, back there in the Sixties, [Rabbit] couldn't let go of Him and now . . . he can't

get it up for Him. He is like a friend you've had so long
you've forgotten what you like about Him. (p. 450)

In the early 1960s, however, when Rabbit first appeared in print,
Updike had not yet made his metaphysical discovery: that God had
died, or at least disappeared form the human scene, and the magic of
religious faith had been replaced by the magic of sex.

By the time of his mid-fifties, Rabbit experiences God primarily
as an absence, a giant void in the cosmos. When he remembers the
bathtub-drowning of his baby daughter thirty years ago, he thought
of the God who wasn't there:

> God hadn't pulled the plug. It would have been so easy for Him,
> who set the stars in place. To have it happen. Or to delete from
> the universe whatever it was that exploded that Pan Am 747
> over Scotland. (p. 10)

When he telephones long distance to speak with his six year old
grandson, the boy's failure to reply reminds him of God.

> "Hi, Roy," Harry says.
> Silence. God on the line again. (p. 497)

For Rabbit, God is so gone that even the imminence of his own
death cannot drive him to find again that piety he knew as a young
man.

For others, however, God seems to be very busy in America at
the end of this century. When Rabbit drives alone from Pennsylvania
to Florida, the car radio keeps him awake with its endless flow of
prayers and hymns and Jesus talk. After his son returns from six
months in a rehabilitation program, he explains to Rabbit the importance of God:

> A day at a time, with the help of a higher power. Once you
> accept that help, Dad, it's amazing how nothing gets you
> down. All these years, I think I've been seriously depressed;
> everything seemed too much. Now I just put it all in God's
> hands, roll over, and go to sleep. You have to keep up the pro-
> gram, of course . . . local meetings, and my therapist at Philly.
> (p. 407)

However much Rabbit wants to say a good word to his son, he finds these little sermons "full of AA bullshit" (p. 408).

His long-term mistress, Thelma, now suffering from lupus, has also discovered God in "one of those new denominations that goes back to fundamentals" (p. 205). On what turned out to be his last visit with her, she admonished him: "Believe in God, darling. It helps" (p. 206). But not for Rabbit. Whatever God may have meant to Rabbit in his youth, or to others now, such talk has lost its power to shape or transform his life. Its magic is gone.

Rabbit hears the most articulate, if painful, description of his social world through the mangled English and self-righteous posture of Mr. Shimada, the representative of Toyota's Mid-Atlantic Division. Before his rehabilitation, Nelson Angstrom managed to steal about $137,000 from Toyota to support his coke habit. The Toyota Company was not pleased to learn this bit of news. Nelson had violated one of the cardinal taboos of the business world, and Toyota sent Mr. Shimada to inform Rabbit of the punishment. He also gave Rabbit a Japanese view of American society.

> In United States, is fascinating for me, struggle between order and freedom. Everybody mention freedom, all papers terevision anchor people everybody. Much rove and talk of freedom. Skateboarders want freedom to use beach boardwalks and knock down poor old people. Brack men with radios want freedom to self-express with super-jumbo noise. Men want freedom to have guns and shoot others on freeways in random sport. In California, dog shit much surprise me. Everywhere, dog shit, dogs must have important freedom to shit everywhere. Dog freedom more important that crean grass and cement pavement. In U. S., Toyota Company hope to make ireands of order in ocean of freedom . . . Too much disorder, too much dog shit. Pay [$137,000 plus interest] by end of August, no prosecution for criminal activities. But no more Toyota franchise at Singer Motors. (p. 392)

God may be gone, but the Toyota Company is alive and well, enforcing economic sanctions upon their self-indulgent American clients. In spite of his individual freedom and relative isolation in society, Rabbit discovers that the sins of the sons may be visited upon their fathers, one of the many developments which speeds him on the way towards his own death.

AN EMBATTLED SELF:
GENDER AND GENERATIONAL CONFLICTS

Updike's vision of family life is not likely to lead anyone to matrimony. The family is nuclear: that is, loaded with a capacity for self-destruction and limited to mother/father, child and (by Rabbit's mid-fifties) his/her offspring. Uncles, aunts, cousins, and other relatives who may buffer such explosions in the real world are nowhere to be found. Rabbit and Janice are either trapped in a gender war from which they cannot escape, or both are consumed by endless conflicts generated by Nelson and his unresolved oedipal bond with Janice. Beyond these two basic conflict patterns of the nuclear family, Updike extends the lines of battle to include Rabbit's grandchildren.

While Rabbit lives within the constraints of a matrilineal economic structure, he also found himself to be the target of attack by the women who were his significant others: for example, his mother; his wife, Janice; his daughter-in-law, Pru; and his eight year old granddaughter, Judy. The story of Rabbit's mother appeared in an earlier volume; nevertheless, while long dead, Janice cannot help but remembering, even as she anticipates Rabbit's death, that "it was hard for him to respect any woman, his mother had done that to him, the hateful woman" (p. 510). Rabbit's problems with Pru will appear later in this essay. Here, our concern is limited to his granddaughter, Judy, and his wife, Janice.

Judy was the youngest member of an intergenerational conspiracy of women dedicated to hunt out Rabbit's weaknesses. While he was too devoted to the task of winning Judy's affection to recognize her guile, the reader perceives her threat to Rabbit from the moment she first appeared in the Florida airport. After Rabbit greets Judy with a kiss, she humiliates him by announcing to all:

> Grandpa has been eating candy again, for shame on him. I could
> smell it, something with peanuts in it, I can tell. He even has
> some little pieces stuck between his teeth. For shame. (p. 13)

Shortly thereafter, she puts Rabbit on the wrack, with much crying and tantrums, because he would not drive them all from Fort Myers to Orlando, to visit Disney World. She also makes certain that Rabbit's substitute treats, such as a visit to the Edison Museum, is a failure. Driven to ever higher standards of entertainment for this fussy young lady, Rabbit arranges to take her sailing on a rented sunfish on the Gulf of Mexico. Short on sailing experience, but desperate to please his granddaughter, Rabbit dumps the sunfish, himself, and his granddaughter into the Gulf of Mexico. With their life jackets and an easy-to-right boat, the experience should have been inconsequential. However, in her swimming class back home, Judy had won a prize for holding her breath the longest under water. So, to trick Grandpa, she hid under the sail, driving Rabbit to a frenzy of exertion and anxiety which triggers his first heart attack.[7]

Like many other middle-aged women of the 1980s, Janice discovered women's liberation and joined a succession of "consciousness-raising" groups. Each of them enhanced her personal sense of power and her independence from Rabbit. Thus, near the end of his life, while she was waiting for Rabbit to emerge from a coma, she tried to pray for him, but instead found herself thinking, "With him gone, she can sell the Park Penn house" (p. 510).

The frequency of her humiliations of him increases as the story progresses: the subscript of the death of Rabbit is the rise of Janice. By the end of the book, she has passed several of the examinations required for her real estate license, her own career. Nelson has returned to manage the lot, in a scaled-down version of Springer Motors without the Toyota franchise, and so Janice informs Rabbit that he is no longer needed at the lot. She also tells him that she has lost her interest in Florida: she needs to stay up north to further her new career in real estate and to manage the new Springer Motor Company with Nelson. Rabbit is left with some bushes to trim in his backyard, and an occasional golf game with a high school chum whose wife (Thelma), recently deceased, was one of Rabbit's long-term sexual partners. While Janice is a bundle of energy in her new life, a veritable "Wonder Woman," Rabbit is in decline, a man without a job, hobby, friends, or a family he can trust (p. 430). As he confesses to Thelma,

> Without Janice, I'm shit. I'm unemployable. I'm too old. All I can be from here on in is her husband. (p. 207)

When the economic power of a matrilineal inheritance system is combined with the personal power of a newly liberated woman, Rabbit can only lose, the victim of a gender war he was never equipped to win.

Updike did not invest much affection in the character of Nelson, Rabbit's son. He is a thoroughly unpleasant person. In the words of his wife, Nelson was

Out all night doing God knows what, then this snivelling and begging for forgiveness afterwards. I hated that worse than the chasing; my father was a boozer and a chaser, but then he wouldn't whine to Mom about it, he'd at least let her do the whining. This immature dependence of Nelson's was totally outside my experience. (p. 342-343)

When Nelson first appears in the story, he is a secret coke addict. While visiting his parents in Florida for a Christmas holiday, he disappears for a day and most of the night, without telling anyone of his whereabouts. When Rabbit questions him about car sales and some fishy financial reports from the "lot," he flees into the kitchen, complaining to Janice that he cannot stand five days of this bugging. Earlier he began this family reunion by accusing his father of kidnapping his daughter, because Rabbit and Judy had not made connections with the rest of the family at the baggage return area.

When the "new" Nelson appears, after rehabilitation, he had ingested such a heavy dose of Twelve-Step-Program talk as to be equally unattractive and unreal. In neither of his roles can Rabbit respond to him with the affection or concern which Nelson seeks to elicit. Indeed, in the whole book, I cannot identify one exchange between father and son which is not hostile, from one side or the other.

Between mother and son, however, there is only empathy and mutual support. They always understand each other, even in their confrontation when Janice demanded that Nelson seek help for his addiction or be fired as manager of Springer Motors. During the Florida visit, Pru and Janice shared many confidences about Nelson's coke habit. Rabbit, in contrast, knew nothing, and Janice never told him. Thelma, his long term mistress, first told him the bad news that his son was hooked on coke. She learned it from her children, Nelson's peers. Rabbit does not learn family secrets from family members.

Nor is Rabbit able to intervene with Janice to alter the course of family events. The only way in which he can convince Janice to take any action vis-a-vis her son is to recruit Charlie Stavos as his ally. Charlie used to sell cars with Rabbit at Springer Motors, and had been a lover of Janice. Rabbit literally begged Charlie to do him the favor of telling Janice the truth about her business. Charlie did and Janice found a new outlet for her empowerment: she sent Nelson on a six-month "rehab" leave. Whether concealing Nelson's coke habit, initiating his rehabilitation program, or dreaming of a post-debt, post-Toyota-franchise business venture, Janice lived in unbroken solidarity with her son. Rabbit was always an outsider to this mother-son team.

SEX AS MAGIC AND TABOO:
COSMIC CONNECTION AND EXCLUSION

Rabbit's perpetual conflict with Janice and Nelson, and their alliance with each other, became more life-threatening when charged with sex and Pru. Before turning to this episode, however, I need to make a few observations about Rabbit's sexuality.

First, I have always read Rabbit as Updike's version of a contemporary male form of sexual desire and imagination. In each of the novels, he linked Rabbit with real consumer products and stereotypical male fears. For example, in his first appearance in this novel, Rabbit is tempted to buy one of the 'girlie' magazines at the airport news counters; his confusion about Nelson repeatedly focuses on his fear that this married son may be homosexual.

Second, in his imagination, sex for Rabbit is pure and uncontaminated by other factors, such as affection, appreciation, and/or interest in another person. It is the f_____ itself that matters, not the talk before or after. Thelma explicitly states the difference between her long-term love for him and Rabbit's sexual desire for her. On the one hand, she knew that "You've never loved me, Harry. You just loved the fact that I loved you" (p. 199). On the other hand, when he asks "why do you think I'm here," she replies for him, "To make love. To screw me. Go ahead" (p. 202).

At the time of Thelma's funeral, her husband, Ronnie, makes the same point in an exchange with Rabbit.

> I don't give a f___ you banged her, what kills me is you did it without giving a shit. She was crazy for you and you just lapped it up . . . She went against everything she wanted to believe in and you didn't even appreciate it, you didn't love her and she knew it, she told me herself.
>
> Rabbit's own throat aches, thinking of Thelma and Ronnie at the last, her betraying her lover when her body had no more love left in it. "Ronnie," he whispers, "I did appreciate her, I did. She was a fantastic lay." (p. 379)

Third, Rabbit's obsession with sex is located more firmly in his head than in his body. This volume reports Rabbit engaged in one

sexual episode, one disappointed try with Janice, and one uncon-
summated encounter with Thelma: not that impressive a record of
activity. But in the head, there is an endless flow of sexual memories
and images, mostly of female genitalia, buttocks, breasts, nipples,
and so forth. Rabbit reviewed all of his prior sexual partners, extending back to the first "whore" who introduced him to sex when he
was an adolescent. Some of them had already died: Peggy Fosnacht,
Jill, maybe the whore in Texas (p. 184). Others are dying, like
Thelma. But whether dead or alive, each of them lived on in the
images of Rabbit's desire, as he recalled and enjoyed the details of
their anatomy, the pleasures of his union with them.

Fourth, sex is not a mere diversion for Rabbit. For him, sex is a
far more serious matter than a moment of pleasure. It is the only
activity, outside of basketball, that made him feel good about himself—good enough to blot out all the bad feelings that were there. Sex
was the magical antidote for all the humiliations and losses he suffered in the rest of his life. He could still remember when he was
eighteen, and not yet a loser, how Mary Ann made him feel about
himself.

> Mary Ann the first woman whose smell he made his own, all of
> her his own, every crevice, every mood, before he went off to do
> his two years in the Army and she without a word of warning
> married somebody else. Maybe she sensed something about
> him. A loser. Though at eighteen he looked like a winner.
> Whenever he went out with Mary Ann, knowing she was his to
> harvest in the warm car, he felt like a winner, offhand, calm,
> his life set at an irresistible forward slant. (p. 187)

Much later, and shortly before his death, he looked back over
the course of his life, at his many sexual experiences with his several
partners and, somewhat like God reviewing His creation on the sev-
enth day, declared that it was all good.

> One thing he knows is if he had to give parts of his life back,
> the last thing he'd give back is the f_____, even that sniffily
> girl in the Polish-American Club, she hardly said two words,
> just took his twenty, a lot of money in those days, and wiped
> her nose with a handkerchief while he was on top of her, but
> nevertheless she showed him something, she took him in,
> where it mattered. A lot of this other stuff you're supposed to
> be grateful for isn't where it matters. (p. 471)

For Rabbit, whose culture left him bereft of symbolic or social bonds, whose family attacked and undermined the minimal self he was driven to defend, a woman's body became his only point of connection with a reality larger than himself.

While living alone in his Florida condominium, he contemplated the sexual possibilities of Mrs. Zabritski, an elderly widow and fellow elevator passenger. True, her body was somewhat the worse for age and a share of suffering greater than her due. But . . .

> all his life seems to have been a journey into the bodies of women, why should his journey end now? (p. 468)

F_____ is the substitute and compensation for all the absent connections of his social world, including the absent God; the self-giving love of a Thelma, who makes herself available to him in f_____, is the substitute and compensation for all the love and care absent from the rest of his life. For Rabbit, sex is a kind of magical Cosmic Connection, not a correction for social pressures, as O'Keefe has suggested, but a substitute for any significant social connections.[8] Living in a cultural wasteland and a battleground of intimacies, the sexual connection is all that is left.

While sex is the antidote for loneliness and depression, it also has its risks. Rabbit knew about AIDS, and did not trust the sexual habits of Ronnie, Thelma's husband. So, to Thelma's offer of sex, he said, "No." But he quickly discovered that the social risks of sex were far more serious than any physical dangers.

It all began quite innocently. Rabbit was coming home from the hospital, having had one of those balloon procedures to clear out the plaque from his arteries. That same evening of his first night home, Janice had a real estate class, and did not want to leave Rabbit at home alone. So, she and Pru agreed, in spite of Rabbit's protest, that he should spend his first day and night in his son's house, not his own.

After much domestic ritual, especially putting the two children to bed, Pru, Rabbit's daughter-in-law, appeared in his bedroom. She just came in for a cigarette "and a little adult company" (p. 342). Since her husband, Nelson, had just left home for the rehabilitation program in Philadelphia, she needed to confide in someone about the miseries of her life with a drug addict. But the bedroom in which Rabbit is installed was small; there was no chair. So, Pru sat on the edge of Rabbit's bed, and began to tell her story. She and Nelson had not had sex for a long time, for several years. She was afraid that he was going to give her AIDS from one of his "coke whores" (p. 343). She sobbed as she described her life as a waste. Rabbit touched her lightly. She "huddles tightly though a blanket and sheet are between them" (p. 345). But shortly thereafter, Rabbit finds himself viewing "a piece of paradise blundered upon, incredible" (p. 346).

For the next six months, the Angstrom clan resumed its peaceful co-existence. Neither Rabbit nor Pru spoke of their incident, nor was the experience repeated. Then, at the end of six months, Nelson returned home, filled with the spirit of confession learned in the Twelve Step Program. As he told Pru and God one horror story after another in their nightly prayer sessions, Pru found herself under increasing pressure to add her little bit of confession. That seemed to be the least she could do to rebuild a lost marriage. Finally, Janice arrived one evening to tell Nelson and Pru her plan for saving Springer Motors: she and Rabbit would sell their $200,000 home in Penn Park to pay back the money owed by the business to the Bank and the Toyota Company; then, she and Rabbit would move into the home of Nelson and Pru, and both families would live under the same roof. To stop this plan and to clear her past, Pru told all.

Back at Penn Park, Rabbit got a call from Janice. After some preliminaries—the news from Pru and Rabbit's half-hearted acknowledgement of it—Janice let the ax fall.

"Oh, Harry. How could you? Your own daughter-in-law. Nelson's wife."

He feels she is beginning to work from a script, saying standard things, and into the vault of his shocked and shamed consciousness a small flaw admits a whiff of boredom.

"This is the worst thing you've ever done, ever, ever," Janice tells him. "The absolute worst. That time you ran away, and then Peggy, my *best* friend, and that poor hippie girl, and Thelma—don't think for one moment I didn't know about Thelma—but now you've done something truly unforgivable."
"Really?"
"I will never forgive you, never."
. . . "We want you over here, Harry."
"Me? Why? It's late," he says. "I'm bushed from all those bushes."
"Don't think you're out of this and can be cute. This is a hideous thing. None of us will ever be the same. . . . Think of

how Nelson feels . . . You have hurt Nelson incredibly much,"
she says. "Anything he does from now on you can't blame him.
I mean, Harry, what you've done is the kind of perverted thing
that makes the newspapers. It was monstrous." (433-445)

Rabbit tried to subvert the power of the taboo against sex with
a daughter-in-law.

"What's this 'perverted'? We weren't at all blood-related.
It was just like a normal one-night stand. She was hard-up and
I was at death's door." (p. 434)

But his efforts were hopeless. He'd been caught, trapped, or
entrapped, and he knows it. Nelson and Janice are the offended victims, and he is the unforgivable pervert or monster. From such a
moral position, he could not fight, so flight became his only option.
He packed his clothes in the Toyota Celica and headed not for
Nelson's house, but for the Florida condominium.

When he left town Rabbit did not know, or would not believe,
the extent of his punishment for breaking the taboo of intra-familial
sex. On the highway to Florida, he began calling Nelson's house,
speaking first with Judy and Pru. Janice, however, would never speak
with him, when he tried to reach her at their home or when she
was at Nelson's during one of his calls. Nor would the enforcer of
morality call him. He had become an outcast, rejected by his wife,
and because of her, abandoned by the rest of the family also. With
one exception, none of them contacted him by phone or mail in the
weeks after his exclusion. While readers might not find the loss of
such a family to be a cause for mourning, they were all Rabbit had.
His death came a few weeks after his expulsion from their midst.

DYING WITH DIGNITY:
WINNING A YOUTH AND LOSING A LIFE

The name of Rabbit's town in Florida is Deleon, "named after
some Spanish explorer." Through most of the book, Rabbit never
found the springs of eternal youth any more than had his Spanish
predecessor, but unlike Ponce, Rabbit did know where to look: on
any playing area with a basket at one end.

On a Monday morning, he found it, in the African-American
neighborhood where he had been going for walks:

> an abandoned high school built about when Brewer High was,
> an ochre-brick edifice with tall gridded windows and a piece of
> Latin in cement over the main entrance, a recreation field—a
> wide tan emptiness under the sun . . . and also of pale tamped
> earth, a basketball court. A backboard and netless hoop lifted
> up on pipe legs preside at either end. (p. 486)

He sat on one of the benches by the side, watching the black kids
play, while making himself as inconspicuous as a six foot three,
two hundred thirty pound older white male could be. He saw no
action himself that first visit, but made a point of memorizing the
street signs so that he could find "this peaceful place again"
(p. 487).

On Wednesday morning, he headed for the playing field he discovered Monday. Three teenage Blacks were shooting baskets in a
game Rabbit used to call HORSE. A couple of their missed passes
ended up by his bench. With the last one, he asked if he could join
their game, and two of the three were obliging. He missed a few
shots,

> but then Rabbit finds a ghost of his old touch and begins to
> dominate. Take a breath of oxygen, keep your eye on the front
> of the rim, and it gets easy. The distance between your hands
> and the hoop get smaller and smaller. You and it, ten feet off
> the ground, above it all. He even shows them a stunt he per-
> fected in the gravel alleys of Mr. Judge, the two-handed back-
> wards set, the basket sighted upside, the head bent way back.
> Seen upside down, how blue and stony-gray the cloudy sky
> appears—an abyss, a swallowing, upheaving kind of earth! He
> sinks the backwards set shot and all three of them laugh . . . by
> doing nothing else from five steps out Rabbit might have
> cleaned up. But, since they were good sports to let him in, he
> lets himself get sloppy-silly on a few one-handers, and Number
> 8 gains back control. (p. 492)

On the walk back to his car, he feels

> purged like those people on the Milk of Magnesia commercials
> who drift around in fuzzy focus in their bathrobes ecstatic at
> having become "regular." His bit of basketball has left him
> feeling cocky. (492-493)

Meanwhile, back at Valhalla Village, the days drift by with no phone calls. The "lonely refugee" lived with "the phone that refuses to ring," "the silence, the presence of absence, the unanswerable question that surrounds his rustling upright stalk of warm blood" (493-494). He called Nelson's house, talked with Pru, Judy, and Roy, but Janice, who was there, would not speak with him. He was still under the curse.

The next day he put on Bermuda shorts and returned to his basketball court. There he found an older boy playing alone, one more experienced and skillful than his opponents of yesterday; his name was Tiger. After some conversation and a few shots by Rabbit, Tiger recognized the old man as a former player. Rabbit suggested they play to twenty-one, and took one of his Nitrostat pills before the game began.

In his early plays, Rabbit used his advantage of height—an inch or two—to drop in a few air balls. Tiger responded by increasing his speed, so that Rabbit had to "kick himself up a notch," aware of his belly bouncing up and down and his breath coming harder as he moved faster. With the score tied at eighteen, Tiger pulled the ball out of play and offered Rabbit a break.

> "Hey man, you all right?"
> "I'm fine."
> "You puffin' pretty bad."
> "You wait. Till you're my age."
> "How about coolin' it? No big deal."
> . . . "Let's keep our bargain. Play to twenty-one. Like we said. Eighteen up, right?" (p. 505)

Rabbit made one more beautiful two-handed set shot, good enough to win the admiration of Tiger: "Man, that is pure bullshit" (p. 506). After Tiger tried the same shot and missed, Rabbit went to the hoop for a shot "he can't miss," then collapsed to the ground unconscious. Tiger fled, but a neighbor watching this strange drama dialed 911.

Winning back a few moments from his youth, Rabbit managed to tear apart his heart, what there was left of it, by literally destroying its muscle, leaving nothing but "a wad of scar tissue": a casualty, at age fifty-six, of a loss of soul from an excess of freedom and absence of others, divine and human, in a society which substituted the magic of sex for the magic of faith.

NOTES

1. Roger A. Johnson is the Elisabeth Luce Moore Professor of Christian Studies at Wellesley College, Wellesley, Massachusetts.

2. John Updike, *Rabbit at Rest* (New York: Alfred A. Knopf, 1990). All page citations are to this volume, unless otherwise indicated.

3. *Rabbit at Rest* required two pages of acknowledgements just to cover the television commercials and popular music quoted in the text.

4. Daniel Lawrence O'Keefe, *Stolen Lightning: The Social Theory of Magic* (New York: Vintage Books, 1982).

5. While not necessary, I will note that Rabbit's voice cannot be identified with that of John Updike, nor do either Rabbit or Updike speak for me. But I do recognize my own affinity with Rabbit which probably accounts for my sympathetic treatment. He and I are of the same age, belong to the same race and ethnic origins, and even have a common religious background. In addition, I grew up in a matrilineal home in which property passed directly from my mother's father through her to her children. I suspect that my sense of identification with Rabbit may account for my original interest in converting a "novel-for-summer-reading" into the subject of this essay. I usually write only in the areas of intellectual and social history, with a focus on religion; exploring novels is a new endeavor.

6. In this essay, I use the term "soul" in the generic sense of the word: that is, as a near equivalent of "spirit," "heart," or "self." I do not use the term with the hierarchical and dualistic meaning of its classical origins: for example, the soul as eternal and master of the transient body. For a critique of this use of the term, see the early writings of Rosemary Radford Reuther, or the more recent work of Catherine Keller. I also do not use the term in its classical or contemporary Gnostic meaning: for example, the soul as a divine spark imprisoned in an alien body, or the soul as an organ of innate spiritual capacity, as in the Southern Baptist doctrine of "soul competency." For a purported description and provocative critique of Gnostic themes in American religion, see Harold Bloom, *The American Religion: The Emergence of the Post-Christian Nation* (New York: Simon and Schuster, 1992).

7. One of the many "cardiac arrests that occur during stress" (O'Keefe 297). Rabbit died from heart failure: still the most frequent cause of death in contemporary America, even with the maze of technological and surgical advances available; and the most symbolically accurate social "cause" of his death, a broken heart, a worn-out heart.

8. O'Keefe, pp. 316ff. Earlier he attributed this view of magic to the Freudian tradition: "Magic is symbolism expropriated to protect the self against the social" (xviii).

9

Desire, Domination, and the Life and Death of the Soul

No. 48
Tennessee Williams said, "Every time I pick someone up on the street, I leave a piece of my heart in the gutter."

No. 49
Oscar Wilde said, "I lie in the gutter, but look up at the stars."

No. 65
Promiscuity fails to satisfy the most basic need—for intimacy, rootedness, shelter.

No. 66
Promiscuity supplies these in small ecstatic doses.
> —Andrew Holleran, "On Promiscuity"[1]

HINTS AND GUESSES: LISTENING FOR THE LANGUAGE OF SOUL

There are two ways one might tackle the theme of "soul death." The first would be to trace out the peculiar intellectual lineage of the term soul death. I will later do a bit of that. The second way, and my own preferred tack into the topic, would be to look for clues to its possible meaning in the ways in which the term may spontaneously arise in common conversation. Alas, in eight months of attentive listening no Groucho Marx parrot has descended rewarding the pronouncement of the magic phrase (a reference perhaps obscure to those too young to remember the early days of television). What I discovered is that the phrase, soul death is, strictly speaking, not part of ordinary parlance. But there are near relatives, and this essay begins by picking up the trail of one of these as given me in a conversation I was privy to this past summer. By unpacking the intuition condensed in a single moment of luminous self-observation casually offered, we may be gradually lead to appreciate the significance of soul death as a profound metaphor for a matter of universal importance: the complex relationship between what we shall call "desire" and "domination."

The conversation was one of those that simply happens in the breezy familiarity of a shared summer house in Provincetown on Cape Cod. A group of gay men, friends, and friends of friends, down from Boston for the Fourth of July long-weekend were talking over morning coffee in the kitchen. The conversation came round to what was known—from that almost impossible-to-recall era before the epidemic—as "recreational sex" or simply, "tricking." At one point, one of the men remarked that quite apart from concerns of health and safety, he had largely given up the practice because he found that the experience of waking up with a relative stranger with whom one has just shared a night of intense sexual intimacy somehow constituted a "wounding of the soul." It was a strikingly serious and surprising turn of phrase, especially coming from a business man of no particular religious or theological orientation. It's reception in the group with a thoughtful silence suggested he had spoken for more than himself. I have pondered for some time the insight compacted in this one comment.

In what consists the wounding of the soul to which my friend made reference? One possibility is that he is speaking of the curious contradiction one finds oneself in of having become vulnerable and exposed in the act of love making to another human being with whom one has no history or horizon of relationship. Though such encounters are not without the possibility of some genuine solace, pleasure, connection, and mutuality—or so my own experience attests—nevertheless there is an almost inherent limitation in the circumstances that simultaneously both evokes and undermines the deeper desiring that drives human sexuality. On the one hand one has been "known" in a singular way—when it comes right down to it there is simply no such thing as "casual" sex.² On the other hand one is left with the vertiginous question, "who was known, and by whom?" It is almost inevitable that two persons under the conditions of such a meeting are responding in large part to their projections of the desired other, and such projections inevitably are challenged by the dawn. In their deconstruction in the lucid light of morning is glimpsed that more awesome, frightening and longed-for possibility: that one might really know and be known by the other. Yet except for those rare and wondrous occasions when these close encounters of the briefer kind actually inaugurate a new love or a sustained relationship—such a mutuality of knowing is not part of this tacit social arrangement. The conventional quip that the benefit of masturbation is that one "doesn't need to figure out what to say over breakfast" is a tip off to the soul-wounding process. Boundaries must be awkwardly reestablished by social habit and conversational ploy. A "self" must be mobilized and reconstituted in two dimensions to meet the self of the other. Two persons hastily re-objectify one another and themselves in some fashion so as to beat a retreat from a meeting that did and did not happen, was and was not desired. Perhaps the wounding of the soul then has something to do with what occurs to the psyche when a desire for mutuality of recognition and the consequent experience of one's own inner intricacy is both stimulated and frustrated, recognized and defended against. Contemporary gay writer Andrew Holleran juxtaposed his aphorisms on promiscuity precisely to highlight just this paradox. The very behavior that regularly and more or less predictably defeats my desire for genuine self-fulfillment is at one and the same time the most profound evidence of the intentionality or conatus of that desiring. To evoke the language of "soul" is to suggest further that what we are examining here goes to the very core of what it means to be a human being.

From Soul Murder to Multiple Personality Disorder:
The Development of an Insight

We have a clue then that at least in our own time the language of soul—its becoming, its wounding, its death—is implicated in those processes whereby persons achieve a felt-sense of inner complexity or intricacy, a rich and vital internal world, and a wide repertoire of affective responses to the "outer" world. It has to do with "becoming real" and that viewed as a profoundly interpersonal as much as an inter-psychic process. Thus we speak of persons as "thin of soul" whose affective engagement with other persons and situations we judge to be constricted, limited, or "shallow." We acknowledge "soul music" and describe works of art that are deeply emotionally resonant as "soulful." A recent book by psychotherapist Thomas Moore, is entitled *Care of the Soul: A Guide for Cultivating Depth and Sacredness in Everyday Life*.[3] Written in the form of popular spiritual self-help books, it loosely evokes the unpretentious, eminently practical Renaissance and late Medieval versions of that genre. What is obvious in a scan of the book is that for its author, a former Roman Catholic religious, the care of the soul is emphatically not about the cultivation of some inner spiritual entity whose perfection is ultimately to be realized in some eschatalogical world-transcending moment. The dust cover of Moore's book displays the domestic serenity of nineteenth century painter Edouard Vuillard's "Woman Sewing Before a Garden Window." The suggestion is clear: the making and tending of the soul is a down-to-earth, "homely" business, using the term with its original old English connotations of receptiveness, welcome, and hospitality.[4] Soul has to do with how hospitality is offered to the "other" in daily life, and this as a function of the hospitality one has oneself been extended by those others into whose care we were ourselves first given (or sentenced).

With this latter observation I have already telegraphed the move I want to work out in this essay: regrounding the discourse of soul in an experience-near account of the formation of our sense of self and other, and finding a route back to soul's transcendent function only by way of this humanward path. But it is useful here perhaps to take note of the ways in which my friend's intuitions about the wounding of the soul as involving the diminishment or distortion of the self-in-relationship are convergent with the original use of the term soul death or "soul murder."

Leonard Shengold has carefully traced the phrase "soul murder" back to a gruesome account of a case of protracted child abuse written by a German jurist, von Freurbach and originally published in 1832 as *Kaspar Hauser: Beispiel eines Verbrecherens am Seelenleben des Menschen (Kaspar Hauser: An Instance of a Crime against the Life of the Soul of Man)*.[5] Kaspar Hauser was a young man who had apparently been imprisoned from early childhood until the age of seventeen in a dark cellar by an identified adult male whom he referred to only as "the Man who was always there." When Hauser was eventually discovered and released he displayed profound cognitive developmental deficits which he very quickly overcame by a voracious desire to learn. More horrifying to his patron and protector,

Judge von Freurbach, however was the irreversible wounding of the young man's capacity for the experience of normal human affectivity (anger, resentment, passion, joy). Hauser appeared to be permanently cut off from the emotional memory of his own abuse and thus ultimately and tragically was also unable to manage adjustment to the world he was lately born into. Von Freurbach wrote of Hauser, "How long soever he may live, he must forever remain a man without childhood and boyhood, a monstrous being, who, contrary to the usual course of nature, only began to live in the middle of his life. Inasmuch as all the earlier part of his life was thus taken from him, he may be said to have been the subject of a partial soul murder . . . the life of a human soul was mutilated at its commencement."[6]

Von Freurbach advances an insight here which can be tracked through the literature on child abuse down to the contemporary resurgence of interest in the phenomenon of post-traumatic stress disorder and multiple personality disorder. Something is done to the child early in life which functions to separate him from some vital center of emotional energy by stealing from the child his own unique experience of childhood. The more profound the abuse and the deeper the alienation from inner experience, the more the individual is unaware of what she has been robbed of. Shengold quotes Nietszche in this regard, that the worst form of slavery is to have lost knowledge of being a slave.

Soul murder appears again in the writings of Freud's most famous psychotic non-patient, Daniel Paul Schreber, who recorded his paranoid fantasies of being a soul murdered by God. Shengold highlights the work of William Niederland who investigated the actual circumstances of Schreber's childhood and discovered there the unmistakable evidence of a pattern of psychological and physical abuse at the hand of Schreber's famous father, a prominent expert on child rearing and discipline. Niederland shows how Schreber's father tried out on his son all manner of innovative pedagogical experiments for breaking the stubborn and "perverse" will and sexual impluses of children and conforming them to the will of God as represented by the authority of the father. He argues convincingly that Schreber's elaborate delusions are psychotic expressions of his childhood experience of being the object of the cruel and irrational behavior of his simultaneously feared and idealized/longed-for father. In this Niederland anticipates the general move within (and sometimes against) psychoanalytic theory towards regarding with greater seriousness the impact of the child's imaginatively elaborated experience of the way in which he was actually responded to by the significant adults of his childhood, primally the parents.

The most extreme and perhaps most publicized critique of psychoanalysis as having avoided the hard and uncomfortable evidence of real childhood sexual and emotional abuse as a pathogenic factor is the case made by Jeffrey Masson.[7] It was Masson who believed he found hard evidence that Freud deliberately and knowingly retreated from his own clinical data regarding incest and parental seduction and elaborated a theory of childhood sexuality instead. The often bitter controversy around Masson's writings may obscure the fact that psychoanalysts as far back as British analysts Michael Balint and D. W. Winnicott have tried to take into account, in theory and in practice, the way in which the psychic life of the child is formed and deformed by the quality and character of the parent-child interaction. Indeed, over the last fifteen years the theoretical integration of the "reconstructed infant of psychoanalysis" with the "observed infant" of increasingly sophisticated studies in early infant development has produced nothing less than a paradigm shift in our model of the human person.[8] In broadest strokes, the shift is one away from an essentially one-person model of a psychological system composed of "hard-wired" endogenous drives or instincts, towards a more thorough-going "two person" model of the psyche in which all desire must be understood as patterned by relationships. Because this gradually emerging new paradigm of the human psyche has such substantive implications for our understanding of soul death it would be helpful to elaborate it in some greater specificity.

Soul Death Psychologically Described

The Swiss psychoanalyst Alice Miller, in her book *The Drama of the Gifted Child*, has written arguably the most accessible and widely influential accounts of how children may suffer a version of "soul death" as a result of a pattern of familial interaction that is more subtle and yet potentially as destructive as that found in the more dramatic cases of abuse and neglect that stand at the head of this literature. In this book she examines what happens when a human child is born into a network of relationships with persons who, by reason of the vicissitudes of their own interpersonal histories, are not prepared to offer the infant the kind of empathic responsiveness which would permit the child to learn the value of his or her own distinctive self-experience. Miller's argument goes that parents who themselves are so narcissistically wounded that they must seduce, coerce or cajole certain responses from the child inorder to enhance their own sense of self-esteem and value create the conditions for the creation of a "false self personality." This term, originally coined by British pediatrician and analyst, D. W. Winnicott, has proven a provocative one in the imaginations of those of many of us encountering this literature.

Winnicott's "false self" is a term that echoes what Helena Deutsch refered to as an "as if" personality.She employed that language to describe the situation of a person who is so attuned to the emotional needs of the others, whether individually or in a social situation, that she in effect is capable of performing as if she really felt the emotions demanded by the other, but without them proceeding from some authentic core of self-hood. The give away is that persons who are most deeply embedded in a false self organization are little aware of any intention to dissemble or pretend. The clue to the disease that drives them is that after even the most successful social performance they are left with a nagging, aching sense of somehow being empty and unsatisfied in their lives and relationships. Like Woody Allen's character Leonard Zelig, the human chameleon, they can be marvelously adaptive to social situations, but sometimes desperately unable to answer convincingly the question, "but what do you want or desire?" More deeply disturbing, Alice Miller felt, was that children grown to adulthood in such families lacked the capacity to empathize with their own childhood selves that were the victims of abuse and neglect. Such a failure of empathy sets them up to identify with their aggressors (who after all usually inflicted pain or neglect with the claim this is "for your own good"). Alternatively, such children in adult years might be found to seek out and repeat relationships that replicate the original conditions of childhood since these represent the only form of love they were able to believe in. Thus when von Freurbach expressed his dismay that the severely neglected Kaspar should express a desire to return to the "man who was always there," Kaspar protested, "Man not bad, man me no bad done."[9] Von Freurbach was incredulous—sadly, we are not. It does not take much of a stretch for most of us to hear in these words the echo of comments frequently voiced by survivors of abusive marriages or relationships, "but he (she) really loved me!"

This description of a profound and prevasive woundedness in our capacity for spontaneous, creative and self-originating human gesture and for genuine self-regard, and its argued linkage with a pattern of early familial interaction, has evoked broad recognition in some sectors of American culture. At a popular level, the now wide-spread discussion of "dysfunctional" families and the powerful response evoked by the books and lectures of John Bradshaw, for example, alert us that this description hits a very live psychic nerve in the body

politic. If there is a problem with the current discourse on "dysfunctionality" it is, from my perspective, that it is not yet radical and
thorough going enough in its critique of culture. To say this is to take
a quite different position than some critics who charge that the definition of dysfunctionality informing the rapidly growing recovery
movement is so broadly drawn that it excludes virtually no one—a
point humorously made in a recent cartoon that shows a nearly empty
convention hall overhung with the banner, "Annual Meeting of Adult
Children of Normal Families." Now one could conclude dismissively
that so inclusive an analysis must lack real meaning and significance.
Or, contrastingly, one could choose to see in its sweep evidence of
an attempt to name a human problematic so foundational as somehow
to bear upon all of our lives. The latter I believe is closer to the mark.

To be thoroughly convincing on this point, however, we need
a more developed analysis of the underlying psychological and spiritual dynamics of soul death than that provided by Alice Miller. It is
true that her vision of the near inevitability of narcissistic injury
and false self formation has grown progressively darker in more
recent works, particularly as she has explored the collusion of religious, political and social science ideologies in processes of abuse and
denial.[10] Yet what remains to be understood and explored is how
deeply set into the structure of culture and social arrangement might
be those conditions that eventuate in the deformation of the self we
have named soul death. If an exploration of those processes should
further show them to be inextricably involved with those essential
and sui generis longings that constitute us as human beings, then our
investigation of soul death may necessarily have to engage that
dimension of living which has been called "the spiritual." In what
remains of this essay I would like to sketch out just this line of analysis by reference to the work of two provocative contemporary psychoanalytic thinkers , Jessica Benjamin and Emmanuel Ghent, and to
the imagery of soul and of death found in another "overheard" conversation, this one with D. H. Lawrence.

Desire and Domination: Untangling the Bonds of Love

Jessica Benjamin in her book, *Bonds of Love: Psychoanalysis,
Feminism and the Problem of Domination*, has argued for a significant corrective to the formulations of psychoanalytic object relations theory, one that advances psychoanalytic theory in the direction of becoming a more genuinely intersubjective and not simply an
inter-psychic account of human mental life.[11] She points out quite

rightly that the British independent school of psychoanalysis have, as noted above, attempted to give proper place in theory and practice to the fundamental motivating need of human beings for relationship with other persons. Yet such formulations as this theory has produced, its language of "internalization" and "mirroring" for example, do not succeed in liberating psychoanalytic theory from what Benjamin calls the "solipsistic omnipotence of the single psyche."[12] Internalization language as commonly used, for example, still suggests the activity of an individual psyche that must "take in" the attentive ministrations of the other for the sake of the self-regulation of affect states. Benjamin observes that running thoughout the models for psychological development presented by contemporary psychoanalytic theorists is the notion that normative psychic development demands "differentiation" and that therefore the interpersonal interactions of childhood are primally significant in terms of how they "build up" an internal world capable of sustaining the individual as a discrete, separate, and independent person. Even the metaphor of empathic mirroring introduced by Heinz Kohut can be understood to imply that the "good enough" mother simply reflects back to the child his or her own behaviors and affects in such a fashion as to permit the crystalization of internal self-structures. The "good enough" parent (Winnicott) permits him/herself to be "used" in that function by the child for the sake of this crucial development. In spite of the accumulating research data suggesting that the human infant, from virtually the beginning of post-partum life, is capable of recognizing and responding to the separateness and distinctiveness of her primary caretakers, the notion lingers that development is all about disentangling the baby from some kind undifferentiated state of oneness or fusion.[13] What holds this idea intransigent, all evidence to the contrary, is a fateful set of gender defined polarities which Benjamin argues are based ultimately on the social/biological assignment of "mothering" to women and the denial of a fully valued subjectivity to women in general and in that maternal role in particular. The polarities run something like this:

female = fusion / lack of boundaries = irrationality = passivity = submission

versus

male = separateness / boundaries = rationality = agency = domination

What is missing in this dichotomization, with its clearly implied superiority of the "male" mode of being over the "female," is a whole range of experience which Benjamin holds to be powerfully and primally motivating in human development. Specifically what such a dichotomization ignores is the human being's innate pleasure and delight precisely in mutual recognition, "the joy of discovering the other, the agency of the self, and the outsideness of the other."[14] There is ample evidence that this intentionality towards the other qua other is present from the beginning of life. As one small example, Benjamin cites the mother-infant interaction research which finds that infants respond most positively and attentively to responses which do not replicate exactly the infants own sounds or gestures but which are a little "off," sufficiently different to be the response of an other and not simply an echo or a reflection in a mirror. From these and other studies the hypothesis is built up that the capacity for "intersubjectivity," the experience of separate minds sharing the same affective state, may be understood to be the normative goal of human development. The experience of communion, connection, or "merger," therefore, is not a matter of regression back to some undifferentiated pre-oedipal state, but is rather a developmental accomplishment along the trajectory of a desire which is foundational to human being. As Benjamin insists:

> Experiences of 'being with' are predicated on a continually evolving awareness of difference, on a sense of intimacy felt as occuring between 'the two of us.' The fact that self and other are not merged is precisely what makes the experiences of merging have such high emotional impact. The externality of the other makes one feel one is truely being 'fed,' getting nourishment from the outside, rather than supplying everything for oneself."[15]

Jessica Benjamin is not the first psychoanalyst, of course, to observe the intricate ballet of recognition and response between parent and child which constitutes us as selves, or which in repeated misstep hobbles future development. Erik Erikson, for example, observed in the playful ritual of greeting between parent and child the wonder of "separateness transcended yet also a distinctiveness confirmed."[16] Yet even in Erikson's formulation of this process it is the distinctiveness of the child that is being affirmed in this interaction. Benjamin balances the dance by seeing that it is also the parent's distinctiveness, recognized as nonthreatening and enhancing by the child, which is equally in play in "play." It was of course Erikson's moral agenda to find in the ritualizations of childhood the basis for the adult's capacity to nonviolently negotiate conflict. Benjamin has substantively deepened this analyis and advanced this agenda by suggesting how this ability to feel the self enhanced and more "real" by the experience of "being with" the other is the ground of social solidarity and compassion.

The identification with the other person occurs through the sharing of similar states, rather than through reversal (i.e., taking turns at being active or passive, etc.). Being with breaks down the oppositions between powerful and helpless, active and passive, it counteracts the tendency to objectify and deny recognition to those weaker or different—to the other. It forms the basis for compassion—what Milan Kundera called 'co-feeling,' "the ability to share feelings and intentions without demanding control, to experience sameness without obliterating difference."[17]

In reading Benjamin, one finds oneself wondering whether she has offered a diagnosis of our human condition and a vision of what health might look like, without a clear prescription as to how this might be realized. It is a question she raises herself. To the extent that she answers it she does so by pointing us to the need to address the social, cultural, and psychological impediments to the full and mutual encounter of women and men as partners in dialogue and equally valued subjectivities.

To halt this cycle of domination, I have argued, the other must make a difference. This means that women must claim their subjectivity and so be able to survive destruction. They must thus offer men a new possibility of colliding with the outside and becoming alive in the presence of an equal other. The vision of recognition between equal subjects gives rise to a new logic—the logic of paradox, of sustaining the tension between contradictory forces. Perhaps the most fateful paradox is the one posed by our simultaneous need for recognition and independence: that the other subject is outside our control and yet we need him. To embrace this paradox is the first step towards unraveling the bonds of love. This means not to undo our ties to others, but rather to disentangle them; to make of them not shackles but circuits of recognition.[18]

I am convinced that this proposal is essentially on target. The realization of authentic human freedom will involve the progressive evolution of social forms in which not only men and women but all persons across whatever gradients of domination and difference, can experience "colliding with the outside and becoming alive in the presence of an equal other." But perhaps we should not limit the "outside" to that particular human subject whom I encounter, important and even indispensible as that person is. Just as Erik Erikson, in his discussion of the conditions necessary for the parent to evoke a sense of "basic trust" within the child, spoke of the parent's felt relationship to some super-ordinate or ultimate environment that was itself trustworthy, might we not ask whether mutual recognition between two human persons requires one or both of them to have engaged their own relationship with the transcendent dimension of human existence, "that which exceeds us utterly."[19]

Clues to the Transcendent:
The Longing for Surrender and Its Disguises

Again following the "bottom up" strategy of this essay, I would have us find our way into a discussion of the transcendent by way of a more experience-near psychological analysis. Our guide here is Emmanuel Ghent, psychoanalyst and author of a remarkable paper entitled, "Masochism, Submission, Surrender: Masochism as a Perversion of Surrender."[20] In his paper, Ghent proposes that we think of the desire to be known by the other as the longing to "come clean," to drop the pretense of false self-structure and be recognized and loved for who we are and how we are by an other whom we also recognize and love. "Surrender," Ghent argues, "has nothing to do with hoisting the white flag; in fact, rather than carrying a connotation of defeat, the term will convey a quality of liberation and expansion of the self as a corollary to the letting down of defensive barriers."[21] For Ghent the inner drive to surrender is the functional equivalent of Benjamin's desire for mutual recognition, a universal human need, the fortunes of which can be traced over the life cycle and the frustration of which is our heart's greatest sorrow. Where for Benjamin "domination" describes the distortion of the desire for mutual recognition under the conditions of patriarchy, for Ghent, "submission" or "masochism" represent the expression of the longing for surrender under circumstances where the courage, trust, reciprocity, or love is lacking that would sponsor genuine surrender.[22]

The contribution of Ghent to our investigation of the notion of soul death is two-fold. First of all he allows a generous and uncondescending understanding of the motive forces which lead persons into relationships of domination and submission, abuser and abused. Submission or masochism, he argues, is the ever available counterfeit of the deeper longing to be known by a loved other. But similarly, in at least some cases, sadism may be the channel through which is acted out the correlative human desire to know the other, to penetrate to the reality of the other, to generate a response and a reaction that convinces one that real contact has been made. The developmental histories that lead particular individuals to one set of behaviors over another may vary greatly, but at base the motive force is the same. Ghent writes of this with a degree of sympathy rare in clinical writing on the topic:

> The main hypothesis of this paper is that it is this passionate longing to surrender that comes into play in at least some instances of masochism. Submission, losing oneself in the power of the other, becoming enslaved in one or other way to the master, is the ever available look alike to surrender. It holds out the promise, seduces, excites, enslaves, and in the end, cheats the seeker-turned-victim out of his cherished goal, offering in its place only the security of bondage and an ever amplified sense of futility. By substituting the appearance and trappings of surrender for the authentic experience, an agonizing, though at times temporarily exciting, masquerade of surrender occurs; a self-negating submissive experience in which the person is enthralled by the other. The intensity of the masochism is a living testimonial of the urgency with which some buried part of the personality is screaming to be exhumed. This is not to be minimized as an expression of the longing to be healed, although so often we bear witness to its recurring miscarriage.[23]

Ghent's perception of the paradox involved in "soul wounding" behaviors is akin to the insight Andrew Holleran suggests in linking together the two epigrams by Oscar Wilde and Tennessee Williams that began this paper. Sexual activity, particularly that which pushes the boundary of what a culture may regard as proper and appropriate may often be understood to reflect an unconscious desire, self subverting perhaps and unevenly successful, for ex-stasis, for an experience of the self-in-relationship that breaks through isolation and the numbness of false self organization.

The other contribution of Emmanuel Ghent to our topic is the explicit way in which he considers the act of surrender to involve us in the gestures and substance of religion. In his discussion of the felt-sense of the false self, that which we are pointing to with the language of soul-wounding, he describes it as a matter of "missing the mark," of failing to realize something essentially, even ontically true about the self. He is quite aware that this same language has been used to define what the Judeo-Christian tradition has meant by "sin." "The cure of missing is to become whole through surrender; the cure for sinning, in this sense, is to come alive, to be present in full awareness, authentic, centered in true self, holy."[24]

What Ghent seems to imply here is what my English Benedictine colleague, Dom Sebastian Moore made explicit in his ongoing efforts to write a soteriology and a Christology that begins with the vision of the self emergent in the work of the neo-psycho-analytic theorists like Alice Miller, Jessica Benjamin and others. The primary and irreducible proposition about human beings, Moore wrote, is that "we all desire to be desired by the one we desire."[25] But it is also the case that our very capacity for self-transcending reflection carries our questioning to the limit conditions of our existence. The outside with which we collide and in relationship we desire to be most real reveals the finiteness and mystery, depth and greatness of that which is "verily other" than ourselves. It is this fact which causes Moore to assert: "The only serious form of the religious question today is: Is human self-awareness, when it finds its fulfillment in love, resonating, albeit faintly, with an origin that 'behaves,' infinitely and all-constitutingly, as love behaves?"[26] To ask this question in the poetry of the biblical tradition, "Does God have regard for me?" or "Am I a source of delight to the Source of my delight?"

A project for research and investigation that continued along the trajectory outlined in this essay would want to return to the territory of the earlier literature on soul death, the religious fantasies of Schreber, but with different interpretive tools and sensibilities. One would want to be prepared to find evidence not only for how the representations of God conspire in the processes of self-destruction and falsification, but also how an experienced mutuality with an Other, mediated imaginally or interpersonally, may be healing of the wounds of the soul. Perhaps alongside Schreber we might look at the autobiography of Antoin Boisen or more currently Marie Balter's moving account of her own twenty year sojourn in mental illness, *No Body's Child.*[27] Yet it may also be the case that outside of the hidden world of therapy, or spiritual direction, or counseling, the most complete and most accessible accounts of this process will be found in great literature. On that premise I would conclude this essay simply by noticing how one modern writer has addressed both the death of the soul, and its recovery.

In a condensed but illuminating form, the processes of both this soul wounding and this healing have been masterfully described in the work of D. H. Lawrence. In his novel, The Rainbow, written between 1913 and 1915, Lawrence writes about how a father's brutal scolding of his young daughter generates a psychological defense that bears all the signs of the kind of pathological narcissism and psychic self-mutilation of which the analysts have been speaking. The father in the story spots the foot prints of his small daughter where she had thoughtlessly run across his newly seeded garden to pick flowers she had spotted on the other side of the yard. He screams at her for following her "own greedy nose."[28]

No Alice Miller could more powerfully describe the process whereby a child begins to "harden herself upon her own being." Yet what is remarkable in Lawrence are the ways in which he has also attempted to put into language what may be the numinous experience of the breakdown and breakthrough of the character armor of the false self. For this he has almost necessarily had to turn to poetry. In his long poem, New Heaven and New Earth, Lawrence follows as it were the soul-wounded child described in The Rainbow into an unhappy adulthood.[29] In harrowing imagery he evokes the psychic hell of a kind of narcissistic implosion, the condition of someone whose defenses against the risks of mutuality and relationship have sealed him into self-sufficiency and splendid isolation. The poem suggests as well what happens when the ideology of domination , as reified and politically realized in the masculine cultures of science and technology, runs to its desperate limits.

In another movement of the poem there is a violent evocation of the "goodness" of war and murder and the relief of death. It is suggestive both of Emmanuel Ghent's contention that sadism may disguise the desire to see if there is any other that can withstand and survive my self-isolating rage and desperate desire for connection, and also of the notion that there is that in us which desires to destroy or deconstruct the false self that keeps us from newness of life.[30]

What acccomplishes this resurrection for the persona of the poem is an encounter with the "otherness" of another person, the poet's wife who suddenly and miraculously presents in Benjamin's words, "a new possibility of colliding with the outside and becoming alive in the presence of an equal other."

I would suggest that here in D. H. Lawrence's poem is expressed the hope and yearning for newness of life and mutuality of recognition that flings people into the turbulant waters of all manner of relationships, encounters, sexual adventures, and passionate commitments. Here too is the promise claimed that those graced meetings which renew the spirit and heal the soul are not just accidents of happy circumstance, provisional and tentative and doomed by time, but rather bear that signature of an "origin" that "behaves infinitely and all-constitutingly as love behaves." Thus Lawrence ends his poem, and I end this essay, with something of a prayer of surrender, a deliberate giving up of control and domination.

NOTES

1. Andrew Holleran, *Ground Zero* (New York: Dutton), 1978.

2. What my friend is realizing here is what many of us resist recognizing, namely that *psychically* "safe sex" may be an oxymoron. It is an observation which Canon Alan Jones mischievously makes in suggesting that perhaps our uptight Victorian ancestors were alive to something about this business of sexual encounter that we have congratulated ourselves on forgetting, "Great sex on a Victorian sofa is far more awkward than sex atop a Sealy posturepedic king-size mattress, but . . . those violently contorted Victorian lovers know by their cracked skulls and bumped shins that what they have engaged in is something and not nothing; hard not soft; risky not safe; productive of long and dire consequences, not immediately dismissed in a cloud of smoke from a cigarette ironically named 'True'." Alan Jones, *Passion for Pilgrimage* (Harper, 1989), p. 27.

3. Thomas Moore, *Care of the Soul: A Guide for Cultivating Depth and Sacredness in Everyday Life* (New York: Harper & Row), 1992.

4. An example of this usage is found in the visionary writing of the English anchorite Julian of Norwich, for example, who is fond of refering to the "homeliness" of her God.

5. Leonard Shengold, *Soul Murder: The Effects of Childhood Abuse and Deprivation* (New Haven: Yale University Press, 1989).

6. Quoted in Shengold, *ibid*, p. 18. For Shengold's own account of the case of Kaspar Hauser, see Shengold, 1988.

7. Jeffrey Masson, *Freud: The Assault on Truth* (London: Faber & Faber), 1983, and *Against Therapy* (London: Collins), 1989.

8. See Stephen Mitchell, *Relational Concepts in Psychoanalysis* (Cambridge: Harvard University Press), 1988.

9. Shengold, op. cit., p. 18.

10. See Alice Miller, *For Your Own Good: The Hidden Cruelty in Child Rearing and the Roots of Violence* (New York: Farrar, Straus and Giroux), 1983; and *Thou Shalt Not Be Aware: Society's Betrayal of the Child* (New York: Meridian), 1986.

11. Jessica Benjamin, *Bonds of Love: Psychoanalysis, Feminism and the Problem of Domination* (New York: Pantheon Books), 1988.

12. Benjamin, ibid. p. 46.

13. This evidence is brilliantly assembled and summarized in Daniel Stern 's book *The Interpersonal World of the Child: A View from Psychoanalysis and Developmental Psychology* (New York: Basic Books), 1985.

14. Benjamin, p. 43.

15. Benjamin, p. 46.

16. Erik Erikson, *Toys and Reasons: Stages in the Ritualization of Experience* (New York: W. W. Norton), 1977, p. 90. Note that Erikson explicitly identifies this early childhood experience as a proto experience of the "numinous."

17. Benjamin, p. 48.

18. Stern, p. 221.

19. Louis Dupre, *Transcendent Selfhood, The Loss and Recovery of the Inner Life* (NY: Seabury Press), 1976.

20. Emmanuel Ghent, "Masochism, Submission, Surrender: Masochism as a Perversion of Surrender," *Contemporary Psychoanalysis.* Vol. 26, no. 1 (1990) 108-136.

21. Ibid., p. 108.

22. "Surrender might be thought of as reflective of some 'force' towards growth, for which, interestingly, no satisfactory word in English exists. Submission,on the other hand, either operates in the service of resistance, or is at best adaptive as an expedient. The superstructure of defensiveness, the protection against anxiety, shame, guilt, anger, are in a way, all deceptions, whether they take the form of denial, splitting, repression, rationalizations, evasions. Is it possible that deep down we long to give this up, to 'come clean,' as part of an even more general longing to be known, recognized? Might not this longing also be joined by a corresponding wish to known and recognize the other? As to the developmental origins of such longings I would locate them as being rooted in the primacy of object seeking as a cental motivational thrust in human beings." Ibid., p. 110.

23. Ghent, p. 116.

24. Ghent, p. 110.

25. Sebastian Moore, OSB, *The Fire and the Rose Are One,* (New York: Seabury), 1980, p. 11. For other serious efforts to ground a soteriology in this psychological analysis see Rita Nakashima Brock, *Journey By Heart: A Christology of Erotic Power* (New York: Crossroads), 1978; and Don Capps, *The Depleted Self: Sin in a Narcissistic Age* (Minneapolis: Fortress), 1993.

26. Moore, p. 15.

27. Anton Boisen, *Out of the Depths,* 1960; Marie Balter & Richard Katz, *No Body's Child,* 1989.

28. D. H. Lawrence, *The Rainbow* (Cambridge: Cambridge University Press), 1987.

29. D. H. Lawrence, *The Complete Poems of D. H. Lawrence,* Vivian De Sola Pinto & Warren Roberts, eds. (New York: Viking Press), 1971.

30. "Certainly some patients seem to be aware, dimly or increasingly, of a force in them to do with growth, growth towards their own shape, also as something that seemed to be sensed as driving them to break down false inner organizations which do not really belong to them; something which can also be deeply feared, as a kind of creative fury that will not let them rest content with a merely compliant adaptation; and also feared because of the temporary chaos it must cause when the integrations on a false basis are in process of being broken down in order that a better one may emerge." Marion Milner, *The Birth of the Living God* (New York: International University Press), 1969, p. 348. See also John McDargh, "The Deep Structure of Religious Representations: A Case Study," in Mark Finn & John Gartner, eds. *Object Relations Theory and Religion: Clinical Applications* (New York: Praeger Press) 1992.

10

Soul-Loss Revisited

Speaking of the fifth century B.C., the historian Bremmer writes:

> After the end of that century there is no longer the whole com-
> plex of the dualistic concept of the soul: a free soul representing
> the individuality in sleep, swoons, and trance without any con-
> tact with the ego souls, *thymos, noos,* and *menos*. This does
> not mean to say that in some parts of Greece elements of 'prim-
> itive' soul belief could not have lingered on. In modern Europe,
> too, elements of primitive soul belief persist in tales of biloca-
> tion and the soul wandering off during sleep . . . It does mean,
> however, that if these elements lingered on, they existed along-
> side a different concept of the soul, the unitary one, a concept
> absent in the period before systematic reflection on the soul
> began." (Bremmer 1983, 69)

I am arguing that the soul emerges in rituals that dramatize
the dilemmas of the ego. On the one hand, the ego buys time by

drawing on the vitality and permanence of the social order. On the other hand, however, the ego must pay, sooner or later, for the attempt to borrow credit and sustenance from society. The ego that recovers its emotional investment from the family and the community in order to have a life of its own must also pay for this withdrawal of libido. For instance, in folklore, the myth of Psyche requires her to undergo a funeral rite as part of her transformation. Bettini speaks of

> the light and delicate flight that moves Psyche from the funereal context of her deathlike wedding to her new state as bride, no less, of the god of love . . . Gently gathered up by Zephyr, with garments rippling here and there like the light wings of a moth, it is truly a *psyche*, in the three senses of 'soul' and 'moth' and character in the story that flies toward further narrative development." (1991, 205-206)

In rituals of transformation, the ego's own dilemma is compounded by the weight of social obligation. If the ego must repay others for living psychologically at their expense, the self also must pay its social debt both for being granted a reprieve from running out of time and for the right to enter into a life of its own. That is why the moth, as a symbol of the soul, is also associated with "black magic," for example, with death, evil, destruction, the savage, and the fierce (Bettini 1991, 203ff.). Black magic defends the self against social pressures which represent a fundamental threat to the life of the soul. As I have noted, individuals most subject to what O'Keefe (1983, 296) calls "the moral weight of society" are in danger of dying from the weight of social life impressed on the very soul of the individual. To defend the self from that excruciating source of pressure requires that one break the spell; one needs countervailing magic (O'Keefe 1983, 297).

The point of magic is that, as O'Keefe puts it, "it is something to *do*" and thus wards off the feeling of helplessness when faced with disapproval, rejection, hate, and even threats of death itself. Slaves, for instance, were placed under the spell of rites that demanded total helplessness on their part in return for a reprieve of the death sentence. No wonder they were particularly susceptible to pathological anxiety stemming from that helplessness. Added to their chronic submission and hopelessness was the threat to the slave's soul implicit in "dying" to one's former life. Guilt at having to renounce one's family and communal identity would be compounded by rage at separation from the slave's former associations. One would therefore expect slaves to be among the population most receptive to magical defenses against social pressures and the loss of the soul.

Nonetheless, by turning to magic the individual merely perpetuates the state of helplessness that initiates the desperate search for supernatural help in the struggle of the soul against social pressure. Too little magic is as dangerous as too much:

> Immoderate magical resistance to social life can lead to complete disconnection and the psychic death of schizophrenia. But inadequate magical defenses make the individual susceptible to voodoo death . . . the struggle is over the will to live. And it is a moral struggle . . . Magic is by nature a kind of avoidance behavior, so it can seldom solve anything, but it can buy time. *Historically, magic bought time for the Individual to emerge and develop more lasting defenses for the self.* (O'Keefe 1983, 316-317; emphasis added)

In this chapter I wish to extend my argument that ritual has been a means by which individuals are enabled to fortify themselves in the face of the unbearable prospect of death and to maintain their sense of their own being in the otherwise overwhelming presence of powerful and captivating forces and figures. Ritual also exacts a price, however, for buying time for the ego. The price is the sacrifice of the individual's own sense of priority and the willingness to accept a secondary position in social hierarchies of deference and control.

There are thus two transformations accomplished through ritual. In the first, the individual's insubstantial and provisional presence in the world is changed into a presence that can withstand the encounter with hostile presence and the unbearable prospect of death itself. In the second, individuals who have undergone such dangers surrender a sense of their own priority to the larger society.

Death, of course, is not the only unbearable prospect that can paralyze or disrupt the soul. The sight of foreigners and their styles of dress, their peculiar equipment, and the symbols of their power can have the same effect on the member of a community undergoing cultural colonization. Speaking of Greeks and Agamemnon, Bettini notes that they were virtually frozen by the sight of Aeneas's armor:

> The voice is weak; the threat sketched out dies in the throat and fails. Nor could one say if the most cruel detail is being

unable even to shout (I see no question about the painfully
dreamlike character of this), or if it is the fear felt by once brave
warriors at the mere sight of arms. Loss of courage, powerlessness to speak, as in a nightmare: among the indirect descrip-
tions of death, among its mythic phantasms, this is one of the
most terrible. (1991, 223)

Ritual does evoke the nature of a dream and evokes a consciousness somewhere between sleeping and wakening, but those
who might otherwise be speechless at the prospect of death are given
words that must be said; those who might lose their voice are
required to shout. Some ask for and receive oracles and predictions.
Words foretelling the future, however, must be followed with firm
response. Thus rituals of initiation also require individuals to make
promises and to swear oaths that bind them to the vision that has
been foretold. If these first-order transformations are successful, they
will be blessed, but they will indeed be cursed if they fail to complete
their transformations: condemned perhaps to be insubstantial and
empty souls, inarticulate and immobile, wandering in a place where
souls can be lost forever.

When individuals are immobilized by the prospect of death,
they may simulate that state in their own bodies. Sacrificial rites
therefore give them something that must be done so that they will
not remain passive and immobilized. In the Passover rite, indeed, the
killing and eating must be done swiftly and completely, so that one
can then depart on one's own journey into unknown territory where
the prospects are both terrible and sublime. For fear that one's own
life will thus be taken, one is required to take life. For fear that one
will lose speech, vitality, force, and substance, one is required to
utter powerful oaths and promises or to consume that which is purified and confers spiritual substance. These observances mobilize
and sustain the individual at a level of self-awareness that can resist
both panic and desire. The soul begins to emerge in the individual's
capacity to face an otherwise unbearable encounter with the prospect
of death. Without the support of ritual, that encounter will cause the
soul to resemble the shadowy and pathetic images of Hades or to
wander forever in Sheol.

The prospect of death can produce the sensations of soul-loss:
speechlessness, paralysis, immobility, emptiness. In the myth of
Hades, however, it is not the experience of soul-loss but the place of
lost souls that must be feared. The experience of soul-loss in this
world is transposed to the underworld, where one encounters souls

who are unable to speak except for a bat-like squeaking sound. In Hades souls are unable to move except for flitting about like a moth or a bat; the soul is shadowy, dim, tired, and empty (Bettini 1991, 220ff.). The experience of the ego, that it is running out of time, is thus transformed by myth into a spatial metaphor: a place where the lost souls of the dead can at least be found, even if they are in a nearly lifeless state.

Myth also has a way of keeping open the possibilities that are foreclosed by death. Indeed, Psyche herself is made to undergo her own funeral before she can become a truly liberated soul uplifted by her own wings and sustained by the zephyrs of the god of love (i.e., by Zephyr himself; cf. Bettini 1991, 205-206). That effortless sort of buoyancy and elevation is reserved for those souls who have survived their encounter with death.

Ritual thus makes it possible to keep open various possibilities that life and death otherwise would foreclose. Through ritual, the individual's experience of what lies 'before' is transformed into a sense of what lies 'behind.' The inexorable approach of death, which lies before every individual, is now placed behind the one thus transformed. Good Friday becomes Easter, year after year. Thus the future becomes, through the magic of ritual, the past. One will be gathered into one's ancestors: restored to Paradise, allowed to enter a new creation, or taken home once again and allowed to meet those who have gone before.

So far I have been speaking only of first-order transformations, in which the individual is transformed through the ritualized encounter with death. The rite or journey once completed, the fearsome prospect of what had been lying ahead can now be regarded as being behind the transformed individual. There is, however, a second order transformation of the individual's experience of time. As Bettini (1991, 158ff.) notes, every culture has its own notions of what is before and 'after.' Notions of what is 'first' and 'second.' These cultural criteria of priority stipulate what is most to be honored along with what is entitled only to honorable mention. Typically, Bettini (1991, 167ff.) argues, what is beforehand in the list of honors has priority and will thus be coded as being 'higher' than the rest; at least this is true of Roman antiquity. I would argue, furthermore, that these societal codes for priority require that the individual sacrifice his or her own sense of priority, even at the moment that the individual passes through the gates that separate the child from the adult, the single from the married, and the living from the dead. It is precisely at those moments, in which the individual has gone 'ahead,' that societal claims to priority are asserted with renewed force. Those assertions can take their own toll on the vitality of the soul.

Because societies embody time, they can represent their priorities to the individual in the form of what is lasting and will stand the test of time. Therefore in accepting and entering into societal representations of time, the individual can be persuaded that he or she now participates in the future and can discern both its benign and its more frightening features. As Bettini (1991, 169ff.) notes of the Roman aristocracy's funeral cortege, ritual can thus take the terror of the unknown, of death and the future, and turn it into an embodiment of a past that is extended indefinitely, through the individual's own life and progeny, into the future itself. The funeral cortege not only projects the survival of the individual, but establishes the society's notions of priority. Inevitably, the living appear to be relatively minor when compared with those who have come first and have gone before.

The first-order transformations of ritual, then, enable the individual to place death behind the self and thus to buy time; the second-order transformations pay for this infusion of grace, as it were, by sacrificing the individual's own sense of priority in favor of the social order itself. In rituals such as the Passover, for instance, the sense of priority gained by being permitted to survive the passage of death is renounced in the sacrifice of the first-born of the flock. Other peoples as well have found the sacrifice of the first-born to be a crucial piece of their own mythology (Bettini 1991, 211).

The mythological bee stands for the successful transformation of the soul in the face of death and for the ego's subservience to the social order. In ideology the bee is a creature of the social order: industrious and domesticated. As Bettini points out, for Pliny it is the bee who is productive and filled with virtue in the works of the day, as opposed to the moth who is canonically assigned to the ranks of the "lazy," the "predator," the "ignominious," and to the world of darkness (1991, 203ff.).[1] The moth is typical of the images assigned minors, the inadequately disciplined or schooled, and those who lack priority because they are peripheral to the major institutions for production and social control. The bee is an excellent ideological model, as it were, for the soul that is safely contained by the larger society and that lends its energies to works that improve and perpetuate the social order.

Even the bee, however, is likely to escape the hive; it must be persuaded to stay or be restrained from departure. Indeed, Bettini

(1991, 207ff.) describes at length a ritual, the *begonia,* in which bees are intended to be created from the rotting viscera of a bull or heifer slain for the purpose of effecting this transformation from animal to spiritual. The orifices of the animal must be closed, just as a hive can be smeared with dung, in order to prevent the bees from departing from their natural habitat, which is the viscera. As Bettini (1991, 211) goes on to note, it is the dung of a first-born bull that can best serve this purpose. Sacrifice thus prevents the bee from fleeing the social order represented by the hive, from which all exits are closed.

In folklore, however, the bee is quite a free spirit indeed; it can wander, come and go, colonize and be a guide to those intent on colonizing, and it is always associated not with the domestic but the unfamiliar and foreign (Bettini, 216-218). Clearly in popular rather than canonical myth, the bee is a soul that may be difficult to domesticate; it is more, one might say, like a hornet or a wasp. These latter insects were associated with barbarians and whatever was destructive of social order (Bettini 1991, 213). Popular mythology, in other words, is well aware that social transformations have their limits, and that rituals may not always be legitimate or effective in subordinating the individual's desires to the priorities of the larger society.

If souls may wander freely of their own accord, it is in the interest of the custodians of social order to control departures and to turn wandering from a right into a punishment. Banishment was precisely a punishment for individuals who adhered to illegitimate notions of their own priority. Cain was therefore forced to wander, as was Esau. Banishment places the soul outside the sphere of salvation in a place where time is forever running out. In Sheol and Hades souls wander without any hope of having an effective presence of their own.

A successful ritual requires that the individual be fully released from previous bonds of duty in order to undertake new obligations. Myth remembers the moth-like Psyche, whose wedding was like a funeral and who therefore entered into genuine exaltation of the soul, but myth also remembers the bat whose flights are far less ethereal and whose relation to the earth remains correspondingly intimate and degrading. As Bettini recounts the myth, it is only after Psyche's parents are in full mourning, and after she is both desolate and abandoned that her transformation occurs; she turns into a moth-like "soul-girl" who symbolizes the wings of love: incorporeal, ethereal, and light. Contrast Bettini's description of the bat in classic mythology: "bats were associated with souls caught up by mad love for corporeal life; like bats, these souls have 'corporeal wings, thick and earthy,' (Proclus, *Comm. in Plat. Resp. 1.120, 5-10; Kroll*" 1991, 225). The bat is associated with dreams, the nether-world, Hades, and the loss of one's own voice: that is, with the loss of soul. To be transformed from a bat to a moth requires powerful rites indeed.

Rituals mimic magic by claiming to release the soul from the heavy duties that weigh it down to this earth and its obligations. Only such a transformed soul is capable of transcending death: Thus Psyche must have her funeral before she can have her wedding: shed old burdens before assuming new, however lighter obligations.[2] Not all the participants in a ritual, however, will be so inclined or exalted by their encounter with the prospect of death. Some, like bats, will cling to their earthly attachments and prefer mortal pleasures to all others.

As we have seen in our discussion of Bettini, the Homeric soul was often weighed down, attached to earth, driven by passions like love and cruelty, and closely associated with death: in a word, a bat-like soul. The moth would have been a simile for a soul more liber-ated from such attachments and passions and yet required, like Psyche herself, to be transformed through close encounters with the terrors of death before being exalted. According to Bremmer (1983, 29), moreover, in the Homeric period the soul was conceived in terms of several bodily entities or spirits that could be released or driven from a person in various adversities.

It is only after the Homeric epic that ancient Greece depicted the soul itself as free to travel, whether or not the individual was able to move. This is the discovery, Bremmer argues, of the "free soul": a development that incorporated many aspects of the vital or bodily soul, and of the psychological experience of the individual, but which also transcended them. For such a soul, I would argue, the bee is an apt simile because it represents freedom and control: productive and yet free to leave the hive.

Between the "soul-bat" and the "soul-bee," Bettini (1991, 226) argues, is "an anthropological gap of very great import." That gap was filled, I would suggest, with rituals that attempted to forge a soul with the bee's will to live and with its potential freedom, yet tempered by the bee's industry and potential for citizenship. Ritual was required not only to enable the soul to survive the encounter with death, however exhausted the soul may be, but to become, like the bee, "eternal and purified." The bee would have emerged as an ideological symbol for a soul free enough to leave the classical city, and yet also capable of embodying the virtues of the industrious and faithful citizen.

Finally, the notion of a "unitary" soul emerges:

> It is only in fifth-century Athens that we start to find the idea that the citizen can determine his own, independent course of action. By the end of that century *psyche* became the center of consciousness, a development not yet fully explained but upon which, most likely, a strong influence was exerted by the rise of literacy and the growth of political consciousness. And it seems likely that the systematic reflection on the soul started precisely at the end of that century because the *psyche* had become the center of consciousness and for that reason would have provoked a much stronger interest than before. (Bremmer 1983, 69)

If Bremmer is right, the notion of the soul as unitary, a single entity identified with the whole person and embodying the individual per se, emerged during the height of Athenian self-consciousness. That is, the emergence of the polis appears to have coincided with the development of a notion of the *psyche*, not as some bat-like or moth-like, ephemeral and fleeting aspect of the individual but of the quintessential person capable, like the bee, of emerging intact from encounters with death: free, purified, and independent, but also capable like the colonizer of transcending the barriers of time and place in the service of a new social order. What Bettini would call the "ideological" aspects of the myth of the soul are here clearly entwined with those deriving from folklore and the existential encounter of the individual with death. The triumph of the unitary soul, as Bremmer calls it, over the 'free' soul reflects the success of rituals of transformation in modeling and monopolizing the magic by which the ego buys time for itself.

It was left for folklore to remember the psyche as able to travel to the past and to the future: that is, to return to places once enjoyed and perceive the future (Bremmer 1983, 41,51).[3] According to Bremmer (1983, 32), the soul that is thus capable of uniting the past and the future in the present typifies individuals who are dreaming, or in a trance, or who are at the point of death: all conditions under which the soul was believed to be free to leave the body.

An illustration may help to make the point clearer. According to Appolonius, Bremmer writes, a man named Hermotimos used to enter death-like trances that lasted for so long, and left him so immobile and inert, that he would seem virtually dead. In these trances, however, he would be able to foretell various natural disasters such as earthquakes, plagues, droughts, and floods. Space, here, is thus a metaphor for time, and wandering in space is a literary analogy for the experience of the soul as being coeval with other times (and, hence other places). In later accounts, (by Pliny rather than by Appolonius), the temporal reference is lost, and Hermotimos is regarded as being a witness merely to distant rather than to future events (Bremmer 1983, 27). The projection of the self over space has superseded the projection of the self over time.

To summarize: Not only soul-girls, moths, and the dead were called _psychai_, but also the industrious and colonizing bee. In ideological terms the free soul would remain either too ephemeral or too likely to cling to its attachments, while the bee-like soul, I have noted, was essential to the city but had to be watched carefully lest it leave under its own recognizance. Insects like the moth and the bat were precisely the right analogues for a soul unsure of its place and uncertain in its flight. They were also the right analogues for the presence of others—the living and the dead—experienced as being unreliable and dangerous.

As the polis developed at last into a community of souls, rituals linked the individual's entrance into the land of the dead with the individual's participation in the community of the living. Indeed, as Bremmer points out,

> The funeral rites of the Greeks functioned as a rite of passage for the soul from the world of the living to the afterlife. Souls of those who died without being full members of the social order such as criminals, children, and adolescents were not given full funeral rites and were not thought to enter fully into the world of the dead. Yet, as we shall see, there is little evidence that those who died outside the ordered social world remained to haunt the living as ghosts or revenants. (1983, 73-74)

Without ritualized transformations, individuals could hardly be said to have souls of their own.

Thus, in ideological terms, the more advanced, unitary soul emerges only when recognized by the community into which the child is born and is later to be initiated. Levy-Bruhl (1966, 208-211) points out in some detail how the very young infant, the newborn in particular, has at best only a provisional soul: the soul of an ancestor, perhaps, but none the less a soul waiting to be discovered and named on the occasion of the infant's initiation into the community. The length of time required for that initiation may vary from one community to another, yet time is of the essence at the very beginning of life. Those children who die before they are initiated were therefore thought never to have possessed a soul of their very own. Their essence remained in doubt.

Later initiations often tell the same story; the young are not fully in possession of their souls until they possess a "a public social name," and to discover that name requires consensus and, often enough, divination. Some initiations are not over until marriage, and for some communities marriages are not complete until a child is born (Levy-Bruhl 1966, 214-215). The point is simply that for one to possess a soul one must have stood not only the test of time but attained full access to the social order.

To be fully present in the community clearly therefore requires certain rites of passage, just as funeral rites are required to ensure the passage of the dead into the afterlife. The community consists not only of the living but of the dead whose entrances and passages have conformed to the temporal order of the larger society. Only then can they be considered to have gone before into the after life, where they will have become part of the community's future and be remembered. Thus rituals of transformation score a victory over time by preventing time from effacing the image of the dead. Indeed, there is some evidence that funeral rites may have included the making of a double of the departed, in the same way that even in modern cemeteries photographs of the deceased may preserve their image on their gravestones.

Vernant argues, for instance, that the ancient Greeks seemed to be able to embody the presence of the deceased in stone funeral monuments that bore "a permanent witness to the identity of a being who, together with his body, finds his end in definite absence" (1991, 40). The rites were thus double-coded, as it were, and pointed to a presence that was contingent upon its absence. With the development of funerary statues, furthermore, a more substantive expression of the virtues of the deceased took over: a development not known until the sixth century. By that time, I would suggest, it has become possible to think in terms of an immortal soul that was not merely a principle embodied in the individual, a 'protective genius,' or a 'phantom,' but of a soul that was a permanent member of the social order.

Certainly Hart (1992, 121) asserts that there is a strong similarity between the fate of the soul celebrated in Eleusinian mysteries and the soul as understood by contemporary Orthodoxy in rural Greece. She points out that the songs and laments of contemporary Greek funerary rites are not merely communal and ecclesiastical; these hymns and songs are extensions of the liturgy into the everyday life of the individual and the household (Hart 1992, 130ff.). As such they also break down the barriers between the living and the dead. In this way everyday life, for a period of mourning that lasts variously from two to five years, becomes a sort of limbo: a purgatorial period in which the fate of the living is still attached to that of the departed. More intense is the period of forty days after the death of an individual; in that time the prayers of the living are believed to be indeed fateful for the final disposition of the souls of those who have died. Such prayers and songs, I am suggesting, are perhaps our most direct point of entry into the world of antiquity.

These funereal rites carry on the notion of the advanced or unitary soul: the soul as an independent, inner principle. Such a soul takes precedence over the individual's protective genius or phantasmal double. The primitive or free soul, folklore's "protecting genius" or the magical self, (cf. Levy-Bruhl 1966, 244), is degraded to an illusion. By the time of Plato, according to Vernant, the Greeks had largely dispelled that illusion:

> In the ghostly world of appearances, the body is 'that which is made to look like the semblance of the soul.' No longer are there . . . phantoms of those whose bodies have been reduced to ashes on the funerary pyre; rather, it is 'the bodies of the deceased (their corpses) which are the *eidola* of those who are dead. We have thus passed from the soul, ghostly double of the body, to the body as a ghostly reflection of the soul. (Vernant 1991, 190; quotations in this excerpt are from Plato, *Laws*, 959b1-3).

Otherwise, the dead become shadowy images and lose their voices; they become shades that flit and squeak. As modern political rhetoric would put it, they lack a voice in the social system. Those who have not been fully incorporated into the community of the living and the dead, for example, children and criminals, are thus most likely to have their images effaced by the inexorable passage of time.

On the one hand, then, ideological views of the soul have long argued that the selfhood of the individual is distorted and incomplete until it is subordinated to the priorities of the larger society. In honoring those who have gone before, the soul finds itself not only completed but corrected: saved from the errors and distortions of what has come to be known pejoratively as 'individualism.' On this view the soul's very being is derived from a larger entity more enduring and more real than the individual will ever be: from the larger society, from nature, or from divinity itself. In entering into its heritage, as it were, the soul comes to its senses. It becomes the unitary soul: part citizen, part free spirit, like the bee. Such a compromise formation should not surprise a civilization that understands with Freud the compromises required of the psyche if it is to be allowed to live.

On the other hand, however, folklore has maintained hope for the 'free' soul: the soul that can escape from the demands and constraints of the larger society. Such a soul may travel and thus be in two places at one time; it may seek the company of the invisible. The soul that is not too earthbound can even find itself caught up in the arms of love, but it will first, of course, have to suffer. Many souls may be called to the higher reaches of spiritual freedom, but in the West relatively few have been chosen for this redemption from the ordinary and from the chains of duty. They are considered to be virtuosos and charismatics: fascinating but a bit dangerous, and thus worthy of continued sociological and psychological investigation.

NOTES

1. Because Bettini is working from a Levy-Straussian interest in opposition, he focuses on the contrast between the bee and the moth in classical folklore, although he does take note of variations within the characterization of the moth. Such an analysis tends to underestimate the importance of the ambiguous and ambivalent values placed on the same symbol by what I am calling first- and second-order transformations.

2. Indeed, Bettini (1991, 226) expressly deplores attempts such as this to make any other sense of the imagery than can be developed from the ancient texts themselves, to the reading of which he claims to have added only a knowledge of syntax and grammar, so to speak. In fact, as he would no doubt agree, he is also applying the logic of a structuralist anthropology after the manner of Levi-Strauss. That logic, I am suggesting, is not necessary for the sort of reading that I am applying here: informed as it is by a sense of what transformations ritual can sometimes, but not always, accomplish.

3. The individual was also believed to be able to be in two places at once, like the "primitive" soul referred to in the above quotation from Bremmer. Bilocation, I have argued, is really the capability to unite in the

self the experience of different times. The spatial reference in bilocation is a metaphor for time. Remember, for instance, the shaman who is able to foresee who—or what—is coming (in the future, and not merely from afar).

REFERENCES

Bettini, Maurizio. 1991. *Kinship, Time, Images of the Soul*. Baltimore and London: Johns Hopkins University Press.

Bremmer, Jan. 1983. *The Early Greek* Concept of the Soul. Princeton, NJ: Princeton University Press.

Hart, Laurie. 1992. *Time, Religion, and Social Experience in Rural Greece*. Lanham, MD: Rowman and Littlefield.

Levy-Bruhl, Lucien. 1966. *The 'Soul' of the Primitive*. New York, Frederick A. Praeger Publishers.

Vernant, Jean-Pierre. 1991. *Mortals and Immortals*. Collected Essays, Froma I. Zeitliln, editor, Princeton: Princeton University Press.

Index

A

Abel, 5
Adam, 98, 100, 111, 114
Aeneas, 233
Agamemnon, 233
Alamogordo, N.M., 161
Allen, Woody, 219
Alline, Henry, 172
Angstrom, Rabbit (fic.), 18-19, 195-212
Appolonius, 239-40
Ashbery, John, 161
Athens, 31
Auden, W. H., 90, 93, 95
Augustine, Saint, 98, 112
Auschwitz, 126

B

Baghdad, 162
Balint, M., 218
Balter, M., 226, 230
Baltimore, MD, 180-81, 183
Balzac, 132
Barber, Carrie, 175
Barber, Jack, 175
Becker, E., 186, 190
Becket, Thomas, 14-16
Beechey, V., 77, 95
Bellah, R. N., 156, 167
Benjamin, J., 90-91, 95, 116, 220-24, 226-27, 229
Berger, P., 65, 81-82

Bettelheim, B., 1, 17, 138-40, 167, 171, 190
Bettini, M., 232-33, 235-39, 243
Bloch, M., 16
Bloom, A., 126, 135
Bloom, H., 212
Bloom, Leonard (fic?), 73
Bly, Robert, 162
Boisen, A., 226, 230
Bourdieu, P., 27
Bradshaw, J., 219
Bradstreet, A., 161
Brasilia (Brazil), 45, 48-50, 53-55
Brazil, 15, 17, 41-42, 65
Breger, L., 121, 135
Bremmer, J., 231, 238-40, 243
Brewer, PA, 195, 198
Brock, R. N., 102, 112, 115-16, 230
Brown, P., 99
Brown, L., 136
Bryant, Wm. Cullen, 161
Bunyan, John, 157-58, 172
Burke, Kenneth, 161
Burton, R., 151, 155, 167
Bush, George, 163, 165-66, 196, 199

C

Cain, 5, 237
Campbell, B., 74, 85, 94-95
Camus, 122
Campinas (Brazil), 40, 45, 49, 52-53, 60, 62, 66
Cape Cod, MA, 214